D0414665

Donald L. DeWitt
Editor

Going Digital: Strategies for Access, Preservation, and Conversion of Collections to a Digital Format

Going Digital: Strategies for Access, Preservation, and Conversion of Collections to a Digital Format has been co-published simultaneously as *Collection Management*, Volume 22, Numbers 3/4 1998.

Going Digital:
Strategies for Access,
Preservation, and Conversion
of Collections
to a Digital Format

Going Digital: Strategies for Access, Preservation, and Conversion of Collections to a Digital Format has been co-published simultaneously as *Collection Management*, Volume 22, Numbers 3/4 1998.

Collection Management Monographs/"Separates"

The State of Western European Studies: Implications for Collection Development, edited by Anthony M. Angiletta, Martha L. Brogan, Charles S. Fineman, and Clara M. Lovett

Collection Management for School Library Media Centers, edited by Brenda H. White

Reading and the Art of Librarianship: Selected Essays of John B. Nicholson, Jr., edited by Paul Z. DuBois and Dean H. Keller

International Conference on Research Library Cooperation, edited by The Research Libraries Group, Inc.

Euro-Librarianship: Shared Resources, Shared Responsibilities, edited by Assunta Pisani

Access Services in Libraries: New Solutions for Collection Management, edited by Gregg Sapp

Practical Issues in Collection Development and Collection Access, edited by Katina Strauch, Sally Somers, Susan Zappen, and Anne Jennings

Electronic Resources: Implications for Collection Management, edited by Genevieve S. Owens

Collection Development: Past and Future, edited by Maureen Pastine

Collection Development: Access in the Virtual Library, edited by Maureen Pastine

Going Digital: Strategies for Access, Preservation, and Conversion of Collections to a Digital Format, edited by Donald L. DeWitt

Going Digital:
Strategies for Access, Preservation, and Conversion of Collections to a Digital Format

Donald L. DeWitt
Editor

Going Digital: Strategies for Access, Preservation, and Conversion of Collections to a Digital Format has been co-published simultaneously as *Collection Management*, Volume 22, Numbers 3/4 1998.

The Haworth Press, Inc.
New York • London

The Research Libraries Group (RLG) retains copyright for all articles appearing in this volume, except the following: "Introduction," by Donald L. DeWitt, ©1998 The Haworth Press, Inc., and "The Copyright Context," by Robert L. Oakley, ©1995 Robert L. Oakley.

Going Digital: Strategies for Access, Preservation, and Conversion of Collections to a Digital Format has been co-published simultaneously as *Collection Management*, Volume 22, Numbers 3/4 1998.

The development, preparation, and publication of this work has been undertaken with great care. However, the publisher, employees, editors, and agents of The Haworth Press and all imprints of The Haworth Press, Inc., including The Haworth Medical Press and The Pharmaceutical Products Press, are not responsible for any errors contained herein or for consequences that may ensue from use of materials or information contained in this work. Opinions expressed by the author(s) are not necessarily those of The Haworth Press, Inc.

Cover design by Thomas J. Mayshock Jr.

Library of Congress Cataloging-in-Publication Data

Going digital : strategies for access, preservation, and conversion of collections to a digital format / Donald L. DeWitt, editor.
    p. cm.
    "Co-published simultaneously as Collection management, volume 22, numbers 3/4, 1998."
    Includes bibliographical references and index.
    ISBN 0-7890-0521-2 (alk. paper)
    1. Libraries–United States–Special collections–Electronic information resources–Congresses. 2. Digital preservation–United States–Congresses. 3. Research libraries–United States–Congresses. I. DeWitt, Donald L., 1938- . II. Collections management.
    Z692.C65G65 1998
    025.8'4'0285–dc21
                                                98-6626
                                                 CIP

INDEXING & ABSTRACTING

Contributions to this publication are selectively indexed or abstracted in print, electronic, online, or CD-ROM version(s) of the reference tools and information services listed below. This list is current as of the copyright date of this publication. See the end of this section for additional notes.

- *Central Library & Documentation Bureau International Labour Office,* CH-1211 Geneva 22, Switzerland

- *CNPIEC Reference Guide: Chinese National Directory of Foreign Periodicals*, P.O. Box 88, Beijing, People's Republic of China

- *Combined Health Information Database (CHID),* National Institutes of Health, 3 Information Way, Bethesda, MD 20892-3580

- *Current Awareness Abstracts,* Association for Information Management, Information House, 20-24 Old Street, London, EC1V 9AP, England

- *IBZ International Bibliography of Periodical Literature*, Zeller Verlag GmbH & Co., P.O.B. 1949, d-49009 Osnabruck, Germany

- *Index to Periodical Articles Related to Law,* University of Texas, 727 East 26th Street, Austin, TX 78705

- *Information Reports & Bibliographies,* Science Associates International, Inc., 6 Hastings Road, Marlboro, NJ 07746-1313

- *Information Science Abstracts,* Plenum Publishing Company, 233 Spring Street, New York, NY 10013-1578

- *Informed Librarian, The,* Infosources Publishing, 140 Norma Road, Teaneck, NJ 07666

(continued)

- *INTERNET ACCESS (& additional networks) Bulletin Board for Libraries ("BUBL") coverage of information resources on INTERNET, JANET, and other networks.*
  - <URL:http://bubl.ac.uk/>
  - The new locations will be found under <URL:http://bubl.ac.uk.link/>.
  - Any existing BUBL users who have problems finding information on the new service should contact the BUBL help line by sending e-mail to <bubl@bubl.ac.uk>.

  The Andersonian Library, Curran Building, 101 St. James Road, Glasgow G4 0NS, Scotland

- *Journal of Academic Librarianship: Guide to Professional Literature, The,* Grad School of Library & Information Science/Simmons College, 300 The Fenway, Boston, MA 02115-5898

- *Konyvtari Figyelo–Library Review,* National Szechenyi Library, Centre for Library and Information Science, H-1827 Budapest, Hungary

- *Library & Information Science Abstracts (LISA),* Bowker-Saur Limited, Maypole House, Maypole Road, East Grinstead, West Sussex, RH19 1HH, England

- *Library and Information Science Annual (LISCA),* Libraries Unlimited, P.O. Box 6633, Englewood, CO 80155-6633. Further information is available at www.lu.com/arba

- *Library Hi Tech News,* Pierian Press, P.O. Box 1808, Ann Arbor, MI 48106

- *Library Literature,* The H.W. Wilson Company, 950 University Avenue, Bronx, NY 10452

- *OT BibSys,* American Occupational Therapy Foundation, P.O. Box 31220, Rockville, MD 20824-1220

- *PASCAL, c/o Institute de L'Information Scientifique et Technique. Cross-discipinary electronic database covering the fields of science, technology & medicine. Also available on CD-ROM, and can generate customized retrospective searches. For more information: INIST, Customer Desk, 2, alee du Parc de Brabois, F-54514 Vandoeuvre Cedex, France; http//www.inist.fr,* INIST/CNRS-Service Gestion des Documents Primaires, 2, allee du Parc de Brabois, F-54514 Vandoeuvre-les-Nancy, Cedex, France

(continued)

- *Referativnyi Zhurnal (Abstracts Journal of the All-Russian Institute of Scientific and Technical Information),* 20 Usievich Street, Moscow 125219, Russia

Book reviews are selectively excerpted by the Guide to Professional Literature of the Journal of Academic Librarianship.

SPECIAL BIBLIOGRAPHIC NOTES

related to special journal issues (separates) and indexing /abstracting

- ❏ indexing/abstracting services in this list will also cover material in any "separate" that is co-published simultaneously with Haworth's special thematic journal issue or DocuSerial. Indexing/abstracting usually covers material at the article/chapter level.

- ❏ monographic co-editions are intended for either non-subscribers or libraries which intend to purchase a second copy for their circulating collections.

- ❏ monographic co-editions are reported to all jobbers/wholesalers/approval plans. The source journal is listed as the "series" to assist the prevention of duplicate purchasing in the same manner utilized for books-in-series.

- ❏ to facilitate user/access services all indexing/abstracting services are encouraged to utilize the co-indexing entry note indicated at the bottom of the first page of each article/chapter/contribution.

- ❏ this is intended to assist a library user of any reference tool (whether print, electronic, online, or CD-ROM) to locate the monographic version if the library has purchased this version but not a subscription to the source journal.

- ❏ individual articles/chapters in any Haworth publication are also available through the Haworth Document Delivery Service (HDDS).

Going Digital: Strategies for Access, Preservation, and Conversion of Collections to a Digital Format

CONTENTS

ABOUT THE EDITOR

Donald L. DeWitt, PhD, is curator of the Western History Collections at the University of Oklahoma. An archivist and manuscript curator for over 25 years, he is the author of several articles and five book-length guides on archivist administration. Dr. DeWitt is currently involved in a pilot project to digitize selected photographs from the Western History Collections at the University.

Introduction

Donald L. DeWitt

Most observers of the library scene acknowledge that the proliferation of digital information resources has brought about dramatic changes in librarianship during the 1990s. The shift to digital information has affected nearly all departments in the traditional academic library and none, perhaps, more noticeably than collection development. With the availability of digital resources have come a number of different perspectives on how library collections should be developed, managed, and preserved. This series of essays represents a multiyear examination of some of the challenges and decisions for collection managers who want to improve their library's access to digital information or to preserve collections digitally.

The articles appearing in this volume were presented originally at a series of five symposiums on digital resources sponsored by the Research Libraries Group (RLG) of Mountain View, California, between 1993 and 1995. Over the years, RLG has earned a reputation for addressing key issues in the field of librarianship. It is a proven leader in fostering collaborative programs in resource sharing and preservation, developing improved access to scholarly databases, and harnessing the power of digital technology to build new information resources. In the years since these symposiums took place, RLG and its members have applied the lessons learned and are implementing projects and programs based on the sum of what digital technology currently offers.

Since RLG held its first "digital" symposium in 1993, experience has grown and options have broadened, but these papers continue to offer valuable ideas and experience. Presenters were from the front rank of library and information field leaders, and their comments represented some of the best thinking available on digital resources. The papers

[Haworth co-indexing entry note]: "Introduction." DeWitt, Donald L. Co-published simultaneously in *Collection Management* (The Haworth Press, Inc.) Vol. 22, No. 3/4, 1998, pp. 1-7; and: *Going Digital: Strategies for Access, Preservation, and Conversion of Collections to a Digital Format* (ed: Donald L. DeWitt) The Haworth Press, Inc., 1998, pp. 1-7. Single or multiple copies of this article are available for a fee from The Haworth Document Delivery Service [1-800-342-9678, 9:00 a.m. - 5:00 p.m. (EST). E-mail address: getinfo@haworth.com].

selected for this volume are those most directly related to collection management. They fall into three categories: (1) integration of digital resources into traditional library collections; (2) preservation of digital resources; and (3) selection and conversion of print and graphic materials to a digital format.

This selection, then, may be considered as a sampler of the published proceedings. Those who are interested in other digital themes, especially the technical aspects of digital information, should review the entire five-volume set.[1]

The first symposium, *Electronic Access to Information: A New Service Paradigm*, took place in Palo Alto, California, in July 1993. It explored avenues for cooperative action between libraries, especially RLG members, and how libraries might develop strategies to use digital resources. For Part 1 of this volume, I selected three of its six presentations as the most useful for collection managers and added another essay with a similar theme that appeared two years later at the May 1995 symposium *Scholarship in the New Information Environment* held at Harvard University. Part 1 concludes with four additional essays on digital resources and preservation drawn from the March 1994 symposium *Digital Imaging Technology for Preservation* held at Cornell University, Ithaca, New York.

The papers from the first symposium all recognize that unprecedented change is at hand in research libraries. They also agree that librarians must take charge of digital information sources and organize them, just as they have done with paper resources. They also identify a shift that has occurred in the focus of collection development. That is, with the coming of electronic resources and rapid access to digital collections, libraries have changed the way they consider acquisitions of research materials. They no longer acquire materials solely based upon anticipated need. Instead, they acquire and develop collections based upon what researchers want now. This shift has given the researcher or user a much more active role in the collection development process of academic libraries.

In fact, the first article, by Robert C. Berring, declares the digital revolution already over and suggests that librarians are behind the adjustment curve. He urges them to regain the initiative by assuming a leadership role in managing information and forming new alliances with traditional vendors who, he claims, have an equal stake in managing digital resources. Berring's sense of urgency sets the stage for this series of assessments of the progress and possibilities of digital information in libraries.

Nancy M. Cline gives an overview of electronic options for librarians working through the conversion from traditional print information sources to digital ones. She puts the scholar/user first, suggesting that consideration of user needs should be the primary motive when selecting electronic resources for the library. Libraries must shift their service commitments and resources to what the user wants, not just what librarians believe the user wants. Throughout her presentation, Cline poses questions collection development librarians should consider before making decisions concerning digital resources.

Jerry D. Campbell's essay on creating the new library also places the user at the center when deciding what technologies are to be selected and utilized. He bases his paper upon a survey done at Duke University which confirmed that library users wanted and expected rapid, remote, and full-text access to digital sources. Clearly, digital resources have brought changes in the way scholars do research and in their expectations of what libraries should offer. While noting that expectations may exceed libraries' financial or technological abilities to deliver, Campbell concludes that opportunities to develop a new type of library are at hand.

In the fourth essay, written two years later, Douglas Greenberg looks at how a private research library/archives like the Chicago Historical Society is working to meet the challenges of digital information. He concludes that his institution must not only continue to collect as it has in the past, but also now acquire electronic resources, provide electronic access to similar holdings elsewhere, and even convert its own holdings to a digital format. Greenberg notes that incorporation of digital resources into an institution's holdings has brought new economic challenges. For most libraries, there will only be enough funding for judicious collection development decisions based upon user needs and recommendations. Greenberg's presentation infers that libraries, archives, and museums need to look beyond traditional funding sources to meet the electronic information challenge.

Preservation of collections remains an ongoing problem for libraries. Advancing digital technology, allowing conversion of print and graphic collections to digital formats, promises some relief for hard-pressed libraries. But M. Stuart Lynn, while recognizing the potential of digital conversion for preservation, cautions that the labor intensiveness of digital scanning, issues of long-term preservation, and the need for hardware and software systems stand in the way of rapid or large-scale conversion of print materials to digital resources. Lynn's article is especially useful for its comparison of microfilming preservation to digital conversion, noting that microfliming has the advantages of higher resolution, accepted standards, and a known archival life, while digital preservation offers superior access to data.

In the sixth essay, Anne R. Kenney and Paul Conway, two recognized leaders in preservation and digital conversion, continue the preservation discussion. Conway focuses on choosing the right hardware and software for the job while Kenney elaborates on the advantages and disadvantages of digital conversion. Next, Peter S. Graham addresses the subject of long-term preservation of digital products. Graham identifies two problem areas: guaranteeing the authenticity of digital documentation and providing access to digital collections for indefinite periods. He suggests that technological advances may solve the problem of authenticity of digital reproductions. However, decisions to preserve digital research collections for extended periods require commitments based upon a library's mission and collection management philosophy.

In the closing essay of Part 1, Donald J. Waters recognizes the multiple factors of change and focuses his discussion on what he calls "the political economy" of libraries as they struggle to make a transition to digital resources. Waters makes useful cost comparisons between digital and hardcopy resources.

All the papers in Part 1 suggest that the process of moving a library toward a digital research collection requires dramatic changes in collection management policies and allocation of resources. They argue that librarians must make changes in their attitudes, reexamine the criteria for selection of resources, and give the library user a more active role in collection building. They also look at the conversion of traditional collections into digital formats for increased access and preservation. It is the digital conversion process that provides the bridge to Part 2 of this volume with fourteen articles discussing issues central to selecting collections for digital conversion.

The first two articles are from *RLG Digital Image Access Project*, the proceedings of a March 1995 symposium held in Mountain View, California. Both papers discuss issues that are critical to an institution's decision to digitize collections that it holds. In 1994, nine RLG libraries and Stokes Imaging Services of Austin, Texas, teamed up to select and digitize 9,000 architectural drawings, photographs, and prints relating to a preselected theme, "The Urban Landscape." Based on this experience, Hinda F. Sklar poses and answers some fundamental questions about why collections might be converted to a digital format and Ricky L. Erway discusses many operational issues inherent in a digital conversion project. Sklar and Erway provide a useful background for the twelve essays chosen from the November 1995 RLG symposium entitled *Selecting Library and Archive Collections for Digital Reformatting*, held in Washington, D.C.

This fifth symposium explored strategies for choosing a collection or collections for digital conversion. All the presenters were from institutions that were early participants in digital projects and had a wealth of practical experience to share. They examined the selection process as a special project, with the assumption that archival collections conversion will become an ongoing component of collection management. This examination includes considerations of access, public service, technological requirements, and preservation.

Clifford A. Lynch opens the discussion acknowledging that digital conversion projects are becoming more prevalent in research libraries and reviewing some strategies that must be considered when selecting collections for digitization. Samuel Demas, a collection development specialist, cotinues the discussion by reviewing collection development decisions for print and microfilm collections and suggesting ways to expand those applications to digital collections. Demas urges that the collection development process for selection of digital resources must move past the local perspective to regional and national ones, and beyond the piecemeal, single collection approach to include genres or whole field and discipline concepts. He declares it the obligation of collection managers to use their expertise to influence the selection process of collections for digitization.

Ricky L. Erway, making her second appearance in this set of essays, agrees that librarians and archivists, when working with digital projects, must build upon their experience with traditional formats. At the same time, she acknowledges some of the limitations to what librarians and their institutions can do in the way of digitizing. Erway's article explores what is needed and what decisions must be made in the technical arena for successful digital conversion projects.

Dale Flecker also addresses the technological issues of digital conversion. All projects, he observes, must keep the user in mind by being aware of the hardware and software requirements for access to the digital product. Flecker identifies other cost and access factors to consider when choosing materials for digital conversion.

Despite technological advances and declining hardware costs, funding for digital conversion remains a substantial challenge. It is not a problem, however, unique to the digital preservation format. Nancy E. Gwinn suggests that project directors and library collection managers look to microfilming models for guidance in building the funding needed for digital conversion. Libraries, she points out, have been leaders in convincing outside funding agencies to finance microfilm preservation and they can play a similar role in securing ongoing funding for digital conversion projects.

When choosing collections for digitization, there are "no easy decisions," as Linda M. Matthews observes. She identifies ten factors to consider while making selections. Her views are expanded upon by public service specialists Margo Crist and John Price-Wilkin. They point out that access to information affects the way and extent that library patrons use information and, consequently, access to digital information should be a key factor in determining what collections to convert to digital formats. Crist and Price-Wilkin suggest that digital access should follow the line of traditional print organization by giving users a choice of seeing either selected parts of the work or the whole. They conclude by describing some electronic access tools that offer promise in this area. Karin Trainer underscores the user's centrality to the selection process. Those involved in selecting collections for digital conversion, she emphasizes, must learn more about those who will be using the finished product.

Because of the speed and ease with which print materials can now be copied, copyright infringement has been a longstanding concern for libraries. With the coming of digital technology the copyright issue has taken new twists as Robert L. Oakley explains. He explores conditions under which collections may be digitized and offers some suggestions on how institutions may work with copyright holders.

Criteria for selecting collections for digital conversion also must take into account preservation goals. In the past, decisions for choosing collections for preservation largely focused on deteriorating physical condition, but now, as Tamara Swora asserts, access and informational values should be equal factors for selection. Barclay W. Ogden continues the digital preservation discussion by commenting on the long-term retention of resources in a digital format and the process of converting textual documents to a digital format.

Nancy S. Allen concludes the series of articles with her paper about making digital conversion an on-going institutional commitment. Again, using the analogy of preservation microfilming projects, Allen reviews the components necessary to incorporate digital conversion into an institution's planning.

The essays included in Part 2 confirm that technology and digital resources are bringing libraries improved access to materials, new possibilities for preservation, and opportunities to make their unpublished collections accessible on a scale not before thought possible. Opposing these advantages are the challenges of high costs for staffing and equipment for digital access and conversion projects and the problem of long-term preservation of digital products. High costs and preservation needs, however, are not new. Collection managers have wrestled with these problems throughout their careers. Frequently, it comes down to setting priorities for acquisitions and making hard decisions about what to preserve immediately and what to defer for the future. From this perspective, the incorporation of digital materials into collections is much the same as adding or deferring print and microform materials. Librarians must continue to use the resources they have as efficiently as possible.

These essays offer the reader an opportunity to see how other collection managers have responded to the integration of digital resources into their collections. The papers included provide insights on the costs, problems, and opportunities for digitization as a preservation measure, and they review the questions that must be asked when selecting collections to digitize. Their value lies in the guidance offered to readers who are responsible for managing digital collections or considering their own digital conversion projects.

NOTE

1. The five RLG publications drawn from are: (1) *Electronic Access to Information: A New Service Paradigm. Proceedings from a Symposium Held July 23 through 24, 1993 Palo Alto, California*. Edited by Win-Shin S. Chiang and Nancy E. Elkington. Mountain View, Calif.: The Research Libraries Group, Inc. 1994. 83p. (2) *Digital Imaging Technology for Preservation. Proceedings from an RLG Symposium Held March 17 and 18, 1994 Cornell University, Ithaca, New York*. Edited by Nancy E. Elkington. Mountain View, Calif.: The Research Libraries Group, Inc. 1994. 139p. (3) *RLG Digital Image Access Project. Proceedings from an RLG Symposium Held March 31 and April 1, 1995 Palo Alto, California*. Edited by Patricia A. McClung. Mountain View, Calif.: The Research Libraries Group, Inc. 1995. 104p. (4) *Scholarship in the New Information Environment. Proceedings from an RLG Symposium Held May 1-3, 1995 at Harvard University*. Edited by Carol Hughes. Mountain View, Calif.: The Research Libraries Group, Inc. 76p. (5) *Selecting Library and Archive Collections for Digital Reformatting. Proceedings from an RLG Symposium Held November 5-6, 1995 in Washington, D.C.* Edited by Ricky Erway. Mountain View, Calif.: The Research Libraries Group, Inc. 1996. 170p. Copies may be purchased via RLG's World Wide Web site: http://www.rlg.org/pub.html.

PART 1.
STRATEGIES FOR ACCESS
AND PRESERVATION

Partners and Alliances

Robert C. Berring

The theme of this conference is digital information and the future. It brings together librarians, vendors, and information specialists. The opportunity for both reflection on the past and projection into the future is irresistible. My topic, the potential for future cooperation between librarians and vendors, seems the perfect taking-off point.

My talk is divided into two parts. The first consists of three premises that describe the situation today. The second offers an assessment of where the future may take us.

The premises are three crucial facts we must assume if the purpose of this symposium—indeed, if the field of librarianship—is to move forward. Some may question the truth of one or more of the premises, but we no longer have the time to argue about them. If you disagree with one or more, if I cannot convince you of the validity of each one, there is little point in continuing the discussion. Time is too precious.

Rather than dispute one or more of the premises, one might instead

---

Robert C. Berring is Professor and Law Librarian at the School of Law, University of California at Berkeley.

[Haworth co-indexing entry note]: "Partners and Alliances." Berring, Robert C. Co-published simultaneously in *Collection Management* (The Haworth Press, Inc.) Vol. 22, No. 3/4, 1998, pp. 9-20; and: *Going Digital: Strategies for Access, Preservation, and Conversion of Collections to a Digital Format* (ed: Donald L. DeWitt) The Haworth Press, Inc., 1998, pp. 9-20.

criticize them as self-evident. Such criticism may be valid since basic premises by their very nature should be clear. But there is still virtue in restating the foundations of the current situation in information. If we can agree upon them, we will have a basis for moving forward.

The second part of the paper concerns the paths that are open to librarianship. It will set out alternative responses to the future and alternative futures. It will search for the best strategy for coping with the future.

Before beginning the discussion, however, it is important to address the question of the intended audience for this paper. This is a paper by a librarian written primarily for librarians. Its context will be a colloquy among colleagues. Rather than assuming a neutral, objective stance, the paper will be subjective and blunt. The times dictate prompt action.

THREE PREMISES

1. The Digital Revolution Is Over

Given the trenchant immediacy of Douglas Van Houweling's paper,[1] this may be the simplest of the three premises to accept. He painted a compelling picture of the digital revolution and the fact that it is upon us. His picture of a seamless, easy-to-use information universe is one that every librarian should take to heart.

Librarians are the information professionals. For millennia, they have gathered, organized, and protected information. They have been the forces in society that have preserved the cultural heritage, protecting it sometimes from the very society they served. At the most basic level, librarians are guardians. They guard the treasures of the society.

Much of this function is built around the physical nature of the books and manuscripts librarians are preserving. Books are much more than vehicles for the delivery of information; they are cultural icons. They symbolize more than just data; they symbolize knowledge and culture. A person who holds a book is not just holding a collection of data encoded on paper and bound together; the person is holding a symbol of learning and intellectual progress.

Three quick examples make the point. First, consider the emotional baggage that travels with the words *book burning*, a term that has taken on such power in society that it is even applied to the destruction of nonbook media. To charge someone with being a book burner is to make an emotionally charged statement. The accused is someone who is vilifying culture and meaning. The book burner is a barbarian.

Second, consider the fact that many religions build dogma around a book. The book becomes the expression of the words of the deity made tangible. The book takes on an existence of its own. To destroy it is blasphemy, to alter it a sin. This sanctity of the written word affects the general perception of the book as well.

Third, consider the way our language uses the book as a metaphor for knowledge and meaning. A bookish person is one who is learned, a scholar. The book is a symbol of great power.

This feeling about books is part of the old paradigm of information. It is part of the life of most people in this room, and is likely a part of the experience of most people reading this essay. It is generational. I understand this feeling at a very personal level. I love books.

The love of books awakened in me in my early years has only grown with the passage of time. I love to read, and I collect books as a hobby. What can give greater pleasure than to hold the first edition of a great work like *Blackstone's Commentaries on the Laws of England* in one's hands, to know that it was issued when Blackstone was still alive, and to think of the owner reading it in the late 18th century?

It is that love, that irrational attachment, that seems so natural to those who grew up as a part of the book-based culture that is now on the road to extinction. The law students I teach consider information on a computer screen as completely natural. They are comfortable at a keyboard, and much of the accouterment of book research–indexes and tables of contents–and the inconveniences imposed by the physical attributes of a book–its limitations–seem to them not the necessary parts of a central element in life but the unfortunate drawbacks of an old form of information. They do not hate books, but books do not hold magic for them.

For those of us on the book side of the generation gap, this may be difficult to understand. Some of us see books as having inherent intellectual legitimacy. Digital information is associated with television and low-brow or, at best, middle-brow culture. How many conversations have I had with faculty about the comparative merits of digital- and paper-based information, conversations in which I could demonstrate that one can accomplish digitally everything that can be accomplished with paper that ended with the faculty member simply saying, "Well, it just isn't right to only do it electronically"? And to each of them I reply that of course they are correct–for them, for their part of the generation gap. One learns the habits of research in one's youth, and for most it is very hard to change. But the change is coming.

As a law librarian I have had a chance to see this principle in application. Two commercial databases, LEXIS and WESTLAW, have made the full text of most relevant legal information available online. The amount of information, legal and nonlegal, that is available in full text in each of these systems boggles the mind. When one turns on a terminal and logs on to either system, one has access to the virtual equivalent of the old Harvard Law Library ideal: everything.

Both systems enable the full text of these materials to be searched through a variety of methods ranging from Boolean searching to WEST-LAW's new system that allows natural language queries. Even more important, as a marketing maneuver, both database producers give a free, 24-hour dial-up access number to all law students at accredited law schools. If the student has a modem, he or she can use the databases at any time. They can download information as well. The vendors provide a wide range of training materials, research manuals, in-person tutorials, and even an 800 telephone number that students can call anytime to ask for research help.

For the database vendors this massive investment is part of a marketing campaign, but for those who watch information and its use, it is an experiment of enormous proportions. There are more than 120,000 law students currently enrolled in accredited law schools. Each one has unlimited personal access to a system of legal information that begins to approximate some of the capacities that Dr. Van Houweling described. The systems are relatively easy to use, and the information is valuable.

The students do use the systems. For many law students–in fact, most–the search strategy of choice is to go online. In the advanced legal research course I teach, I see some 120 law students a year. I assign them open-ended research problems. Their default search is an on-line search. I can design a problem that compels them to use paper sources, but if I let them choose, they use online sources. They see the online systems as more efficient and much easier to use than traditional book-based sources.

This is especially telling because law was perhaps the most book-centered discipline. Legal education is consciously built around the use of the law library. Since Christopher Columbus Langdell, the Harvard Law School dean who created the modern form of legal education, declared in 1870 that the law library was the laboratory of the law, this has been the case. Legal publishers developed intricate systems of information organization and retrieval for print sources that were without rival. Therefore, it is significant that in this most traditional and book-oriented of disciplines, the change in information format would come first.

The change is generational. Older lawyers are still attached to the book. Some still view digital information as somehow suspicious or illegitimate. But the change is here. One still hears objections that the price of digital information is too much. Part of this problem can be laid at the feet of LEXIS and WESTLAW. When the systems were first marketed to law firms, the database vendors suggested that these systems did not replace books but were add-ons. They told law firms that the costs of using the systems could be passed on to clients, perhaps even surcharged. Thus, the new systems were not seen as central but as Cadillac systems capable of paying for themselves. When the market for legal services changed and clients grew unwilling to pay for add-on charges, law firms began to view the online systems as costly toys. But the systems are faster, and they produce qualitatively better results when used intelligently. The market will adjust to this fact; indeed, it is adjusting. Law libraries are beginning to cut journal and series subscriptions, and books are being taken off the shelves. The digital databases are becoming part of the center, not toys. If price is the only barrier, then one only has to adjust it and the change is here. The adjustments are being made.

The revolution is over. There will be years of adjustment to come, but the corner has been turned. Digital information is here.

2. Librarianship Is in Peril

These are difficult days for librarianship. Times of economic distress always press hardest on professions that cannot protect themselves with economic or political power, and librarianship finds itself with precious little of either. Librarianship suffers because it is one of the "helping" professions–a service-oriented profession, largely female in composition, that has been undercompensated and undervalued for years. This is not the time or place to analyze how this came about. The point is that many in librarianship are beginning to lose heart. The reasons are easy to see and merit mention if only as place markers.

Librarianship's flagship schools are closing. Columbia University's library school, the school founded by Melvyl Dewey, the creator of the modern American profession of librarianship, is closed. The University of Chicago's library school, long a legend for its demanding curriculum and high-achieving graduates, is closed. The schools at UCLA and Berkeley, both pioneers in integrating technology into the curriculum, both homes of some of modern librarianship's great thinkers, are on the verge of extinction. What does this tell us? It is not the first time a professional school has closed, but it is the first time the most famous, the most prestigious of a profession's schools have shut down. There is no greater threat to a profession than to close down its elite academies.

It is also important to note that these schools were not closed down because of lack of interest by prospective students. More people than ever were applying to the School of Library and Information Studies at Berkeley. Nor are the schools being closed because of atrophy in the subject area. Issues of information are at the forefront of our social agenda. The future of information is the subject of cover stories in *Time*, *Newsweek*, and other popular mass information publications. The vice-president of the United States has a pointed agenda that included information policy. Indeed, this is information's day in the sun. What happened to the librarians?

The problem runs beyond the fate of library schools. It touches on the image of librarians. At a time when information is hot, librarians are not. Librarians have always been identified with books and buildings. Indeed, librarians have named their professional organizations after the buildings in which they work. It is not the American Librarians Association, it is the American Library Association. That identification with an edifice, with a building that is a repository of books, has linked the librarians of today with the books of yesterday.

Librarians have not penetrated the popular culture of today. If you disagree, take this test. Ask someone you know to name a librarian, real or fictional, that they do not know personally. Most Americans would fail to identify a single one. Some very informed folks might recall that James Billington is the Librarian of Congress, but those in the profession know that he is not really a librarian at all. The position Librarian of Congress is too important to be held by a librarian. If any one fictional figure is named, it might be Marian, the librarian from Meredith Willson's *The Music Man*. This musical, though extremely dated, contains the most recent librarian of importance in popular culture.

But the profession's problems are more than ones of popular perception. These are grim days for many organizations. Budget axes are out, and the green gimlet eyes of downsizing gaze upon almost every organization. Libraries, with their big collections, large overheads, and identification with the old system, are natural targets. We see them being trimmed on campuses and in organizations around the country.

Worse, librarians are losing control of their own fate. A new layer of administrative control is appearing in many organizations. As the function of information has risen in importance, structures have changed, but in many organizations, the restructuring has reflected the importance of information but the irrelevance of librarians. Nonlibrarians are brought in to manage things. An excellent example is our keynote speaker at this symposium. Dr. Van Houweling is in charge of information systems at the University of Michigan. He is not a librarian. Note carefully how in some parts of his speech he talked about *us* and at other points he talked about *you*. For all his talent and his marvelous speech, he is not a librarian. Twenty years ago if you had invited the person at the University of Michigan who was in charge of information to come speak, the librarian would have shown up.

The point is that a new layer of professionals is working with information. Librarians may remain the foot soldiers, but we have not been given command of troops, let alone foreign policy. Thus, librarianship is in peril.

3. Librarianship Has Value

Librarianship has value. Is this a controversial statement? There was something special, something different about this profession that called us to it. At the annual meeting of the American Association of Law Libraries last summer in Boston I met with an old friend from my college days. On our way to dinner we stopped at a large reception. My friend, a successful lawyer, was introduced to several law librarians. When we left, he commented, "That must be the largest group of people I've ever seen where they each could make more money doing something else."

His remarks struck home because so much now is based upon money. Success, even happiness, is judged by how much one makes. But librarians have chosen a different course. And there is something that unites us, some spirit of equity and service, some desire to get things done and move the ball along. Those great old guardian librarians that I spoke of protected society from itself. Librarians have always tried to help. Even those who worked in private sector positions were oriented toward service, toward hooking up the person who needed information and the information that was needed. We have always identified with the user. We have fought to keep books on the shelf for him, and we have tried to help him use them.

Some may cringe at this laudatory description of librarianship but, then, feeling uneasy with praise is typically librarian. I say these things and emphasize them here because it is vital for the profession of librarianship to realize that it has a core of values that is worth fighting for, because if the profession is to survive, it will have to fight. Librarians have sometimes turned away from the fight because it was unseemly or too dirty. But the only option is to lose. And the professions that would replace librarianship do not have the core of service values just discussed.

Librarians are the good guys in this movie, but they are surrounded and outnumbered. If librarians are to fight, it will have to be with the knowledge that librarianship is worth fighting for.

PREPARATION FOR BATTLE

Identify Your Allies–The People We Cannot Expect to Help

We cannot win this fight without allies. Librarianship is dying on its own. The professional organizations cannot save us either. They are too big, too bureaucratic, too immersed in their own rules and inner squabbles. In the hope that professional organizations did hold promise I became president of the American Association of Law Libraries. But while I trust my presidency accomplished a few good things, I soon realized my term was too short and the membership too hard to mobilize to take on these larger problems. The professional library organizations will not be librarianship's salvation. There is hope for smaller groups within cities or even within organizations to have influence and sufficient shared interests to work together, but these will not be enough for the profession as a whole.

Nor can librarians look within their own institutions for help. In academic institutions librarians will find little assistance. The brittle status system of academia relegates librarians to a level lower than the faculty. On most university campuses the faculty are the royalty, the students are the yeoman, and the staff are the serfs. The librarians are the faithful retainers. We model ourselves on the faculty; we wish to be like them. Evidence the long battle to win mock forms of faculty status. Yet librarians are not and will never be faculty on most campuses, and when the budget reaper comes calling, like all faithful retainers, librarians will be expected to give up life for the masters. The other staff, long envious of the resources devoted to librarians, will offer little help.

The situation is no better in the private sector. The functions that librarians provide best are often difficult to quantify in terms of the modern "bottom line," and the funds consumed by information always seem so large and so alluring a target when it comes time for budget cuts. Librarians must constantly justify themselves and what they do to the organizational powers in the private sector. These are not likely allies.

Will the public rise up to fight for libraries? With a few heartening exceptions the answer is surely no. Librarians have made the mistake of hiding their costs. When Jerry Campbell discussed his user survey at this symposium, one point rang out loud and clear. His patrons want everything, they want it now, and they would be aghast if they had to pay for it.

Consider this hypothetical: my library has a terrible physical plant. If I attempted to solve this problem by charging admission to my reading room, swearing that the money would go to improving the physical facilities, there would be a holy war. The students see the library as free. But I wager that if a commercial enterprise set up shop across the street from the library, called itself Study Halls R Us, and charged students a $2 entry fee, promising to provide a clean, quiet study environment and perhaps even a small collection of course books to use, the students would use it and pay for it. They would see it as providing a service, a service they were willing to pay for.

This scenario is useful because it shows we have failed to communicate our value to our patrons. The same is true of librarians in every environment. They have endeavored to serve yet never conveyed the value of the service provided. This can be bemoaned, but it is the case, and for that reason our patrons will not save us.

Identify Your Allies–The People Who Might Help

The group most likely to help are the information vendors. Librarians have always regarded the vendor community with healthy skepticism. Vendors merit suspicion because they are concerned with profit, because they want to sell things to librarians. Yet vendors may be librarians' last allies. How can this be? There are three important reasons: first, librarians and vendors have shared interests; second, vendors have resources; and third, vendors value our input.

The vendors share the librarians' problems with the paradigm shift in information from paper to digital. Just as librarians must struggle to accommodate decision makers who are part of the old world while serving increasingly demanding patrons who are part of the new, vendors must struggle to develop and market digital products that are ready for the shift but that do not anticipate it by too much. They see the change and are wrestling with ways to manage it. They are wrestling with issues of intellectual property just as librarians are. Kathryn Downing's[2] presentation was right on point. The vendors are struggling to develop some workable mechanism for getting information distributed and the products paid for. Just as librarians are long identified with guarding books, vendors are identified with selling books in old patterns, through old systems. They too must change. Ms. Downing was refreshing in the honesty of her description of the problems that publishers are working through today. These are many of the same problems librarians face.

One factor is both different and attractive about the vendors: they have resources. Living in a world where most resource pies are shrinking, each of us is constantly searching for potential sources of money and support. If librarians are going to save themselves in this digital world, it will take money. When it comes to money, there is only one pocket available–the vendors'. Though vendors too are downsizing and cutting back, they are eager to build in new markets, and they know that money must be invested.

The example of the law schools may help. Here LEXIS and WEST-LAW have been willing to invest enormous sums in training law students to use full-text online legal research systems. They have achieved a level of penetration into the law school community that has never before been reached. The money they spend on law school programs totals more than all of our law school training budgets combined. Of course they anticipate the money will be made back, but they are willing to invest upfront at a level that none of our institutions can match. How we deal with this phenomenon and our deeply ingrained suspicion of it will be covered in the next section. At this point, simply note that the vendors have resources.

The third and most crucial factor is that the vendors are open to us. They are willing to listen; they want our help. Reflect on what has transpired at this symposium. James Michalko, president of RLG, has been here to talk with us. Kathryn Downing, president of Lawyers Cooperative Publishing, is here. If one goes to an American Association of Law Libraries meeting now, one will find the CEOs of LEXIS and WESTLAW as well as senior management there. These folks are not there to sell; they are there to talk and listen. They see we have interests in common and want to work with us.

This symposium is a perfect example. RLG has brought us together to discuss the future. RLG sees the change in information. Just as librarians are trying to cope with the change, RLG is attempting to retool itself to make its services more useful, more a part of the new world of information.

RLG is an example of how librarians and vendors can work together. The organization grew out of the cooperation of great research libraries and the vision of some librarians who saw that cooperation could serve the interests of their own libraries and others as well. It is an early example of solving problems through blending the role of librarians and the spirit of creative entrepreneurship. RLG is a product of this synergy and a potential partner for cooperation. The organization solicits our advice. One cannot imagine a vendor more open, more creative. RLG is not alone; other vendors are ready and waiting.

It is an unparalleled opportunity for librarians, and it will not last. During the change to digital information many things will be fluid. The vendors *need* allies. Once the change is in place, a new pecking order will exist. The vendors will not need our help. The new paradigm will be set. This is librarians' last brave moment in the sun. We potentially have powerful allies. Let us use them.

THE BATTLE PLAN

Once the allies have been identified, the question becomes, what do we do? The answer is so plain that one might miss it. Librarians must manage the change. Many components will be in sore need of management. The change will not occur for everyone at the same time or pace.

I visualize information users as a great herd of cattle. There are adventurous cattle far ahead of the herd, the ones who lead, who take chances. These are the hackers and database specialists–the people who take apart a computer and reassemble it for fun. They are far ahead of most of us at this symposium, though I suspect a few are lurking in our midst.

After that comes the rest of the herd–the great middle group that will need to be carefully led, prevented from panicking, and kept on the right track. The stragglers are at the back–the ones who will have to be guided the whole way.

It is not news that most middle managers, most decision-makers, are in the middle of the herd at best. They will need help. Librarians must deliver that help. We must be the cowboys–the ones who lead and guide the herd. And this is where the vendors come in. They want this change to be managed, and we can help them manage it. We understand our patrons; we have always understood how to train people in using information. We understand the way people think when they use information tools. This is an asset with value. We can use our expertise, our position, to help bring the change about.

This means articulating the needs of our patrons, getting involved with vendors as they design systems, making sure the systems are good ones, and then bringing them to our patrons, to our organizations, and helping to put them in place.

Too often the librarian is the protector, the one who fends off the vendor. We must become partners with vendors. This will be hard to swallow for some. A few years ago, suggesting to librarians that they work closely with vendors would have been like suggesting they go camping with a bear. While librarians should keep in mind that every sane vendor is self-interested, they should also realize that vendors can be cultivated for our mutual benefit.

The plan is to go back and build bridges. Within each institution represented at this conference, within each organization that librarians belong to, we must be creating mechanisms to facilitate cooperation between librarians and vendors in the development and marketing of the new digital products. RLG may be an especially opportune place to begin. The act of hosting this symposium is invitation enough. If librarians can build on this foundation, perhaps with RLG as a first partner, there can be a brighter future for all concerned. The time is now; the moment of opportunity will not linger. Let us recognize the value of librarianship and the reality of the digital revolution and build something wonderful.

NOTES

1. Dr. Van Houweling, vice provost for information technology at the University of Michigan, gave the opening address at the 1993 symposium entitled *Electronic Access to Information: A New Service Paradigm*.

2. Kathryn Downing, president and chief executive officer of Lawyers Cooperative Publishing, spoke at the 1993 symposium on the concept of fair use.

Local or Remote Access: Choices and Issues

Nancy M. Cline

As research libraries move toward a new service paradigm, there is increasing discussion of *local systems* and *remote users* and growing confusion about what these phrases mean as we work to provide more electronic resources to our users.

The need to access more–and more diverse types–of electronic information resources is introducing as many new issues for library management teams as it does for users. There is, for example, heightened concern that in purchasing electronic access we will be eroding the basis by which we evaluate research libraries–namely, the collections; concern that we are paying money for things that do not ultimately exist as objects in our institutions' inventories; concern that we will be overwhelmed with new or additional users, or that users will no longer need our services and will seek direct access to what they need. And there is simply the increasing anxiety that relates to the phenomenal rate of change affecting research libraries today.

We are faced with more choices, and there are many significant components of the decision-making process. Our enterprise–academic and research libraries–is undergoing rapid and important change. It is important that we engage fully in the process to make certain that the outcomes benefit our students, faculty, and others we serve.

To lease or buy? This question surfaces constantly in terms of automobiles and housing, and has now become inescapable in libraries as we look to fulfilling the information needs of our respective clientele. The question

Nancy M. Cline is Roy E. Larsen Librarian of Harvard College, Harvard University, formerly Dean of University Libraries at The Pennsylvania State University.

[Haworth co-indexing entry note]: "Local or Remote Access: Choices and Issues." Cline, Nancy M. Co-published simultaneously in *Collection Management* (The Haworth Press, Inc.) Vol. 22, No. 3/4, 1998, pp. 21-29; and: *Going Digital: Strategies for Access, Preservation, and Conversion of Collections to a Digital Format* (ed: Donald L. DeWitt) The Haworth Press, Inc., 1998, pp. 21-29.

takes on larger dimensions as we consider whether an electronic information resource should be made available *locally* or accessed *remotely.* In the contemporary information context, we are seeing these words lose their meanings.

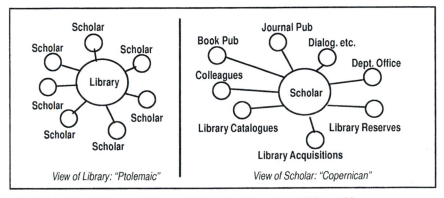

View of Library: "Ptolemaic"   View of Scholar: "Copernican"

Sack. John R., *College and Research Libraries,* November 1986, p. 539.

I use here an illustration from John Sack's article "Open Systems for Open Minds: Building the Library Without Walls," published eight years ago. It challenges us to rethink the expectations of scholars as we move away from the "library as a place" to interacting with users in the electronic setting. It is useful as a concept, an image, as we think about the changing paradigm for services.

TWO PERSPECTIVES: THE ELECTRONIC RESOURCE AND THE USER

The question of local versus remote can be considered from two completely different perspectives–the electronic resource itself or the scholar, the user. Let us first explore these perspectives because they are important in our planning.

From the perspective of the electronic resource, it may be considered local when it is physically acquired by the institution and made available as (a) a stand-alone system (e.g., CD-ROM database); (b) a CD-ROM database on a LAN; (c) a networked CD-ROM within a library; or (d) a tape file loaded on the library's computer or campus network. However, with exception of the stand-alone CD-ROM, these configurations may support remote user access, e.g., through dial-up access to a CD-ROM network.

An electronic resource may be considered remote when it is used through a contract arrangement but is housed offsite and accessed by a variety of means (e.g., phone lines, public access network, multiple institution networks, or the Internet). However, the institution may require its users to be onsite to access the resource and may choose not to provide remote user access where access is beyond the confines of the library. At Penn State, an example would be the Dow Jones News Retrieval Services; the electronic resource is remote since it resides on the Dow Jones computer, but the access is limited to local use from a dedicated terminal in a library reference room.

From the user perspective, however, an electronic resource may be considered local when access is tied to a precise physical location (e.g., terminals within the library). It may be considered remote when access is available from a number of physical locations—meaning that one can use it remotely from the comfort of home, the residence hall, an office, etc.

At the outset, we already have the potential for added confusion in the simplest of terms—remote and local. In planning and budgeting discussions, it is important that we have a common understanding of which perspective we are considering when discussing the choices between local and remote access. For today's discussion, I maintain we must think in terms of the user. As we move to a new paradigm of service, the scholar must be placed at the center of our thinking.

What do we already know about user needs and expectations? What does the feedback from users indicate? Almost without exception, they tell us they want more access, both in terms of the scope of electronic choices and the diversity of access points to those resources. They are clearly in favor of having more information resources accessible locally, e.g., from wherever they are working!

User Needs and Satisfaction

In most cases, the choices which libraries make regarding electronic resources are tied to perceptions of user needs and satisfaction. Issues such as reliability, speed of response, hours of access, hours of availability, level of detail, and ease of use are often cited as key factors.

Products and the Operating Environment

Next we can look at another array of choices—those describing the environment in which a product can be used. Often, at least in the current marketplace, the product itself dictates constraints. There may be limits to the technology, limits to the software and networking capabilities, or limits which the producer chooses to put in place, such as the number of concurrent users. These choices of an operating environment can range from stand-alone systems; local area networks in a closely defined physical setting; local area networks in a physically distributed setting; institutional networks (single campus and multiple campus); access from remote sites into an institutional network; public access networks; multiple institution networks; the Internet, etc.

How many different types of information resources can be used in the current computing and networking environment? How many do you intend to offer? There is a growing array, including OPACs, bibliographic and indexing tools, statistical resources, and full text, image, and audio databases. How these resources are made available can include a range of options from open sharing among network participants (following the basis of the traditional library model) to the pay-as-you-use models. So, not only the type of information resource but also cost issues will be factors in determining whether to mount resources locally or to rely upon a database that is mounted at another site.

Many of the constraints result from the manner in which the information providers choose to sell or lease the information resources. The question may be less one of location of the resources and more one of who controls the pricing structure. Achieving reasonable agreements for the use of electronic information resources takes negotiation and compromise.

Service and User Populations

Finally, and perhaps foremost, there are decisions about who will be served. Who will be provided access to these resources? How many can be accommodated? As libraries make choices about which information resources to provide in networked settings, we are finding that we must often make choices or determine priorities among the constituencies served by our institutional budgets. For academic libraries, students and faculty lead the list. For other research libraries, the clientele may be different. For all of us, there is a growing set of questions about how broad a base of users can be served. And there is growing concern that the needs of independent scholars, those without specific institutional affiliations, could be overlooked in the planning of networked libraries.

All these factors represent choices facing our libraries. Each category needs careful deliberation in the context of the institution's mission, its organizational characteristics, and its budget.

COSTS–OBVIOUS AND NOT SO OBVIOUS

The total costs are often hard to determine. To acquire a specific database product for use only at one's own institution may appear the simplest route, but even in this instance, there are often complicated variables to assess.

If one is planning to acquire a database for mounting on a local system, costs will include, for example, the cost of the database, of storage on the system, and of indexing or mounting special software. They will also include staff costs in developing access capabilities, preparing instructional materials, etc. On the other hand, if one plans to access the database via another facility, many costs will be determined by fees set by the provider.

For libraries, it is critical to identify a predictable annual cost in order to manage budgets for these resources (since costs are not typically passed on to users). The costs of people–staff and librarians–throughout the process will be among the hardest to determine.

Another difficult cost to compute is the cost borne by users. The productivity of faculty and students is a very real factor in a research context. Saving them from hours of labor is a significant factor, but not one that shows tip on the budget sheets in our libraries or even academic departments!

PENN STATE–CASES IN POINT

I would like to address a specific set of choices we have been struggling with at Penn State.

MathSci. In the past academic year, the Penn State mathematicians have been bombarding the libraries with requests to put the MathSci database online as a part of the resources accessed through LIAS (Penn State's campuswide information network). This resource is needed at nearly all our campuses, of which there are 21 scattered across the state, and the math faculty want desktop access. So far, we have only the CD-ROM version available in the Math Library at University Park. It is possible to acquire a license and some hardware so that this database could be provided on a local area network at the University Park campus only, but this would not fulfill the needs of the 20 other campuses.

We are not particularly interested in acquiring the raw data files of MathSci and developing our own search software because there are some special searching characteristics that are essential to the successful use of this database. The development costs to do our own local search software would be out of line. In addition, we are aware that the American Mathematical Society is looking into other options for providing access to this resource. We have decided, despite very reasonable requests from the faculty and our interest in providing good service to the math community, to delay in the hope that other options for institutionwide access will be developed.

Medline. Another example is the Medline database as we have implemented it at Penn State. Medline had long been identified as a resource for which there was significant interest and an expressed demand from users. The various criteria considered in arriving at our choice of how to provide it included the special searching characteristics associated with this database, the need to deliver access to multiple Penn State campus locations across the state; the need to support authorized users in dial-up access; the desire to avoid issuing passwords; the compatibility with existing hardware; and the need to predict future costs. A team of librarians and computer professionals worked on the recommendations. Ultimately, we implemented the CD PLUSNet system, mounting the datafiles on an IBM RS 6000 that is fully accessible by the libraries and the campus networks.

Z39.50. For several other databases, we had the choice to offer a gateway to the RLG Eureka interface to a suite of databases or to implement a Z39.50 server that would preserve the native searching features of the LIAS system. The implementation of Z39.50 has certainly reframed our decision-making at Penn State. Only a year ago we had to mount a resource locally in order to be able to use the LIAS search commands. Now, with Z39.50, the searching can occur with LIAS commands running against a database held at another location, so long as the remote database supports the Z39.50 protocol as well. With a student population of over 70,000—most of them undergraduates—it is important to capitalize on their LIAS search skills. At the same time, we can avoid the costs associated with local loading of the database. We recognize that at some point we may reach a level of usage where it becomes more economical for us to mount some of these databases locally. This decision will require monitoring over the next few years.

Change is constant. Decisions reached today will have to be reconsidered periodically since conditions and costs will inevitably change. Predicting usage of new systems and new databases is an art, not a science. Providing new tools and new capabilities for users will change patterns of behavior, precipitating new and different usage patterns.

ERIC. We had been using the ERIC database on CD-ROM at the University Park campus. Nearly every other campus expressed a need for this, but we had no idea of the volume of unfulfilled needs. We recently mounted the ERIC database on the library computer, making it network accessible to all library locations and searchable through LIAS. Users took to it with ease. In one of the first months of its availability on the network, there were nearly 60,000 searches, and use continues to grow. We also experienced an unexpected doubling of the use of the microfiche collection!

USER-CENTERED SERVICES

Research libraries must continually assess the electronic resources and make strategic choices of which to buy, which to license, and which to access cooperatively with colleague institutions. Choices will be tied to the institution's plans, values, and mission. Clearly attention must be paid to all the prevailing laws, regulations, and policies. Librarians will need a high tolerance for ambiguity in this rapidly changing context, and interaction with users will take on new dimensions since more and more of them will be using our resources remotely.

I will restate my remarks from a recent ALA program: "As we redefine academic libraries, embracing a different balance of electronic resources, we have a provocative opportunity to put the scholar at the center of our focus. . . . If we emphasize user-centered services and programs, we may do a better job in developing strategies for the future."

In this symposium, as we address a new paradigm for services relating to electronic resources, we have an excellent opportunity to bring that focus on the user into our planning for change within our research libraries.

As we do so, we must learn more about what we call scholarly communication: we need to look at how scholars work, to understand how they use information, how they create or share, seek or ignore information. We need to listen more carefully to what users, our scholars, are seeking.

Document delivery capabilities will be very important to our clienteles. There will probably need to be a range of choices, from the rather ordinary to the more refined and elegant services. The technology available to the user will shape the choice of product (photocopy, fax, electronic copy, etc.), and the providers will range from libraries, personal collections, electronic copy shops, to custom document delivery service providers.

One of the challenges for librarians and information professionals will be to catalog and identify discrete units of information in ways that will accommodate systems for document delivery. For example, we will need to make certain that the delivery of an article, as we have known it, includes the image blocks that are integral to it, even though they may be stored in different formats in separate places in the systems. Books, portions of books, segments of audio files (oral histories or speeches), images–all these will require identification as to their place of storage in order to provide the distribution capability for document delivery.

Regardless of where something is physically/electronically stored, we must know who is responsible for the authentication of the item and how it will be accessed and shared. The lines are blurring in terms of local ownership and remote use, but for those responsible for acquiring the goods or the access to them, it is a time to plan for responsible choices and to make certain that we can collaborate effectively as the paradigm shifts.

Let me take a minute to discuss a recent decision made for Penn State's libraries. We have been providing access to a table-of-contents database, CARL Uncover, through Internet access using a fixed number of passwords. User feedback revealed various pros and cons of this particular resource. We have also been reviewing the options for a table-of-contents database, notably Faxon Finder and OCLC's ContentsFirst. A task force was charged with evaluating the options. Among their major considerations were the extent of control over the communications network environment; the number of simultaneous users that can access this increasingly popular type of resource; the costs for tapes versus the costs for access and service; the scope of the database (coverage of journals); the ability to tailor the display with local information such as our own call numbers; and the type of electronic forms that could support both interlibrary loan processes and document delivery.

The desire to have locally mounted data evolved from problems that were being experienced with response time using the current vendor and the Internet. The institutional network provides a better, more responsive environment. A locally mounted database would be searchable using the LIAS search engine, and thousands of students would not need to learn separate search conventions but would build upon their LIAS skills. We would not have to restrict the number of users so that more people would be able to concurrently access the database whenever needed at all locations of the university. The recommendation also included an assessment of the specific number and types of journals included in each database as well as the depth of the indexing provided. The task force also placed a priority on the ability to develop a document delivery capability that would be responsive to our users' needs. The task force did not recommend the least costly option in terms of stated price but instead recommended an option that offers the maximum benefit for students and faculty and that provides a strategic direction upon which we will build related services.

COLLABORATION, BOLD THINKING

Alliances will be increasingly important to libraries in the networked environment. We need to cultivate more alliances/partnerships/collaborative ventures among libraries and also with our teaching departments, research centers, and the telecommunications and computing organizations. We will also have to learn how to collaborate effectively while fostering healthy competition (grants, industry funding, etc.) in order to continue improving the complex systems through which we provide electronic resources.

Strategic planning for our institutions becomes increasingly important. It is important to know where we intend to go. It is also important to think boldly and strategically since so many of the details and variables will continue to change. We should focus attention on defining strategies–and remain flexible with some specific shorter-term objectives.

I have certainly not outlined a *single* well-defined pathway. My intent today was to present the full range of choices so that we can develop strategies appropriate for our own institutions. It is not a simple matter of choosing between local and remote access. Local resources will begin to look just like the remote systems and vice versa. The matter grows increasingly complex every week as new options reach our desktops. And, while the choices may become more complex, the interface for users must become smoother.

Risks will need to be taken–particularly if we place the user at the center of our planning and decision-making. The choices are complex and require continuous monitoring. And the choices taken will be more visible to more people than any single serial title, any major reference book ever was!

The paradigm shift opens exciting opportunities. It is time for us to take hold of our enterprise, to redesign academic and research libraries, and to ensure our continued and vital role in education and research. It is a time in which we must use change to our advantage, to lead change, and to thrive on it.

Building Xanadu:
Creating the New Library Paradise

Jerry D. Campbell

Weave a circle round him thrice,
And close your eyes with holy dread,
For he on honey-dew hath fed,
And drunk the milk of Paradise.[1]

In addressing the topic of new service opportunities that come with new access choices in the changing library environment, I want to begin with some general observations. It is my intention by means of these observations to help establish a perspective from which we might begin to explore new opportunities. Such perspective is important because it will inevitably shape the outcome.

Even the believer finds it difficult to sustain enthusiasm for that which is prophesied when the gulf between prophecy and fulfillment spans too many years. The prophetic act, or making predictions, strikes quickly. A few words spoken or typed and it is done. Computers, the dreamers have long told us, will change virtually everything about libraries and the knowledge environments of our universities. Meanwhile, the years have come and gone. And that which is predicted, even if it eventually becomes reality in some recognizable form, occurs slowly, incrementally over a generation. Small changes happen around us continually. We get accustomed to them, and from morning to morning things appear stable, almost unchanging.

At the same time, prophecy rarely deals with details or provides a

Jerry D. Campbell is Chief Information Officer, University of Southern California, formerly Vice Provost for Library Affairs and University Librarian at Duke University.

[Haworth co-indexing entry note]: "Building Xanadu: Creating the New Library Paradise." Campbell, Jerry D. Co-published simultaneously in *Collection Management* (The Haworth Press, Inc.) Vol. 22, No. 3/4, 1998, pp. 31-40; and: *Going Digital: Strategies for Access, Preservation, and Conversion of Collections to a Digital Format* (ed: Donald L. DeWitt) The Haworth Press, Inc., 1998, pp. 31-40.

blueprint to the future. It attempts, rather, to see far ahead, to point the way with generalities, to identify trends, to draw out implications. By so doing, it seeks to give us momentum in seizing opportunities and creating the best of futures. It seeks also to give us a head start at recognizing and avoiding potential problems. But it does so without many specifics.

No wonder even those who hope in the dream can become disillusioned. Not only do the years pass, encouraging the scoffers and nay-sayers, not to mention those who dislike the dream, but we do not know with precision what we should do next. Every day presents new choices, each of which will alter the outcome in its own way (a chaos theory of life, if you like). We can achieve the impossible or we can fail in the sure thing. Those who dream dreams and make predictions leave reality to others. In other words, what actually happens is all up to us.

Eventually some dreams do come to pass; the longest night ends in dawn. And the best of dreams appear suddenly to take some particular shape. All those small, incremental changes achieve critical mass. So it is with the effect of computers on higher education and research libraries. After 20 years of expecting too much, *too much* is now actually possible. Just last week I heard Cornelius Pings, the president of the Association of American Universities, say in a moment of reflection, "The long promised revolution is at hand."[2] It now seems that all we ever dreamed and more are possible. We might observe that just because it was predicted did not mean that it would not come true.

ALL YOU EVER DREAMED AND MORE

If a new and different knowledge environment is, indeed, emerging, how will libraries (and librarians) be affected? At least in the print-on-paper era, we all–students, faculty, and staff alike–had become familiar with how the system worked. We knew that bibliographic storage and retrieval functioned within certain almost universal parameters. We could go from library to library and know basically what to expect. We were also conditioned to expect that our own preferences as users were not likely to have any success in altering those universal parameters. The new knowledge environment, however, is just emerging. This means that it is necessarily incomplete; the parameters are not yet fixed. The revolution may be at hand, but it is far from over. So no one knows exactly what to expect, but everyone has an opinion about how he or she prefers to retrieve information. And our users may be expecting more than we can deliver–a veritable information Xanadu.

Such a fluid situation presents us with a great opportunity. For the first time in many years (a century really), we have the chance to redesign our libraries, or rather, the whole campus knowledge environment, in fundamental and pervasive ways. We also have the opportunity and means to involve our users in the process. Indeed, if we can rise above the natural temptation to think that we, as experts, already know what is best and, instead, become experts on discovering and delivering what our researchers want, perhaps we can create the ideal user-centered library. User involvement is also crucial because in the new knowledge environment it is possible that our libraries will have information competitors. We may no longer be insulated from user concerns because they are captive audiences. This means that it is all the more necessary for us to understand the preferences and expectations of our users in creating the new library paradise.

User Preferences and Expectations

But, then, how do we find out what our users are dreaming? To some degree, this is new territory for us as research librarians. Only in a limited sense have we been involved in what the commercial world calls consumer analysis.[3] Many of us have the feeling that user needs and certainly their expectations are changing today, but we really have little sense of this change and virtually no historical data by which to measure it. So this in itself, learning more about our users' preferences and expectations, constitutes one new service opportunity, and we need to explore it and get better at it.

For purposes of illustration, let me share with you some information about users' expectations at Duke. In so doing, I am not suggesting that the findings can be generalized but am suggesting that the process may be helpful. Two of our reference staff members, Ken Berger and Rich Hines, recently undertook and completed a project to learn more about the emerging attitudes of Duke library users about library services in the growing electronic library environment. Their project began with a position paper setting forth their concept of the Duke library in the year 2010. The year was pushed out to 2010 so that the description of the library would not be unduly threatening to us in the present. After all, 2010 is a long way off. The paper was used to generate discussion and develop a series of questions designed to elicit opinions and preferences about the library of the future.

The second stage of the project involved retaining an external marketing firm to refine the questions further by conducting focus groups among all major elements of our campus constituency. In the third stage, these refinements were worked into a set of questionnaires which were administered to the appropriate groups on campus. The questionnaires were designed to provide us with dependable information about our users' opinions and interests in this transition toward the library of the year 2010.

The final stage of the project, in process at the time of this symposium, consists of understanding and evaluating the implications of the findings. This last part, of course, is a most interesting and vital undertaking.

The full results of the project will be published, so you will have an opportunity to see them if you wish. For this occasion, however, let me share just a couple of the findings with you. The first of these relates to the second objective noted above, that of determining the expectations for a computerized library. The information was collected by asking respondents how critical certain characteristics would be to the ideal library of the future. Specifically, the question read, "Each member of the university community has different information needs. When considering your needs, please tell us how important each of the following features of an ideal library would be to you." Response was given in the form of a five-point scale, 1 being "not at all important" and 5 being "critically important."

Quick and Complete Access

Among those items that rated a "critically important" score with a significant portion of our users was the element of speed. While speed has been a factor in past years, this new emphasis represents a quantum change. In the paper environment, delays of days or weeks were not unusual, and user expectations were adjusted accordingly. Now, however, our users have begun to experience the rapidity of electronic access and have readjusted their expectations. The new emphasis on speed has significant implications not only because it must be a factor in the development of new services but also because it is spilling over to user expectations for materials in traditional formats. We are increasingly being asked to develop rapid delivery of books and to fax journal articles to academic departments.

The study cross-checked this emphasis by asking another question: "Please tell us how much you agree or disagree with the following statements about what libraries might be like in the 21st century." This question was tallied on a five-point scale, with 1 being "strongly disagree" and 4 being "strongly agree." Five was reserved for "not sure." Once again, speed was among the categories that dominated the "strongly agree" response. It was joined by the category of completeness. Our users wanted quick and complete access. This confirmed the emphasis on speed and, in addition, revealed the users' interest in electronic access to full documents rather than bibliographies or abstracts only. The question relative to completeness was posed in this fashion: "The ideal information source should provide a means to review topics and abstracts quickly, but also allow access to entire documents when desired." Seventy-three percent of our users strongly agreed.

What emerges from this kind of project is a profile of our specific user community. That profile gives us more insight than we have ever had about their interests, the differences among them, and their expectations. In the matter of making access choices, we now know with some relative accuracy how many of our faculty are active users of electronic information and how many who are not yet active users want to be. We also know how many radically disagree with the whole premise that libraries should change. And in constructing the new knowledge environment on any individual campus, I believe this is essential information to have.

Virtual Presence of Information

Fortunately, the changing needs and expectations of our users are accompanied by and connected to the sweeping changes taking place in computer technology. The only way we can hope to respond to the new expectations is by means of the technology that raised the expectations. Thus it is both a challenge and an opportunity to harness technology for service. This, of course, is nothing new. We have offered technology-assisted service in many ways over the years. We are just called on now to go much further than ever before. We must contemplate reference systems that need little human intervention and access that is provided by software rather than the work of catalogers. It must be our goal to provide access for more people than ever before to more information than ever before by creatively harnessing technology.

Indeed, because of technology, we are increasingly offering large amounts of information to users wherever they are located as long as they have some manner of networked connection to our libraries. We may characterize this as a virtual presence of library materials. While this in itself is a tremendous improvement in our service capacity, it presents even more new service challenges and opportunities. For instance, we are creating a circumstance where our users are not within sight of reference librarians as they encounter the mysteries of research. How will we respond to their questions? Should (and can) we create a virtual presence for information professionals to match the virtual presence of the information? And how will we manage a knowledge environment where our old boundaries of convenience and expertise no longer apply? Suppose a faculty member in Duke's math department consults a government documents database and seeks help from the librarian in the math library. This is a likely scenario, and great numbers of referrals are not desirable. We have begun to redefine the library environment through the use of technology, but we must do more. To stop at this point could leave us and our users with more problems than solutions.

YOUR WORST NIGHTMARE COME TRUE

The most awesome power of technology is its power to drive the imagination wild and stimulate the appetite for everything. Imagine the unrestrained growth of information and database access accompanied by chaotic, haphazard, or nonexistent control mechanisms and finding aids. Imagine the Internet as it now is in a few years. Imagine being asked to make sense of the Internet by virtue of some AACR-2-like manual application of a "bibliographic" record. Worse, imagine a new generation of information users for whom our methods are anachronistic and our information mediation inadequate.

This is to say that we also have the opportunity to make a real mess of reenvisioning the knowledge environment. One way we can do this is to drift into the future, holding on to our old ways and leaving the action up to the commercial world. With this approach, our users will flounder in an increasing assortment of proprietary systems and invisible sources of information. As opposed to *user friendly*, such an environment might be called *user oblivious*. Only the fortunate and the lucky researchers satisfy their information needs in such an environment. If we take this approach, our users will be forced to seek help elsewhere. Remember, we made sense of information in the paper world, and we must apply our skills to do the same in the electronic information world.

While technology is one of the keys to success in creating the new knowledge environment, we can also make a mess of it if we forget or otherwise eradicate the human presence. In the Duke user study referred to above, we asked our users to list for us the characteristics of a good database or information source. One of the characteristics listed by a majority of users was "information professional available." In other words, they told us that a good information source is one that includes a librarian. How we include librarians in an increasingly dehumanized environment is the challenge. If we achieve a virtual presence, it must not be by virtue of automatons with sterile computer "voices." We must convincingly humanize the technological library.

MAKING DREAMS COME TRUE

Even if you suppose that we come to understand what our users want and how to provide it to them in a user-friendly and humane way, there is still the challenge of how to get there from here. Our organizational models evolved from and are consistent with the print-on-paper environment. They correspond to the characteristics of that environment and reflect its peculiarities. And, of course, most of us have specialties in one or another aspect of this environment. The new more technologically based information world, however, not only ignores the old boundaries but crosses them freely, mixing responsibilities, tasks, and territories.

Creative Thinking and Experimentation

It is in responding to and pursuing the new options that our paper-based models often prove inadequate or even detrimental. This is why, in part, many libraries are exploring the methods of total quality management and team-based operations. Such management methods not only focus on the user, but also diminish the hard edges of the old departmental boundaries and foster a systemwide ownership of the new challenges and problems created as we increasingly employ technology to deliver information in new ways to an unseen public.

Achieving success eventually requires that we let go of much that has served us well and develop new organizational and service models to replace it. As one who has often voiced this claim and experienced some professional resentment as a result, I urge Research Libraries Group members to foster among themselves an open and supportive spirit that welcomes, even encourages, creative thinking and experimentation. The prophets who have given us the rough parameters of the dream have left the details of reality up to us. Be bold and let one another be bold in making the dreams come true.

Education for Users and Ourselves

Harnessing technology, understanding our users, learning new systems of management, and developing new organizational models, however, require not only our best efforts but some new skills as well. It is neither a cause for embarrassment nor shame that the challenges of our time require new skills of us. Indeed, most of us expect that if the rate of technological change continues or increases, continuing education will become a routine part of each individual's working life. There is some irony in the fact that, for the most part, we come from institutions whose business is education but that most of us have not established substantial and ongoing staff training programs. Such programs should be provided at library expense, and a specified amount of training each year should be mandatory for each library staff member. It is urgent that we develop staff training programs, as have many progressive industries, if we are to equip ourselves to tackle a daunting agenda.

I believe that we are somewhat better at educating our users than ourselves, though our approach is usually episodic and unsystematic. While we got by with this approach during a time when library procedures were more stable, our efforts in this regard will be severely taxed as changes in the information world pour forth. Thus, new attention to user education is now necessary because of the practical needs in navigating new systems and the public relations damage that may result from surprises (welcome or unwelcome) among the more powerful members of our constituencies.

By user education, I mean something a little different from our customary use of the phrase. What I have in mind is more akin to what the business world means by marketing and sales. I am sorry to borrow again from industry, but we librarians need a better process for introducing new features, products, and services to the research world, and unfortunately, we do not have satisfactory terminology as yet to characterize this process. Because of the rapid changes accompanying technology, we can no longer focus primarily on first-year students or other new members of our communities. With increasing frequency, we need to reach everyone. Sound user education in this sense, therefore, is an essential characteristic of the emerging library.

FINANCING THE DREAM

For most of us, the toughest challenge of creating what I have called the new library paradise really appears with the issue of finance. It is easy to contemplate the new opportunities; it is stimulating to discuss them; but it is hard to pay for them. In this regard, our budgets are like lie detector tests. Regardless of our rhetoric, our budgets reveal our real priorities.

It was unpredictable and unfortunate that the technological challenge for libraries arose as libraries were experiencing the worst period of inflation and constrained resources in memory. Failing in their efforts just to stay current with the development of print-on-paper resources, libraries faced the added challenge of exploring the vast new technological terrain. Declining rates of interest in recent years also reduced the revenues from endowments, further limiting budgets. Efforts to raise money from external sources became a necessity for more libraries than ever before. In other words, there could hardly have been a more frustrating time in the modern history of libraries to have encountered the challenges and opportunities of creating the new library paradise.

Effective Use of Limited Resources

While there is no financial magic to solve this problem of constrained resources, technology itself may offer some relief. If we become proficient at providing better information-related expert systems and if we can discover how to use technology to create the virtual presence of information and information professionals, then perhaps we can use our limited resources in ways that are increasingly effective. Toward this end, as location diminishes in importance, we may explore sharing reference experts (perhaps area specialists) among several institutions by means of networking. Similarly, we may also experiment with acquiring source-specific reference services from publishers and information vendors. Indeed, there are perhaps dozens of such possibilities we have yet to discover and explore, and some of them may offer significant cost effectiveness.

Even so, we still must find a way to begin, and it is difficult to move forward with bold new efforts without using funds already committed to our stewardship. In order to accomplish a transition, even over time, we will have to reallocate dollars previously devoted to long-standing library operations. This means that no matter how great the promise for the new information environment, it must be bought at some price to present research and service. This makes it all the more imperative that we work closely with our users during this time of transition. We must help them understand the issues, the choices, and the tradeoffs, and we must, in turn, be responsive to their concerns as we make fundamental decisions about the library of the future.

While it is unlikely that libraries will experience great budget increases to cover the new costs of technology, they may find some fresh fundraising opportunities. Such opportunities may exist particularly for seed money with which to construct and test new information-related delivery mechanisms. Because of the rapid appearance of technology-related opportunities, this makes the regular governmental and foundation sources of funding seem inordinately slow. Nonetheless, they provide important sources of support for those experiments that can wait for the funding cycles. For this reason and because there is a certain excitement and entrepreneurial flavor associated with ventures in new technology, helping develop the infrastructure for the new information environment may be especially appropriate for individual donors. There are those to whom this challenge might have special appeal.

THE DREAM BECOMES REALITY

The prophets and dreamers were right. Computer technology is in the process of changing libraries in fundamental ways. The new service opportunities inherent in these fundamental changes are vast and largely unexplored. For you and me, this is the great challenge of our age–and an equally great opportunity. If we are wise, diligent, and focused on our users, we indeed have an opportunity to create a new library paradise.

NOTES

1. From Samuel Taylor Coleridge, "Kubla Khan," in Allison et al., editors, *The Norton Anthology of Poetry*, Third Edition. New York: Norton, c1983, pp. 564-5.

2. This remark was made during a conversation with the Board of Directors of the Association of Research Libraries.

3. See my recommendations on this point in "Shaking the Conceptual Foundations of Reference," *Reference Services Review* 20/4(1992): 29-35.

Return to the Valley of the Dolls: Reflections on Changing Lanes Along the Information Superhighway

Douglas Greenberg

Several years ago, I wrote a paper on some of the general problems for humanists associated with the use of technology in teaching and scholarship.[1] The paper contained a fantasy about a next-century scholar who was able to write a major multimedia monograph on that great literary artist, Jacqueline Susann.

I will not subject those of you who escaped that paper to a complete rendition of the fantasy. Through hyperbole it attempted to establish that scholars of the future will have access to amounts and kinds of information of which we can only dream, and that such access will make possible a kind of scholarship and teaching that is quite difficult, if not impossible, to accomplish at present. The title of this paper derives from that other essay, which imagined what sort of work might be done on Susann in the future and how such works of literary genius might be assessed by a technologized, poststructural critique of the genre of popular fiction that she helped

---

Douglas Greenberg is President and Director of the Chicago Historical Society (CHS). He was formerly Vice President of the American Council of Learned Societies. A graduate of Rutgers and Cornell Universities, he was affiliated with Princeton University for over a dozen years, as a faculty member, and, in the mid-1980s, as associate dean of the faculty. Teacher, administrator, speaker, editor, author, board member, he is active in all aspects of the scholarly enterprise, and the recipient of numerous honors and awards for his work. He encourages visits not only to CHS, but to its home page on the World Wide Web (http://www.chicagohs.org/).

Note: A version of this paper will appear in *Biblion*, Spring 1996.

[Haworth co-indexing entry note]: "Return to the Valley of the Dolls: Reflections on Changing Lanes Along the Information Superhighway." Greenberg, Douglas. Co-published simultaneously in *Collection Management* (The Haworth Press, Inc.) Vol. 22, No. 3/4, 1998, pp. 41-53; and: *Going Digital: Strategies for Access, Preservation, and Conversion of Collections to a Digital Format* (ed: Donald L. DeWitt) The Haworth Press, Inc., 1998, pp. 41-53.

to initiate. The title of the resulting imagined monograph was *Valley of the Trash: Jacqueline Susann and the Semiotics of Mediocrity in Late Twentieth-Century American Literature.*

I thought myself rather clever for using an example combining both the power of emerging technologies and important trends in humanistic scholarship and teaching. My intention was only partially satirical, for it seemed to me then–as now–that scholarship in the humanities has significantly broadened and deepened in both method and sources and that this expansion of the ambit of scholarly work is remarkably well-suited to the power the new technologies offer. Name your discipline–social history, literary criticism, art history, philosophy, area studies of any kind–and I think you will agree that what scholars are now doing matches beautifully the capacities of electronic technology to locate information, access it, and analyze it.

The paper was actually quite prescient, if I do say so myself, since it predicted that technologies we now associate with the World Wide Web would soon make images, sound, and full-motion video available to anyone with a desktop computer of reasonable power. Three years later that technology is exploding, and we are only at the beginning! So I can feel quite smug and proud of myself. However, I have also come to recognize that my naivete about the economic context of technological change was much more impressive than my prediction of universal access to the diaries and library check-out cards of Jacqueline Susann.

I understood then that technology is not free. In that paper and in a series of essays on similar subjects I emphasized that the financial resources required both to put such technology on the professorial desktop and to create the electronic information to which it would provide access were not trivial.

I worried aloud a good deal about where the dollars would be found. Now, with the National Endowment for the Humanities on the block and public support for higher education dwindling, I am a good deal more concerned. Technologist friends had assured me that there was nothing to worry about, that everything would soon be so cheap that we would be foolish to be concerned about a phenomenon–the high cost of technology and electronic information–that was likely to be transitory in any case. While I did not accept this argument entirely, it did seem to me that the history of technology indicated that consumer technologies tend to decline in price until they are either replaced or disappear.

IN THE SLOW LANE

At the time, I was vice president of the American Council of Learned Societies. I was also a sometime teacher and writer of history and had spent four years as a dean at an RLG institution with very substantial resources. In all of these capacities, however, I was blissfully unaware of the real, sometimes hidden, costs of technology, despite my concern that it was unevenly distributed among institutions and disciplines. Thus, my little fantasy about Susann, although qualified significantly by what I knew to be the limits of budgets, seemed nonetheless to be within reach and worth spinning out if only to think about what would be possible had we but world enough and time.

I have now changed lanes on that old information superhighway, however, and lead an institution that possesses 20 million of the sort of items I continue to believe will be crucial to humanistic scholarship in the future. These collections include 1.5 million prints and photos, one million books (some quite rare), four million feet of news film, oral history interviews on tape and in transcript, a locomotive, the bed on which Abraham Lincoln died, and the original puppets from and kinescopes of the old Kukla, Fran, and Ollie television program. All should be accessible to scholars or at least findable by scholars over the Internet. At the moment, none of it is. Why that is so and what might be done about it are really my main topics today.

From the vantage point of the (slow) lane I now occupy, the information superhighway is a pretty intimidating sort of roadway. Not only can't I pay the tolls very well, but I don't have the horsepower to stay at the minimum speed, no less keep up with the Maseratis (called universities) that whoosh by me every now and then, not obeying the speed limit since there isn't one; this superhighway is actually a racetrack and those of us driving Model-Ts are having our troubles keeping up. But institutions like mine serve precisely the same constituencies as universities: college- and university-based scholars and their students. In addition, we also must serve the general public, the schools, and businesses that know a good thing when they see it: research resources for which they do not have to pay.

I do not want to exaggerate, however, the difference between universities and the independent and private research institutions of which the Chicago Historical Society (CHS) is only a middling-sized example. The dilemmas I am about to describe inhere in the collection and creation of research information in the electronic age. At one level, I have already described them: money, money, and more money. At another, however, money is not the first issue. For an institution like mine, in fact, even the need for electronic access to the collections is, while one on which we work steadily, not the driving issue that most of us would like it to be.

The reason for this is our very catholic mission with respect to the history of Chicago and the country. Our collection policies prescribe some limits on what we can take into the collection but are (at least for the moment) sensitive enough to the range of things that scholars will likely want that they give us very little guidance about what we can reasonably say "no" to.

I shall return to some of the peculiar problems of private independent research institutions, about which I have learned some hard lessons in the last year, because a significant number of such institutions are part of the RLG community, and we hold precisely the sorts of collections that scholars will be requiring in the future.

NEW TRENDS IN SCHOLARSHIP

But let me turn now to some of the conditions that all repositories of research materials must face. To begin with, transformations of the subjects and objects of humanities research and teaching in the last three decades have dramatically altered what the potential user of research collections is likely to be interested in finding. These transformations are familiar, but a quick sketch may be of some value.

First, scholars in the humanities are now interested in the experience, literary accomplishments, and artistic production of people who were barely a blip on the scholarly horizon 25 years ago. The list of newly included categories is long; although race, class, and gender are a convenient mantra, the actual scholarly work is more subtle and complex than such broad categories imply.

Second (and related), including groups at one time ignored or disparaged by scholarship has opened a new universe of individuals for scholarly study by philosophers, art historians, literary critics, and historians. The brilliant biographical treatment of an 18th-century shoemaker by Alfred Young is just one of innumerable examples.

Third, a slightly different class of scholarship focused on the experience and productions of groups, rather than individuals, has also expanded exponentially. In this sort of work there is relatively little information available about any one member of the group, but cumulative bits and pieces of many lives may help to construct another set of interpretive insights to illuminate social experience or artistic output. One of the early examples of such scholarship was Joan Scott's *The Glassworkers of Carmaux*. The list of significant works that have used this method, termed *prosopography* by Lawrence Stone, is enormous and reaches into every avenue of the humanities.

Fourth, the humanities have also expanded their methodological tool kit to accommodate these new subjects. Since the 1960s, therefore, the application of quantitative methods of analysis and database technologies has swept over all the humanistic disciplines. Although it would be inaccurate to say that the use of computers and quantitative methods has become a prerequisite for scholarship in the humanities, without such methods and technologies humanistic scholarship would be far less rich and productive. Some of the subjects to which I have just referred could not have been studied at all without computers. Humanists rarely used the word *data* when I entered graduate school. Today they not only use it, they analyze it, and they expect research repositories to be able to provide it.

Fifth, in addition to new subjects and methods, recent trends in scholarship have also set researchers to identifying new sorts of materials with which to work. Text–ink on paper (whether in manuscripts or printed sources)–will not always do the trick. At CHS, for example, we are as likely to be asked for photos, prints, textiles, architectural drawings and models, sculptures, radios and jukeboxes, children's games and puppets, as we are for newspapers, books, microfilm, and manuscripts.

And this brings me to my sixth point. Each of these trends–the creation of newly legitimated subjects of humanistic inquiry, the identification of newly significant individuals and groups for study, and the application of new methods of analysis to the work of the scholar–has created a demand that research repositories must be prepared to satisfy.

From the vantage point of the Chicago Historical Society, I am always astounded that our collecting policies in the past have been as farseeing as they have been and that we are able to provide wonderful materials for scholars of the new as well as the old breed. But we do so at great cost and much more slowly than we would like. In addition, our future collection policies are unsettled, given our limited space and even more limited resources to create new space.

Thus, the problem that research repositories face is more than financial; it is also strategic adaptation to new conditions of scholarly and educational work. An important component of those new conditions is the growing capacity of new technologies to carry not only information about scholarly resources (which is primarily what RLIN now does) but the actual resources; that is, not only the catalog entry for an item but an image of the item itself. Technology, joined with the transformation of scholarly work in the last several decades, creates a set of appetites that institutions like mine need to be prepared to satisfy to remain what we are: an essential feature of the infrastructure of North American scholarship in the humanities and social sciences.

NEW CHOICES, NEW PROBLEMS

I am disinclined to say that these two factors, changing scholarship and changing technology, can easily be separated from institutional policy. All libraries, archives, and museums have always had to make tough choices about what to accession and what to reject and deaccession. Hard choices have always been imposed on even the wealthiest institutions regarding where to invest resources for the future. But I believe the simultaneous emergence of powerful technologies for the storage, retrieval, and use of images and text, combined with what can only be called an entirely new set of scholarly disciplines, imposes an agonizingly difficult set of choices and problems on all research libraries, archives, and museums. Let me give you some examples, drawing on the experience of my own institution.

First of all, CHS must continue to do almost everything it has done in the past. That is, we must continue to care for the collections we already have, some requiring very sensitive environmental controls. We can do some deaccessioning, but that is itself an expensive and time-consuming process, not likely to create much by way of economies to apply elsewhere. This general requirement immediately limits my range of choices for the future.

Second, CHS must continue to accept into its collections new materials of a traditional kind: books, manuscripts, ephemera, photographs, museum artifacts, and so on. These materials must be processed and made available for use, a task with which we cannot keep up now.

Third, CHS should begin to digitize materials already in the collection to make them available on the Internet, beyond our own building. Our photos, for example, are a priceless resource on the history of Chicago and the country (just ask Ken Burns), but our cataloging of them is incomplete and difficult to use, and there is no electronic access to them either at CHS or anywhere else, although that will soon change.

Fourth, in addition to doing what we have always done and to digitizing existing holdings and their records, we should be prepared to accept into our collection materials already in electronic formats, whether quantitative or text or image. We are entirely unprepared to cope with either preservation of or access to this entirely new class of research materials, but we have been offered such items and will be offered much more as time goes on.

Each of these tasks is one that a responsible institution ought to regard as a critical part of its responsibility to its user community. To employ an ugly word, I have no idea how to *prioritize* these tasks. (I deliberately use the word *user*, by the way, although I know that the word *reader* is now more in fashion among library folk. We have users; they do not just read–they look, they touch, they examine–and they also read.) In any case, as the English philosopher Mick Jagger once said, What can a poor boy do?

Unfortunately, the problems are even more complex. All that I have outlined here must be accomplished in an institution only now installing a local area network, having no universal staff access to the Internet, even e-mail, and with no online public access catalog. You will not be surprised to learn that I regard the installation of a LAN, Internet access, and an OPAC as essential underpinnings for the future. Nothing else can go forward without them, and they are being installed even as we speak.

But the retarded state of technology I found when I arrived at CHS about 18 months ago is an instructive case that brings me to some of the differences between independent research institutions and universities. Why, I hear you ask, was CHS so backward? Having changed lanes on the information superhighway, I asked the same question. A short story helps illustrate what I learned.

Soon after I came to Chicago I had the opportunity to talk with an unidentified former university president who now heads a nameless federal agency whose initials are NEH. We chatted amiably, and he asked me what sorts of things institutions like mine needed. Newly shocked into reality by the absence of computer terminals in our excellent library, I said immediately that if I could have one item for our research collections, it would be an OPAC. He was shocked to hear that we did not have an online catalog and pointed out that when it became clear that his university needed one, they had regarded it as such a necessity that they simply "found the money" and went ahead.

I responded by asking how much tuition had risen at this university the following year. The answer was 6%. In other words, if we were to think of what we all do as a business (which I know we do not), we would say that the university in question had to make an investment in new equipment in order to remain competitive in the marketplace and that it passed along the cost of this new equipment to its paying customers. That is precisely why CHS has not had an OPAC in the past: We have virtually no paying customers to whom we can pass the cost of investment in new equipment. We must find the resources to do these things within our existing operating funds–hard enough to maintain at current levels, no less to increase.

In this sense, therefore, the situation of independent research institutions is radically different from that of the colleges and universities. Needless to say, such institutions all differ from one another. Many carry on other functions besides their research functions. The Huntington Library has gardens and an art gallery, the Newberry Library has exhibitions and public programs, the Folger Shakespeare Library has theatrical productions, and so on. In our case, we also have a very significant museum. The museum function has tended, for obvious reasons, frequently to overwhelm the research function, and I would bet that there is not one Chicagoan in 100 who knows that we are also a great library.

The museum function is also difficult to fund, and it also ought to be taking better advantage of new technologies. In addition, it also needs to respond more effectively to the latest trends in scholarly work. As a result, as we plan for the future, we must have our eyes on two prizes simultaneously: One is that which all libraries and archives need to address: providing the fullest and most effective access to the largest part of our collections for the largest number of users. The other, however, is closer to what in a university would be an instructional rather than a research goal: to think not merely about access but also about a structure of access for a different sort of collection use that advances our educational mission.

These two items of agenda are not incompatible, but the need to do them both simultaneously complicates our lives considerably and also makes things a lot more expensive. And there are other questions as well. For example, should our future OPAC provide access only to books and manuscripts, making use of one of the standard and proven library systems, or should we attempt to create an integrated catalog for all our collections with one of the less tested, but very powerful Windows- or Mac-based museum systems that tries to do what the sorely missed RLG Archives and Museum Information System project (AMIS) intended? The integrated catalog has great appeal to us and to our researchers, but many of you are veterans of some of the early attempts at library computerization so you know the sort of risk we run.

I also regard presence on the Internet and World Wide Web as vital to our future viability–but not cost free, especially in the need to have staff who provide for the care and feeding of electronic resources (hardware and software are the least of it).

Such considerations apply to other institutions of our type. And the sad lesson of the New-York Historical Society has not been lost on me or my board of trustees. So, the "implications of the new environment for researchers at my institution and for my budget" are significant. Let me say a few words about how these implications might be addressed.

HARD CHOICES, NEW OPPORTUNITIES

The first point is unexceptionable and in the most general sense is not much different for universities and colleges than for research institutions. We cannot do everything; we must therefore be sure that we are doing the right things. Our choices need to be conscious ones, and we must be prepared to do less than we have done in some areas in order to take on a new responsibility.

For example, at CHS, we have been worrying a good deal about cataloging and its impact on staff time. Here is an issue that libraries understand well. As a nonlibrarian, not initiated in the mysteries of MARC records, I suggested to members of my staff that we might be able to find a way to cut down on the length of each catalog record. I was greeted by looks of horror, but I was quite heartened to discover at RLG's Primary Sources Forum in March 1995 that this is not an idea of such terrifying proportions that it must be rejected out of hand.

It is that sort of choice we need to be making as a way of permitting us to do other things. In addition, and this point will undoubtedly disturb some of you, we need to start thinking about our operations as businesses and finding opportunities to turn our collections into income resources. Although I recognize the distaste for that view in some quarters, I want to reiterate to those of you from higher education that I do not have any students whose tuition I can raise, whereas I have lots of faculty members from your institutions clamoring for everything from an OPAC to an Internet connection in the CHS library to everything, in other words, they would have in a university library. To respond I need income streams besides my endowment and other slowly growing sources of income. The occasional corporate or foundation grant, however generous, will not get us where I believe my institution needs to go technologically–on a par with a good university library–because my most basic needs have to do with ongoing digitizing and cataloging rather than with one-time purchases of hardware and software. All this sends me in the direction of marketing my collection.

America Online, CompuServe, and the other online services have machines and wires, but they have very little to load on those machines and send over those wires. They need content, and every institution represented in RLG has loads of it. At CHS, we intend to exploit this advantage in every way we can. Licensing arrangements for use of our materials in publications, sale of our photos in electronic and hard-copy form, opportunities for percentage participation in film and TV projects, educational CD-ROMS, and a pay-for-research business for private-sector companies that use our collections are among the business opportunities we plan to either expand significantly or initiate in the next several years. Other people already make a good deal of money from the use of our collections, and we intend to support the maintenance of scholarly access to our collections by marketing the collection as the content for which electronic information providers are both desperate and willing to pay.

This is a departure for CHS. Like most places, we have always received a trickle of income from licensing fees for use of materials in our collections. What we plan now is something different: We are going out to find the customers, we are signing deals with businesses that are prepared to recognize our intellectual property rights, and we are developing new products and services of our own that will help to pay for the new technologies we must have to do our work properly.

This does not mean, I hasten to add, that a faculty member at a college or university will have to pay for access to our OPAC or to use our library. And those needing reproductions of our photos or photos of our artifacts for their own use will pay a minimal fee to cover our costs. Much of our material will be available over the World Wide Web or whatever comes next; but usable reproductions of high-resolution photos will be costly, and filmmakers and television producers may find us asking for considerably more financial consideration in the future than we have in the past.

I am sensible that many in this room will not share this position. As someone responsible for the health of his institution and the care of its collections, I would only ask those of you who find these ideas disturbing to provide me with an alternative. Again, if you work in a university or college, you are all charging much more for access to your collections than I am charging for mine, but you do it through the mechanism of tuition, which is at least in part a fee paid by students to subsidize not only their own access to your collections but also that of the faculty.

COLLECTION DECISIONS–A KEY ISSUE

When all is said and done, however, efficiencies in cataloging and new income streams will not give me all the breathing room I need to serve our users as effectively as I would like, and I cannot envision any near-term future that will permit people to do the kind of research that I outlined in my original paper and its fantasy on Jacqueline Susann. Now, with a changed perspective, I think that in addition to finding better ways to do things and better things to do, and more money to pay for them, we ought to go back to first principles and think about our collection policies.

The proliferation of new scholarly subjects and methods on the one hand, and the rise of new technologies to facilitate scholarship on the other, does not (as I believed several years ago) really allow us to think very differently about our role as the memory of our civilization. I was naive to think that any library or group of libraries, even rich and technologically sophisticated ones, could afford to expend collecting energies on the perfect Jacqueline Susann research collection or anything of the type. New technologies are already making it much easier for scholars to find what they need, but they need more and more diverse materials than they have ever needed before. The day when libraries and archives can collect everything that any scholar is ever likely to need is not near at hand. It was, in fact, nearer at hand when Harvard was founded in 1636. And while some of us might sympathize with Oliver Wendell Holmes's dictum that "Every library should be complete on something, even if it were only the history of pinheads," the plain fact is that not even the Chicago Historical Society, with far more resources than it has now, will ever be complete on the Great Chicago Fire of 1871, let alone the entire history of the city or all the pinheads in it.

In other words, we need to think hard and be even more clever about what we do and do not accept into collections. This means actually asking our users what they need. It means doing market research. Our users may not for the most part be paying customers, but they are customers and we are in business to serve them. If I once thought that someone would want to preserve all of Jacqueline Susann's drafts of her books, I now think that, while it might be possible and might even serve some useful scholarly purpose, someone will have to choose to do it at the expense of another choice. The most significant change imposed on us by the new technology and the new scholarship is, finally, not so much what technology to use and how to use it, but rather what to collect. Our collection decisions will be more arduous than they have ever been because the range of choice is so much greater.

There are some hopeful things we can say and some constructive things we can do about this rather daunting prospect. We can be more collaborative about collections; we can share technological resources; we can be thoughtful and strategic about what to digitize and for what purposes; we can combine preservation for the future with access for the present; we can establish better cooperative arrangements with other repositories; we can think in terms of access rather than ownership; and we can be willing to provide materials to users just in time rather than have them available just in case. In other words: We need RLG and the promise that is implicit in the consortial arrangement that RLG represents.

RLG is the agency that will make some of these tough decisions easier. At a time when NEH is in danger of disappearing and in a society that has never supported its libraries, museums, archives, and scholars properly, the collective power of the members of RLG should be impressively useful in addressing our common problems–not library problems in some parochial sense but even more fundamental issues having to do with the nature, extent, and character of the research enterprise itself.

Such issues are profound, in other words, in whatever lane you may happen to be traveling on that old information superhighway and however much horsepower you may have under your metaphorical hood.

THE HEART OF THE MATTER–MONEY

But let's not kid ourselves. Behind all our careful contemplation and technological sophistication, the money question still looms. And it looms more seriously now than at any time in my professional life. Before I close, I cannot resist ticking off just a few of the threats that we need to confront:

- In the US, the National Endowment for the Humanities, National Endowment for the Arts, Institute for Museum Services, and National Historical Publications and Records Commission are all in danger of disappearing. At best their budgets will be radically cut. (Where have the presidents of your universities been in defending their centrality to the cultural life of the country? How much more vocal would they have been if it had been the National Science Foundation or the National Institutes of Health rather than NEH on the chopping block?)
- Area studies funds throughout the federal government and especially those on which many university libraries have relied are also at serious risk.
- Public higher education is being eviscerated. (The state of California now spends more money on prisons than on colleges and universities. The City University of New York, one of the great democratic institutions of the country, is being torn apart by shortsighted and simpleminded budget cutting.) And the worst is yet to come.
- Public attitudes towards scholars and scholarship, toward colleges and universities, are at an all-time low.
- Major private research institutions and museums throughout the country are in serious financial difficulty. The New-York Historical Society appears to be the first of many tottering on the brink of collapse.
- Scholarly publishing is at least in the doldrums and, according to some, in a serious financial crisis; this affects all our library budgets and, even more important, will almost certainly eventuate in the closing of several major university presses. The learned societies are only a little healthier and, for the moment, blissfully unaware of the

potential difficulties they will face as electronic publication becomes easier and more effective.

- Museum attendance is down throughout the country. The very idea of scholarship in museums is under attack in no less an institution than the United States Congress, while the American Association of Museums is silent. Competition from the likes of Disney and Nike Town challenges museums daily. Corporate, foundation, and private donor support for basic functions is more and more difficult to come by, while programmatic ambition and financial need grow.

And I could go on.

In short, there is hardly a sector of the nonprofit research arena that can be said to thriving, although some individual institutions are doing quite well. (Or at least that is how it looks from the slow lane.) The simultaneously dwindling support for educational and cultural institutions in the public sector and the private sector should alarm everyone in this room. Reversing this trend is just as or more important than keeping your pedal to the metal on the information superhighway. It is on that somewhat sobering note that I pull onto the exit ramp and close this talk.

NOTE

1. "Get Out of the Way If You Can't Lend a Hand: The Changing Nature of Scholarship and the Significance of Special Collections." *Biblion* 1993;2(1):518. The same fantasy appeared with two others in another paper, "Technology and Its Discontents: Some Problems and Possibilities for the Humanist in the Virtual University," in John Mulvaney and Colin Steele, *Changes in Scholarly Communication Patterns: Australia and the Electronic Library*, Canberra: Australian Academy of the Humanities, 1993, Occasional Paper No. 15, pp. 131-146.

Digital Preservation and Access:
Liberals and Conservatives

M. Stuart Lynn

The sentry in Gilbert and Sullivan's operetta *Iolanthe* noted that he some-times thought it comical that every boy or girl born into the world alive is either a little liberal or else a little conservative.

In the world of digital technologies, every little piece of information is electronically reduced to a collection of liberals and conservatives, other-wise known as 0s and 1s. This almost miraculous world of digital technol-ogies continues its relentless march, what George Gilder termed "the descent into the microcosm." Costs continue to halve every two or three years, or performance or capacity doubles over the same time frame. And there is no end in sight. In recent years, we have seen the compact disk—a digital device—bury the analog long-playing record; newspapers that trans-mit photographs in scanned digital form; and more recently the dramatic shift in the U.S. away from current analog standards of television technol-ogy and towards a digital standard for high definition television (HDTV). And the ways in which we communicate and collaborate are being trans-formed by these same digital technologies.

THE INTERNET PHENOMENON

About a year or so ago, a now famous cartoon of a dog appeared in the *New Yorker* magazine. In that cartoon, the dog was standing before a

M. Stuart Lynn is Associate Vice President for Information Resources and Communications, University of California Office of the President. At the time of this symposium, he was Vice President for Information Technologies at Cornell University.

[Haworth co-indexing entry note]: "Digital Preservation and Access: Liberals and Conservatives." Lynn, M. Stuart. Co-published simultaneously in *Collection Management* (The Haworth Press, Inc.) Vol. 22, No. 3/4, 1998, pp. 55-63; and: *Going Digital: Strategies for Access, Preservation, and Conver-sion of Collections to a Digital Format* (ed: Donald L. DeWitt) The Haworth Press, Inc., 1998, pp. 55-63.

networked personal computer. The caption was, "On the Internet nobody knows you're a dog." I surmise that future linguists will regard that cartoon as the defining point when the word *Internet* fully entered the vernacular. Now we are bombarded with Internet literature, books, and articles in both electronic and paper forms, the latter being out of date by the time they reach the bookstores. Tools such as Gopher and Mosaic are revolutionizing the ways in which we access information across the world's networks. Traffic across the global Internet continues to grow at astounding rates, compounding at over 14 percent per month, and the number of people connected directly or indirectly to the Internet grows at similar rates.

Daily we are bombarded with newspaper articles about the National Information Infrastructure, about mega-mergers among telephone and cable TV companies and network and content providers. Much of this is hoopla that has less to do with dissemination and communication of educational and scholarly information and more to do with how to deliver 500 channels of mud wrestling to the home to feed the world's insatiable appetite for passive entertainment and numbing out. These pastimes mean big money for these large corporations. However, while they talk about what can and should and should not be done, and who should do it and when, and with whom, the Internet continues its relentless march forward. The Internet is where the real action is, fueled by the rapid advances in digital technologies, computers, and communications.

THE SHIFT TO DIGITAL

We are all aware that digital technologies hold great promise for the world's libraries as well as for the publishing industry, revolutionizing how we capture, store, disseminate, and access information and how we cope with the exponential growth of recorded knowledge. This conference focuses on how these technologies can be applied to the preservation of scholarly materials, such as books, serials, photographs, manuscripts, videos, and slides; and to enabling worldwide access to these digitally stored materials across global networks.

Digital technologies decline rapidly in cost and improve in performance. What is not practicable today will be tomorrow. By contrast, the costs of analog technologies such as paper, video, sound—and even microfilm—decline slowly, if at all. In fact, they tend to increase. If cost decreases occur, it is generally because of the economies of scale associated with mass manufacturing, so that, for example, the economics of traditional book and journal publishing are closely tied to the need for large markets.

However, it is not only declining costs that are providing the impetus for the shift to digital. There are other motivators, such as the reliability of reproduction and of transmission at great distances. Photocopies, for example, lose in quality at each successive stage of reproduction, as do microfilms with each generational copy. For these and other reasons, it is only a matter of time before the cost/performance curves cross and digital technologies come to dominate in any given area. Those wretched liberals and conservatives will be everywhere.

MAJOR OBSTACLES

Digital technologies offer the potential for access at a distance to the intellectual resources of our libraries. The rapid—indeed exponential—growth in the reach of the world's open networks, in particular the Internet, opens the door to the realization of Erasmus's 16th-century dream of a library "with no limits other than the world itself."

What are some of the obstacles that inhibit the realization of this dream, that inhibit turning the promise of digital technologies into reality? What do these obstacles mean for preservation and access? I would like to briefly review three major hurdles to be overcome:

- The hurdle of converting between the analog world and the digital world and vice versa, for example, scanning paper books on the one hand and providing access to those scanned images on the other.
- The hurdle of ensuring that these scanned digital images can be stored in a form that will be accessible 500 years from now to meet preservation requirements.
- The hurdle of implementing the storage and distribution systems needed to provide access at a distance across the world's networks.

Analog to Digital and Vice Versa

The reality is that, notwithstanding all the potential advantages of digital technologies, at the level of actual use analog technologies are better suited to the needs of human beings. Unlike computers, we human liberals and conservatives do not think in 1s and 0s but prefer the warm and fuzzy world of paper, sound, and video that we can touch, see, read, and hear. One of the challenges is indeed in how we convert back and forth between the use of digital technologies for storage and transmission and analog technologies for human presentation and interaction.

We can, for example, scan brittle books to convert them to digital images in a number of ways. One way is to scan the books directly using high-resolution production scanning equipment. At Cornell University, in a joint pilot project with the Xerox Corporation and the Commission on Preservation and Access (the CLASS Project), we have scanned over 750,000 pages–or about 2,000 books or book equivalents–in a production setting at moderately high resolution reducing them to digital form. From these digital images we have produced high-quality paper facsimiles, printed on acid-free paper, that should last several hundred years; indeed, our faculty often prefer the crisp new facsimiles to the brittle and often crumbling originals. These facsimiles can be bound and reshelved for traditional forms of access or printed on demand in response to researchers' needs.

We have also prototyped network access to the scanned images from computer workstations located across our campus and across the Internet worldwide. Directly from their desktops, researchers can rapidly access and browse Cornell's embryonic digital library.

Bitmap Images. I must emphasize that we are talking about scanned pages that are essentially digital photographs, or so-called bitmap images. We do not convert these images to machine-readable text through optical character recognition (OCR) technology although we have the option of doing so later. There are several reasons for this:

- OCR technology is not sufficiently accurate without hand editing, which is relatively expensive, particularly when applied to many of the older fonts. Our goal has been to develop a process that is cost competitive with microfilming. As OCR technology improves, it can always be applied later to the scanned bitmap images.
- For preservation purposes, we wish to capture the original format of the book.
- Books contain substantial amounts of image material such as half-tones, engravings, and graphs, not to mention material such as mathematical equations, that do not lend themselves to OCR technology.
- Bitmap image formats provide a lowest common denominator that enables us to capture most classes of materials and freely interchange the digital images among different computer environments.

I suggest that for retrospective digital conversion of books for preservation purposes, image scanning will dominate. Relatively few documents will be converted to structured text formats such as SGML (Standardized

Generalized Markup Language). The costs would be too expensive. This is in contrast to what will dominate for new texts, particularly those that originate in electronic form.

The major component of image capture and storage production costs is the labor cost of handling fragile pages. These production costs are therefore quite comparable to the costs of microfilming. Our studies also show these costs to be less than those of photocopying. Incidentally since the copyright has expired on many if not most embrittled books, we have been able to build much of the infrastructure for the digital library unencumbered by having to address complex issues of control of intellectual properties.

Microfilm and Bitmap Images. We can also produce microfilm—for archival purposes—from the scanned digital images. With today's technologies, the quality of the digitally produced microfilm on the whole might not be as good as that obtained from directly microfilmed books using conventional methods; however, preliminary evidence suggests that it is good enough to meet required standards.

Another way to produce digital images is to microfilm the books first using conventional photographic techniques and later scan the microfilm itself into a digital image whenever the film-scanning technology is adequate. Yale University is undertaking a project testing this approach. The advantage is that to preserve the intellectual content of the book we can exploit the inherently higher resolution and superior archival quality of film, while providing for improved access across digital networks now or at any time in the future. Today, we may scan microfilm in production settings at relatively low resolution at perhaps only a small increment to the original cost of producing the original microfilm. At some point in the future, for the same small incremental cost, we will be able to scan the microfilm at very high resolution that will allow us to capture the fine details of the original document.

The key point is that, either way, we can have our cake and eat it too. Interchanging both ways between the digital world and the analog world of microfilm appears both practical and achievable, the tradeoffs being ones of permanence, resolution, and speed. We can exploit the preservation advantages of microfilm today and the access advantages of digital technologies tomorrow. We can transmit the scanned digital images to distant computer workstations for viewing, and we can print out high-quality paper facsimiles whenever and wherever they are needed.

The world's investment in microfilming for preservation continues to be a wise one, in spite of the emerging advantages of digital technologies.

Microfilming today does not preclude exploiting the advantages of digital access in the future.

Deacidification to slow down the deterioration processes also remains a promising area for investigation, even if only as a holding strategy pending the viable application of digital or other technologies.

Other Applications of Digital Technology in Preservation. The CLASS Project at present only spans monochrome materials less than 8 1/2 × 11 inches in size that contain text, line art, and halftone images. In another collaborative project involving Cornell, the University of Southern California, and the Kodak Corporation, we have studied the application of PhotoCD capture and storage technologies to the digital preservation of continuous-tone monochrome and color imagery and to larger formats.

All of these projects and other related activities reflect the extraordinary versatility of digital technologies. Indeed, Cornell's own investigations parallel other activities, underway or planned, across the world. The extraordinarily impressive task undertaken by Seville's Archivos de los Indios in scanning about 10 percent of their manuscript holdings, or around 10 million images, has also underscored the potential of these technologies. I revisited this project about a month ago, and it was gratifying to watch scholars in their reading room accessing manuscripts at workstations–reducing wear and tear on the originals as well as significantly speeding up access times–and digitally enhancing the manuscripts on the fly to make text legible that had long been obscured by bleed-through or other problems.

The Cost of Conversion. Conversion still remains the expensive part of the process, approximately $100 per book including the costs of selection, regardless of technology used. Let us put this figure in perspective. If there are indeed 11 million unique titles across the research libraries of the U.S. that will become embrittled, the cost of converting these books amounts to about $500,000 per year for 20 years for each of the 120 members of the Association of Research Libraries (ARL) representing about 5,000 books per year per institution. This does not count the costs of long-term storage and delivery systems. Nevertheless, the conversion cost of $500,000 per year can be compared with an average figure of about $4 million per year spent for new acquisitions. I recognize that acquisition budgets are under enormous pressure, and I am certainly not suggesting substitution; however, the decision to reformat a book is almost equal to the decision to buy a new book if the alternative is that the book will become completely unusable. I simply note that the cost of digitally preserving our old library is about 12 percent of the annual cost of acquiring new materials.

I have mainly focused in these remarks on conversion of books, manuscripts, and photographs. But the same essential issues apply to many other formats, such as videotapes, where, I suggest, we are almost compelled to consider digital alternatives because of the rapidity with which these tapes are changing before our eyes.

Ensuring Longevity

The second hurdle to be overcome underscores the wisdom of choosing microfilm as today's basic preservation standard. Unlike microfilm technology, digital technologies change rapidly. The formats in which data are stored are also subject to evolution. Standards are fluid and are often replaced even before they have matured from working to accepted standards. As a result we cannot guarantee that images scanned and stored in digital form today will be accessible even five years from now, let alone 500 years, any more than today we can easily read the punched cards of yesterday.

Keeping Pace with Technology. Contrary to what is often assumed, however, the primary issue is not the longevity of stored images on some given medium. There is no reason to assume that we will want to keep these digital books on the medium of original capture. Today, for example, we could store about 20 scanned books on a compact disk; 100 years from now we will be able to store the entire 5 million volumes of today's Cornell Library in the same physical space. People ask me how long will such-and-such a medium last. My answer is, I hope not longer than 10 years.

Space savings alone, however, will only *encourage* periodic transference to new media. It is the need to keep up with changing formats, software, and other technologies that absolutely *compels* such periodic "refreshing" as an absolute necessity. Fortunately, Cornell's studies suggest that the continuing costs of technology refreshing are more than offset by cost savings associated with space compaction, an attractive feature in the context of the burgeoning costs associated with traditional library growth. It is possible to hypothesize that we will refresh not just because we have to, but because we cannot afford not to. Our challenge is to formalize the task.

Perpetual Technology "Refreshing." In business terms, technology refreshing simply represents a form of continuous inventory management, a task that will of necessity occupy increasing attention of librarians as they struggle to cope with deteriorating analog media, from acidic paper to videotapes. Indeed, the need to institutionalize such technology refreshing–that is, ensure that the means exist to guarantee continuous attention to the need well beyond our lifetimes–is conceptually no different from entrusting microfilm repositories to maintain in perpetuity correct temperature and humidity settings. It may, however, require us to consider the finances of libraries in wholly different ways if libraries are not to implode under the weight of exponential growth.

Indeed, many if not most libraries have already crossed the digital Rubicon of technology refreshing. Digital online catalogs replace analog card catalogs. We entrust our computer centers to maintain such digital catalogs for eternity, refreshing the databases as technologies change. Imagine the consequences to our research libraries if those digital catalogs became inaccessible because of some future disruption in the refreshing process. A library without an index virtually ceases to exist.

Even as digital technologies evolve to provide improved worldwide access, the stable and standardized properties of microfilm continue to demand our attention for preservation reformatting. This will likely continue until we fully come to grips with the issues of how to institutionalize the process of refreshing our stored digital images. However, these issues are not insurmountable, and we may rapidly approach the point where it makes sense to consider digital technologies for preservation–at least in a hybrid partnership with microfilm.

Providing Worldwide Access

Thirdly, there is the issue of access. Research libraries throughout the world justifiably pride themselves on open access, a fundamental underpinning of a democratic society. Open access, however, must not be confused with free access. It is a well-maintained fiction that our libraries are free to all scholars; this is misleading not because it costs to acquire and maintain collections, but because easy or free access is largely limited to those scholars in physical proximity to those collections. It is expensive and time-consuming for scholars to come from a distance. The irony is that in maintaining open access to our "analog" libraries, we may be inhibiting equitable access by scholars and others from institutions across the nation and around the world, who would benefit from open access at a distance to digitized collections.

Equal Access to All. The promise of digital collections is indeed that they can equitably be accessed by scholars from wherever they may be, that is, access from any place and at any time. And not just by scholars, but also by citizens everywhere, from young elementary school students to life-long learners–provided, of course, they are not network-challenged! The further promise is that as we come to implement the necessary infrastructure, the exponentially declining costs of digital technologies will ultimately place such access within the financial range of all scholars everywhere. It has been suggested that scholarship follows access, not collection, and that the greatest collections in the world have diminished scholarly value if access is inhibited.

A Time of Prototypes and Experimentation. The creation of electronic virtual libraries spanning the globe heralds the fulfillment of Erasmus's dream, but there is much to do before we can close the gap between promise and reality. Erasmus may yet have to wait awhile.

We are in the early stages. We still have much to learn about the best ways to store, share, index, and access digital information. Navigation among the growing cornucopia of distributed network resources presents extraordinarily difficult challenges. We still have to agree on standard ways of exchanging digital information. We are only just coming to grips with the complex issues surrounding control of intellectual property and ensuring a fair return to copyright holders.

Rapid progress, however, is being made, both in the private and higher educational sectors. Organizations such as RLG, the Commission on Preservation and Access, OCLC, the Coalition for Networked Information, and professional library associations are leading the way in addressing the complex issues involved. Prototype projects are underway, and rapid progress is now occurring. The projects I have described here and the many others at other institutions more than hint at what is to come, as does the explosive growth worldwide of network-accessible information resources on the Internet. There is a surge in experimentation in creation of electronic journals, even though at this early stage it is not clear how these are to meet the exacting standards of the academy or to become financially self-sustaining. The recent National Science Foundation digital library initiative has stimulated new thinking and creative proposals.

THE BEST OF BOTH WORLDS

Attitudes are changing rapidly. Liberals and conservatives alike–librarians, as well as publishers, scholars, and technologists–no longer view the electronic library in the manner of St. Augustine, who prayed, "Lord, give me chastity–but not yet," but as a concept whose time is upon us, not necessarily to replace the paper library, but to augment it in ways that combine the benefits of both.

Digital technologies, providing access at a distance across the world's electronic highways to our intellectual resources, will realize Erasmus's dream over the coming years and decades. As we move forward in this regard, however, we must be mindful of the primary and urgent need to preserve those intellectual resources and to use the mix of technologies–analog or digital–most appropriate to the task.

From Analog to Digital:
Extending the Preservation Tool Kit

Anne R. Kenney
Paul Conway

DIGITAL IMAGING AND PRESERVATION–
UNCHARTED TERRITORY

[KENNEY] The 1990s have been called by some the decade of the image. For those of us concerned with the preservation and access of research library materials, this claim has a specific meaning tied to the emergence of digital-imaging technology, which represents a powerful new way to manage, store, and retrieve information. Its use stems from a convergence of technological capability and opportunity, including the ubiquitous nature of personal computing, the development of high-speed networks that are accessible to an increasing number of individuals and organizations, the declining cost and increasing capacity of mass storage, and the availability of reasonably priced, high-quality, production scanning systems. By providing for immediate, simultaneous, multiple, and random access to resources located at geographically distant places, digital technology has the potential to expand dramatically the rapid availability of information to users world-wide. Increasingly, business, government,

Anne R. Kenney is Associate Director of the Department of Preservation and Conservation, Olin Library, Cornell University.

Paul Conway is Head of the Preservation Department, Sterling Library, Yale University. Conway was unable to attend the symposium, and his remarks were delivered by Barclay Ogden, Head of the Conservation Department, Doe Library, University of California at Berkeley.

[Haworth co-indexing entry note]: "From Analog to Digital: Extending the Preservation Tool Kit." Kenney, Anne R., and Paul Conway. Co-published simultaneously in *Collection Management* (The Haworth Press, Inc.) Vol. 22, No. 3/4, 1998, pp. 65-79; and: *Going Digital: Strategies for Access, Preservation, and Conversion of Collections to a Digital Format* (ed: Donald L. DeWitt) The Haworth Press, Inc., 1998, pp. 65-79.

industry, and the professional and scientific communities are turning to the use of digital technology to manage information and to make the full text of important sources routinely available.

Scholars in the arts and humanities, however, continue to rely heavily on the books, serials, archives, and special collections materials stored on library shelves. With notable exceptions, few historical sources have been converted to electronic form. It is for this group of users–who incidentally represent the primary beneficiaries of preservation reformatting–that the application of digital-imaging technology could prove most significant.

Indeed, there is a rising level of interest throughout the library community in the use of digital imaging for preservation reformatting as evidenced by the many conferences devoted to this topic over the past several years. Additionally, major funding agencies report receiving an increasing number of proposals for projects that involve the use of information technology to capture and make available research materials.

While interest is high in the use of digital technology, the knowledge base–including the development of commonly accepted protocols and standards for the use of digital technology in a preservation context–is low. As a consequence, funding agencies and research institutions alike are slow to implement programs for scanning and digitization.

An important first step towards the recognition of the value of digital-imaging technology in this context has come in the form of *Considerations for Converting Materials to Electronic Form*, which was recently produced by the Joint Federal Funders Group, representing agencies that make grants relating to archival, library and other primary research materials, including the Department of Education, the National Archives, the National Endowment for the Humanities, and the National Science Foundation. This publication covers some of the major issues associated with conversion that will be addressed during this symposium.

The symposium is designed to provide participants with a baseline level of knowledge about the use of digital-imaging technology for preservation reformatting. Throughout the next several days, we will come to understand that digital reformatting does not end with the conversion process itself, but encompasses a host of related processes associated with imbuing the digital images with "intelligence" and the requirements for associated indexing of structure and content.

The symposium is intended to raise as many questions as it answers. One of the basic truths to remember about this emerging technology is that nothing is as sure as change itself. My rule of thumb is that when I really think I have mastered the situation, I'm in trouble because the ground rules change all the time and my complacency means that I have failed to keep up. I suggest you consider the information presented here as providing a framework for the theoretical as well as the practical–and to recognize that the technical information is but a snapshot of what is available at this particular point. Nonetheless we will begin there. To give you the technical background against which to assess the role and requirements of using digital technology, I turn this presentation over to Paul Conway.

THE RIGHT TOOL FOR THE RIGHT JOB

[CONWAY] A colleague of mine once proposed that when someone goes to the hardware store to buy a 1/4-inch drill bit, they really need a 1/4-inch hole. The more we know about the problem we need to solve and why we need to solve it, the easier it is to select the right tool for the right job. The job that brings us to this symposium is the need to make sure that any investment we make in converting library materials with long-term value to digital image is well spent on behalf of our patrons–present and future.

Digital-imaging technology is a tool with many possible applications. It is only a tool not necessarily a solution, as some vendors would have us believe. In this regard it is extremely important to distinguish between acquiring imaging technology to solve a particular problem on the one hand and adopting it as a preservation option. Acquiring an imaging system primarily to improve access to information now is almost as simple as choosing the right combination of available features to meet immediate management goals. Adopting the technology for preservation, on the other hand, requires a deep and long-standing institutional commitment, the full integration of the technology into our information management procedures and processes, and significant leadership in developing appropriate definitions and standards of quality.

It is our job, then, to reconcile what seems like a fundamental contradiction between our traditional preservation responsibility and the promise of new and emerging, but rapidly changing, information technologies. Library and archival administrators who wish to add digital-imaging technology to their preservation tool kits must take to heart the following statement: the fundamental goal of digital preservation is to preserve continuing access to digital data for as long as that data has value.

Subsumed in the goal statement are assumptions that should be made explicit. Administrators who have responsibility for selecting imaging systems for materials with long-term value also bear responsibility for providing long-term access. This commitment is a continuing one that requires that decisions about preservation and access not be deferred in the hope that technological solutions will emerge. Decisions on the long-term value to researchers and scholars of library and archival collections that may be converted to digital images are made independently of the decision to adopt the technology. Although increased access by image conversion may indeed add value to library holdings, the point of departure must be assessments of the research value of materials in their original format.

The process of converting library materials to an electronic form is distinct from the medium upon which the images are stored. This distinction allows for a continuing commitment to the digitized information while entertaining the possibility that other, more advanced storage media may render today's optical media storage obsolete. The best digital-imaging system is an integrated collection of hardware and software components that may serve short-term functions in addition to the conversion of library materials for long-term retention.

FOUR PRIMARY ISSUES

Four major issues must be considered by library administrators who wish to adopt digital-imaging technology as part of a comprehensive preservation strategy.

1. System functionality over time.
2. Storage media deterioration and migration of data.
3. Digital image data quality.
4. Integrity of information sources.

I should note in passing that the imaging industry has not reached consensus on some of these points, and there is certainly room for other viewpoints.

1. System Functionality Over Time

It is ironic that today's optical media will most likely far outlast the current hardware and software systems that retrieve and interpret the data stored on them. Since libraries and archives can ill-afford to become museums of obsolete computer technology, we must work simultaneously with manufacturers and within our own institutions to maintain the functionality of the systems we acquire and upgrade their capabilities as the technology evolves. There are at least five aspects to this issue.

- *Open Systems Architecture.* Open systems architecture is a systems design approach that permits users to interchange system hardware components with minimal impact on the primary operating software and to upgrade the system over time without significant data loss. Open systems architecture should be required for new digital-imaging applications.

- *Nonproprietary Systems.* One of the keys to open systems is the development of nonproprietary standards. Because the barriers imposed by proprietary system configurations can create serious problems for long-term access to documents stored on optical media, vendors with proprietary products should be required to build linkages to systems with nonproprietary configurations.

- *Backward Compatibility.* A useful way to mitigate the impact of information technology obsolescence is to require that new system generations be *backward compatible*, that is, able to read information written by an older generation of technology and convert it to a newer one.

- *Technical Documentation.* Full technical documentation of system components, application software, and operating systems is essential to facilitating long-term access. Administrators should require the delivery of a complete set of documentation, including source code, object code, and maintenance documentation.

- *Responsible Custody.* Digital-imaging systems cannot solve access problems stemming from inefficient manual or computerized information systems and practices. It is necessary to document all aspects of the design and use, including administrative procedures for imaging, retrieval, and storage; problems encountered over time; and measures taken to address them, including hardware and software modifications. It is our responsibility, rather than that of vendors and manufacturers, to ensure that policies and procedures for long-term access are developed and consistently applied.

2. Storage Media Deterioration and Migration of Data

At the heart of any imaging system's functionality is the ability to retrieve data from optical storage media as reliably as possible for as long as possible. Before data error rates become unacceptable (or even fatal), it is necessary to migrate digital data (and the accompanying index information) to newer generations of imaging systems. Simply refreshing data by copying to new disks, as is typical in a magnetic media arena, is not an acceptable long-term solution when imaging systems themselves are becoming obsolete in three to five years. In the area of media longevity, there are at least five issues to consider.

- *Recording Permanence.* The optical media industry appears to be moving towards adopting rewritable disk technology as the standard. However, WORM technology (Write Once Read Many) offers a greater level of data security. I recommend using WORM technology if possible, unless the system permits read-only limitations and can track the activities of those with write privileges.
- *Optical Disk Size.* Systems that utilize 5-1/4-inch optical disks should be selected unless specific programmatic needs require larger-capacity disks.
- *Durability.* The optical media selected should have a prewrite shelf life of at least five years and a minimum postwrite life of 20 years. There is a need for standardized tests of longevity of optical disks and consistent, open comparisons of vendor products.
- *Storage.* Optical media are not immune to hostile storage environments, particularly high humidity and airborne particles. Media should be stored in areas with stable room temperatures of 65 to 75 degrees Fahrenheit and relative humidity between 30 and 50 percent.
- *Plan for Migration.* Laying the groundwork for near-certain future migration involves planning and budgeting as soon as the original system is acquired. This will include specifying existing and emerging standards, budgeting appropriately for the costs of maintenance and upgrade, and testing and evaluating media and systems on a regular basis. For long-term access, it is wisest to transfer data from an obsolete system to a newly emerging generation, in some cases bypassing the intermediate generation that is mature but at risk of becoming obsolete.

3. Digital Image Data Quality

The digital-imaging market has transformed one of the fundamental goals of preservation—to maintain the highest possible quality over time—to one of finding the minimum level of quality acceptable to system users. We must reclaim image quality as the heart and soul of digital preservation. In the area of image quality, at least four factors are critical.

- *Equipment Calibration.* Regular equipment maintenance and periodic calibration of optical media drives and scanning devices are important process control procedures. Standard test procedures are emerging and should be followed.
- *Resolution.* Image data should be captured at the highest possible level. Three hundred dots per inch (dpi) should be a bare minimum; 600 dpi or more may be necessary to guarantee fidelity to the original.

- *Image Enhancement.* Digital image enhancement results from invoking mathematical formulas that clean up each image by removing data, either selectively or automatically. The extent to which enhancement alters the integrity of the original or merely makes the information more usable must be decided on a document-by-document basis until such time as enhancement standards and guidelines are developed.
- *Compression.* Compression reduces the large volume of image data by means of sophisticated mathematical encoding. Standardized or nonproprietary compression techniques, such as CCITT Group 4 fax standards, are an indispensable part of a migration strategy for documents of long-term value. Ongoing projects in RLG libraries may well result in a new set of quality guidelines.

4. Integrity of Information Sources

Digital images are dumb. They can be located only with the aid of a potentially complex index, unless optical character recognition (OCR) programs have been applied as an additional, and expensive, processing step. Without indexing, digitally converted library materials are simply random collections of files stored and labeled in complex directory systems unintelligible to most users. From a preservation perspective, database management helps guarantee that the structural components of the original sources, indexes, chapter headings, finding aids, etc., are built into imaging systems and that structural indexing is developed according to accepted standards. Preserving the internal structure of books, serials, and primary source materials, however, is only half the battle. The other half is creating and then preserving the necessary linkages between imaging systems and bibliographic and other management information systems. Consider the following two guidelines.

- *Image Headers.* Image file headers are the "envelopes" that describe the contents and structure of an image document. The use of nonproprietary image file header structures is essential. The Tagged Image File Format (TIFF) is one example of an emerging file header standard.
- *Error Detection.* The ability to predict the point at which optical media are no longer readable is critical so that media recopying can take place before a fatal error occurs. Until a consensus develops on the most appropriate approach to accessing error correction data, use the "write and verify" command that is available in the system interface to make sure that accurate data is written initially to the optical media.

FOUR PRIMARY COMMITMENTS

I suggest, therefore, that we need to make four primary commitments if we plan to integrate imaging technology into our preservation programs. We need to:

- Transfer valuable information across technology systems as these systems emerge.
- Deemphasize storage media formats as the central focus of preservation concern.
- Shift that concern to the fundamental challenge of specifying and then obtaining digital image quality.
- Recognize the importance of maintaining structural, that is, contextual, as well as content indexes.

Given these four commitments, imaging technology is not simply another reformatting option. It is far more than that, and we ought to find a new term to describe what imaging is all about for libraries and archives. I suggest that *transformatting* instead of *reformatting* might be a more accurate term. Digital imaging involves transforming the format of information sources, not simply providing a faithful reproduction of these sources on a different medium. The power to enhance, the possibilities for structural indexing, and the mathematics of compression and communication together fundamentally alter the concept of preservation in the electronic era. These capabilities alone, along with the new responsibilities imaging technology places on us as information professionals, will force us to transform our library services and programs in turn.

[KENNEY] Having considered the digital framework, I would like now to turn to preservation's niche in this brave new world. First and foremost, I believe that digital-imaging technology will take its proper place as an alternative or complement to microfilm and photocopy for the reformatting of endangered library materials.

SOME ADVANTAGES OF DIGITAL IMAGING TECHNOLOGY IN PRESERVATION

Duplication Without Degradation

Indeed, digital-imaging technology offers several important preservation advantages over light lens processes. Chief among them is the ability to duplicate without degradation. A digital image can be reproduced over and over again with absolute fidelity; those strings of 0s and 1s replicate remarkably well–in marked contrast to light lens copies, which suffer a 10 to 15 percent informational loss with each succeeding generation of copy.

Ease of Manipulation and Enhancement

Digital technology also offers the ability to manipulate and enhance images in ways not possible with light lens technology. This includes removing stains, underlining, and bleed-through; increasing legibility by heightening contrast between text and background; and, by segmenting an illustrated page, capturing both text and image in a manner that optimizes both–the illustration as gray scale, reproducing much of the subtlety of tone, and the text as high-contrast black and white, ensuring readable clarity. By comparison, high-contrast light lens technology requires one to choose which to optimize: text or illustration. Newer continuous-tone microfilms are coming onto the market, which may ease this situation, but the fact remains that digital imaging provides infinitely more flexibility than do light lens processes.

Preview Capability

Digital technology also offers the advantage of previewing the image before keeping it so that adjustments can be made to the brightness, contrast, and color balance beforehand. With light lens processes, there are no preview capabilities. If the lighting is incorrect or the image out of focus, the image must be retaken at a later point. It is also easy with digital technology to reorder the sequence of images after the fact. By comparison, microfilm requires laborious splicing in of missing or corrected pages.

Relative Permanence

A further preservation advantage is that digital images do not decay with use, unlike microfilm, which can become scratched with improper handling, or books whose bindings fail or paper deteriorates over time. In fact, as Paul indicated, use in the digital world can become an important preservation consideration as digital media can utilize error detection and correction codes when used. The more they are used the higher the rate of accuracy maintained.

Flexibility in Output

Digital-imaging technology offers great flexibility in output and can thus meet a variety of user preferences and equipment constraints. With digital technology, it is possible to separate the medium for preservation (film) from the medium for production (digital files) and use (paper, film, on-screen display, etc). These various outputs need not be created at the same time. For example, it may be the case that microfilm is created for archival purposes from the digital images at the time the book is scanned. At another time, a print-on-demand copy (which is superior to a printout from microfilm) can be made in response to local user needs, or the digital images themselves can be transmitted over national networks to researchers at distant institutions. This flexibility obviates the need to make choices about the final format at the point of preservation. Such choices can be use or convenience driven. Thus, digital technology combines the desirable quality of hardcopy reproduction with microfilm's ease of duplication, long-term stability, and space saving compression.

SOME DISADVANTAGES

However, there are a number of disadvantages associated with the use of this rapidly changing technology, including obsolescence and incompatibility of hardware and software; an absence of standards for image capture, file format, compression, and transmission; and a lack of experience with library/archival applications. Because digital images are not eye readable but are coded representations, we are solely dependent on supporting the system configuration to "read" the digital files and are thus vulnerable to total loss on a number of fronts.

Intensive Maintenance

It is fortunate that digital images can indeed be copied without loss of information because preservation using digital technology will require maintaining access to the information through periodic copying, refreshing, and migrating the data to keep pace with changes in hardware and software that are characteristic of an emerging technology. The system requirements needed to access the images are likely to change several times over during the life span of the digital media, and the data will need to be copied to newer formats long before the medium itself degrades. Given such a period of flux, one must also consider the wisdom of providing a human-readable backup to the digital images themselves, either through maintaining the original or creating a paper or film-based copy either before or after digitizing.

Ever-Changing Technology

As will be seen, digital images are extremely large, and their effective use will not only require large storage capacities but will also affect the requirements for user workstations. Low-end PCs and Macs, for example, will not support their storage, decompression, display and manipulation. In the long run, however, the technology itself is the least of our concerns; storage capacity doubles each year, personal workstations are becoming more powerful, dwarfing the big computers of a decade ago, and the costs of conversion and maintenance will decline over time.

Long-Term Commitment of Funds and Resources

The real problem may lie in adjusting institutional mind sets to accept a long-term commitment of funds and resources to accomplish this task. Libraries and archives, in a period of transition, will have to support two systems—the traditional library and the digital library—and the expense, conflicting requirements, and changes required will be difficult. In this period, the preservation administrator's role will not be so much one of technological guru but of watchdog to keep before the eye of the library administration the need to maintain access to information in digital form over the very long haul.

USE AND EASE OF USE

In this time of uncertainty and flux, I believe the role of preservation will be considerably broadened. As resources for supporting our collections diminish, hard decisions will need to be made about what materials to maintain and at what level to provide access to them. Endangered materials will no longer be defined as just those items printed on acidic paper, but will extend to those that languish from lack of use. As researchers become comfortable with online access to sources, they develop rising expectations for improving access to all information and may become increasingly uninterested in materials that are not easily accessible—to the extent that some will restrict their searches to those materials that are most quickly identified and available.

A telling comment was made by one Cornell faculty member whose reaction to the online catalog was, "Don't tell me about information; give me the information itself. That's when I'll be really interested in what you are doing." It does appear that use and ease of use are highly correlated. Despite claims to the contrary, we have seen this occur when deteriorated materials are converted to microfilm or when paper copies are stored off campus. Their use goes down. It may be an apocryphal story, but our math library has been collecting microforms of material it does not own for the past 20 years and has yet to record a single use of that film. Indeed, there have been instances when the faculty have requested interlibrary loan paper copies for items that are available locally on film!

In the future, materials available in our main research libraries may be considered too hard to access and use in their current formats. This change has already begun in technical, professional, and law libraries where researchers have come to equate nearly instantaneous access with relevancy. The conversion and availability online of retrospective sources could prove critical in revitalizing their use and in providing the needed justification for their share of institutional resources. In the not too distant future, the role of the preservation administrator will take on new meaning as retrospective conversion is extended beyond bibliographic information to the sources themselves.

PRESERVATION ADMINISTRATORS–ARBITERS OF QUALITY

In the present, however, there are immediate demands for preservation administrators to become involved in testing, monitoring, and promoting the use of digital technology for preservation purposes. Chief among the many tasks requiring our expertise is the development of benchmarks for image quality. It will fall to us to define them for a wide variety of source materials.

As will be seen in the tutorials to come, image capture will be affected by the electronic format being used, which in large measure will be dictated by the physical format and condition of the material being scanned. We must come to understand the role of resolution, tonal reproduction, enhancement, and compression in the process of defining quality standards.

The preservation community will also have to consider other variables, such as cost of image capture, institutional capabilities and commitments, the quantity and type of material to be captured, the relevance of current standards for reformatting that have been established for photocopy and microfilm, issues associated with fidelity versus legibility, user requirements and perceptions, and the uses to which this material will be put. The application and intended end products of the reformatting effort should be the driving force in making decisions on image capture. As John Stokes once remarked, the tendency is to define solutions for image management in terms of equipment or process with insufficient thought concerning objectives–current, medium, and long range.

The DPI Question

Some first attempts have been made in defining quality benchmarks for preservation reformatting. At Cornell we have spent the past four years evaluating the quality of high-resolution binary scanning to capture printed text. From the outset we were interested in determining whether the quality of the digital image was comparable to that obtained through conventional reformatting techniques–and at an affordable price.

After considerable experimentation with the Xerox prototype scanner and an analysis of the printing processes used during the 19th and first half of the 20th centuries, we concluded that 600 dpi scanning represents a sufficient resolution to capture the vast majority of printed material published during the period of paper's greatest brittleness. Thus, while 600 dpi scanning does not provide the resolution that can be obtained through microfilming, it will do, given the nature of the material we want to capture. Books published during the 19th and early 20th centuries were produced using metal type, which has a tendency to spread, so printers were limited to how small or closely spaced letters could be. All common typefaces used during this period were produced at 5- or 6-point type and above. Six hundred dpi binary scanning can adequately capture 4-point type and below, including the rendering of fine detail and uneven thickness that characterize typical fonts used during this period, which were prone to elaborate serifed script, italics, and small body heights.

Most scanning projects to date have utilized a lower resolution–in the range of 200 to 400 dpi–with 300 dpi being the most common. While lower-resolution scanning can produce satisfactory copies from modern texts of 6-point type and above, many of the deteriorating volumes in our project contained irregular features typical of the production typography and printing techniques of the past century and a half, or they were heavily illustrated with fine line drawings and halftones, or came in languages such as Japanese where characters comprised of varying strokes are difficult to reproduce at lower resolutions. Over half of the initial 1,000 volumes scanned came from our math library and contained annotations and formulae that were really challenging to capture. The mathematicians insisted, for instance, that we not turn pluses into minuses in the scanning process, which actually occurred in a number of cases when using 300 dpi resolution. The 600 dpi copies successfully captured most of these printing challenges to represent faithful and legible reproductions of the originals.

For printed material, then, which consists largely of text and line art, the key to digital image quality is determined primarily by the capture resolution. The higher the number of dots per inch, the better the reproduction, and we feel confident in calling for 600 dpi as the minimum acceptable resolution for preservation replacement purposes. As higher-resolution production scanning systems come on the market, we may well convert to them, but we will not have to go back and rescan the material already captured. It is a chimera to think that we ever could, and so preservation administrators must take care in defining at the outset quality benchmarks for replacement purposes.

The Success of High-Quality Paper Facsimiles

In addition to a technical assessment, we were interested in a subjective analysis as well. Our faculty advisory committee reviewed paper facsimiles and pronounced them of sufficient quality to replace the deteriorating originals, which in most cases were subsequently discarded. Interestingly, in many cases the faculty preferred the scanned facsimile to the original, finding that the slightly heightened contrast between text and background of the new version made them more readable in the age of bifocals. Faculty acceptance of the printed copy is an important point in that we can move to a single preservation cost for replacement purposes. In microfilming projects at Cornell, we have had to return the original volumes to the shelves to satisfy local users. This has resulted in a substantial additional cost to conserve or protect the originals after filming. It is my belief that the use of digital-imaging technology for preservation and the ability to produce a high-quality printed facsimile will lead to increased scholarly support for the national preservation reformatting effort.

These findings on digital quality requirements come from only one institution. The broader preservation community must determine whether there is general consensus regarding Cornell's position and must also move to determine quality benchmarks for other materials–photographs, both black and white and color; archival sources; and works of art on paper–for which resolution alone will not be the only determinant of image quality. This process must be a collaborative one among preservation administrators, the keepers and users of this material, and the providers of digital-imaging equipment and services.

WORKING WITH VENDORS–CRITICAL TO SUCCESS

Which brings me to my last point: vendor relationships. As mentioned earlier, this technology is an emerging one, and vendor capabilities–for providing scanning services of high quality and low cost as well as storage and maintenance services for digital masters–are rapidly developing. The editor of *Imaging Service Bureau News* estimates there are over 2,000 imaging bureaus in the country, one half of which are using digital technologies. To date, very few have established a relationship with the research library community. But this is a chicken-and-egg phenomenon. While there is a great deal of interest in this technology, libraries and archives have been tentative in its use, citing the lack of standards, quality definitions, system support, funding, and technical expertise. This reluctance quite naturally tends to depress the vendor market. It is time now for us to come to understand the value and uses of digital technology and to work with vendors and service bureaus to ensure that they can understand and meet our needs. This relationship will be critical because the vendor role for services will be large. Few institutions will be able to make an in-house system economically viable, considering the flux associated with changing hardware and software requirements.

Margaret Byrne, head of the preservation section at the National Library of Medicine, addressed the National Preservation Planning for Agriculture Conference in 1991 and identified a number of issues that must be resolved before the use of digital technology can become a viable preservation option. Among them was expertise: "It seems to me that the situation today is very similar to that of ten years ago when cooperative preservation microfilming projects were starting up. Specifications for filming brittle bound materials had to be developed and vendors had to learn new ways of doing things. . . . Today we are facing a similar lack of specifications for scanning brittle library materials or for producing preservation quality film from digital files. And library staff must become much more familiar with hardware, software, image capture, and quality control procedures if they are to communicate successfully with the vendors who will do the work."

We hope this symposium will lay the cornerstone in our quest for building that requisite level of expertise to meet the challenges and opportunities posed by the use of digital technology for preservation of and access to our intellectual heritage.

Long-Term Intellectual Preservation

Peter S. Graham

Long-term intellectual preservation treats the difference between the kinds of information librarians and archivists are used to working with and the new kinds of information sources that we are working with now. Broadly speaking, it is the difference between artifactual information and electronic information. Artifactual information is that kind of information which is associated with a material object (books, for example, or engravings): it has weight and occupies space, so to speak, as we create it and use it. If we have preserved an artifactual object, we have done the job of preserving the ill-formation associated with it. With electronic information, this relation is no longer so true.

What follows focuses first on ideas of authenticity, or intellectual preservation, and then on ideas of longevity, both crucial to preservation of electronic information. This is a symposium on digital-imaging technology, but digital images are a very important subset of electronic information more generally, and the issues of intellectual preservation and longevity are important to both.

ELECTRONIC AUTHENTICITY– INTELLECTUAL PRESERVATION

The advent of electronic information introduces new preservation requirements.[1] For print, manuscript, or original art materials, to preserve the artifact is to preserve the information associated with it. Electronic information is easily separable from its medium with no loss of content, requiring us to

Peter S. Graham is Associate University Librarian for Technical and Networked Information Services at Rutgers, the State University of New Jersey.

[Haworth co-indexing entry note]: "Long-Term Intellectual Preservation." Graham, Peter S. Co-published simultaneously in *Collection Management* (The Haworth Press, Inc.) Vol. 22, No. 3/4, 1998, pp. 81-98; and: *Going Digital: Strategies for Access, Preservation, and Conversion of Collections to a Digital Format* (ed: Donald L. DeWitt) The Haworth Press, Inc., 1998, pp. 81-98.

think differently about its preservation; the medium becomes of less intrinsic interest and preserving the intellectual content becomes more complex.[2]

Medium Preservation and Technology Preservation

Medium preservation has been addressed by some librarians and computing experts in discussions of environmental and handling concerns for tapes, magnetic disks, optical disks, and the like.[3] The preservation of the medium on which the bits and bytes of electronic information are recorded is an important concern. But such solutions will inevitably be short-term and will not in themselves be the means of preserving electronic information over long periods of time. Michael Lesk, in a report for the Commission on Preservation and Access, has urged that the greatest attention should instead be directed to the obsolescence of technologies rather than simply of the media.[4]

Lesk describes the rapid changes in the means of recording, in the storage formats, and in the software that allows electronic information to be of use. Urging what might be called *technology preservation*, he asserts that for electronic information "preservation means copying, not physical preservation." That is, the preservation of electronic information into the indefinite future requires its being "refreshed" from old to new technologies as they become available and as the old technologies cease being supported by vendors and the user community.

Intellectual Preservation

There remains a third preservation requirement, *intellectual preservation*, which addresses the integrity and authenticity of the information as originally recorded. Preservation of the media and of the software technologies will serve only part of the need if the information content has been corrupted from its original form, whether by accident or design. The need for intellectual preservation arises because the great asset of digital information is also its great liability–the ease with which an identical copy can be quickly and flawlessly made is paralleled by the ease with which a change may be undetectably made.

The Problem. The problem may be put in the form of several questions that confront the user of any electronic document (whether text, hypertext, audio, graphic, numeric, or multimedia information):

- How can I be sure that what I am viewing is what I want to see?
- How do I know that the document I have found is the same one that you used and made reference to in your footnote?

- How can I be sure that the document I now use has not been changed since the last time I used it?
- To put it most generally: How can a reader be sure that the document being used is the one intended?

We properly take for granted the fixity of text in the print world. The printed journal article I examine because of your footnote is beyond question the same text that you read. Therefore we have confidence that our discussion is based upon a common foundation. With electronic texts we no longer have that confidence.

Taxonomy of Changes. There are three possibilities for change in electronic texts that confront us with the need for intellectual preservation techniques:

- Accidental change.
- Intentional change that is well-meant.
- Intentional change that is not well-meant; that is, fraud.

Note that backup is not the issue or the solution. The question is how we know what we have (or don't have).

Accidental change: A document can sometimes be damaged accidentally, perhaps by data loss during transfer or through inadvertent mistakes in manipulation; for example, data may be corrupted in being sent over a network or between disks and memory on a computer. This no longer happens often, but it is possible. More frequent is the loss of sections of a document, or a whole version of a document, due to accidents in updating.

Intentional change (well-meant): There are at least two possibilities. New versions and drafts are familiar to us from dealing with authorial texts, for example, or from working with successive book editions, legislative bills, or revisions of working papers. It is desirable to keep track bibliographically of the distinction between one version and another. We are accustomed to visual cues to tell us when a version is different; in addition to explicit numbering, we observe the page format, the typography, the producer's name, the binding, the paper itself. These cues are not available or dependable for distinguishing electronic versions.

Structural updates, changes that are inherent in the document, also cause changes in information content. A dynamic database by its nature is frequently updated: Books in Print, for example, or architectural drawings, or elements of the human genome project, or a university directory. How do we identify a given snapshot and authenticate it as representing a certain time?

Intentional change (fraud): Here there are also two possibilities. The change might be of one's own work to cover one's tracks or to change evidence for a variety of reasons, or it might be damage to the work of another.

In an electronic future the opportunities for a Stalinist revision of history will be multiplied. An unscrupulous researcher could change experimental data without a trace. A financial dealer might wish to cover tracks to hide improper business, or a political figure might wish to hide or modify inconvenient earlier views; this is the *1984* scenario. Imagine if you will that the only evidence of Reagan's Iran–Contra scandal was in electronic mail, or that the only record of Bill Clinton's draft correspondence was in e-mail. Consider the political benefit that might derive if each of the parties could modify its own past correspondence without detection. Then consider the case if each of them could modify the other's correspondence without detection. Society needs a defense against such cases, and the parties involved need also to be able to say, "Here is a true electronic record."

A Potential Solution. The need is to fix, or authenticate, a document so that a user can be sure of the unaltered text when it is needed.[5] Such a technique must be easy to use so that it does not impede creation or access. It must also provide generality, flexibility, openness where possible but document security where desired, be low in cost, and–most of all–be functional over long periods of time on the human scale (meaning longer than our life span).

A solution will have to be algorithmic; that is, it will have to be based on simple software rather than on hardware, which rapidly becomes obsolete. This would seem to be a problem, for software, like documents themselves, can easily be tampered with and modified.

A promising solution has been developed by a small group of researchers. Scott Stornetta and Stuart Haber of Bellcore have named their proposal *digital time-stamping* (DTS).[6] It calls upon the cryptographic technique of one-way hashing and uses the concept of the *widely witnessed event,* and is a means of authenticating not only a particular document but its existence at a specific time. The technique is analogous to rubber-stamping incoming papers with the date and time they are received. In electronic form its use is proposed to be by a document's creator (or other responsible intermediate party), who will set up the necessary conditions for later authentication by an eventual user.[7]

The researchers were initially prompted to develop DTS by charges of intellectual fraud made against a biologist. They became interested in how to demonstrate that there had been no tampering with electronic evidence. In addition, they were aware that the technique could be useful as a means for determining priority of thought (for example, in patents). The technique they developed makes use of cryptographic theory but does not require the encryption of documents.

Hashing. Any document may be viewed by a computer as a collection of numbers. A hash function is an algorithm that converts any collection of numbers into a single, distinct number (perhaps of a score or a hundred digits) that has no meaning in itself but that uniquely represents the set of numbers from which it was derived. A one-way cryptographic hash of a document may be created using mathematically complex, but computationally speedy, techniques. The process ensures the uniqueness of the hash and also its nonreproducibility; that is, it is not humanly or computationally feasible to create another document which would result in the same hash. Therefore it is not possible to change the given document and still to preserve its original hash. The hashing technique is called *one-way* because the original document cannot be recreated if one has only the document's hash.

Note that using this technique, the document itself may be kept private if its creator wishes. However, it need not be, and in many cases would not be. For librarianship and scholarship generally, the public accessibility of documents without human intervention is a necessity, and the one-way hash allows both a document and its hash to be public without fear of change. Note also that the algorithm (software) for creating the hash may also be public; its mechanism need not be private for knowledge of it will not affect the uniqueness nor the one-way nature of the created hash.

The Widely Witnessed Event. For many purposes in librarianship the document and its secure hash will be all that is necessary to assure authentication; one can imagine bibliographic citation formats, for example, which would include a form of the hash as a means of identifying a specific version of a particular work and allowing its authentication.

But one can also imagine situations some years, decades, or centuries from now in which it will be desirable to be assured as to when the document first existed. In patent and contract law which DTS will also serve, this is a daily necessity. In scientific research the need is clear, as it is if one considers stylistic analysis of an author's growth using electronic manuscripts as evidence.

The widely witnessed event is a concept that draws on the difficulty of tampering with a fact that is known to many outside the circle of interested parties. State lotteries prevent both collusion and the appearance of collusion by publicly drawing the winning numbers, often on television. Everyone sees the numbers as they are drawn so that it is not possible for officials of the lottery to arrange the winner in advance.

DTS draws on the principle of the widely witnessed event by openly intertwining the hash of a given document with the hashes of other documents submitted unpredictably by unknown other parties. The combined hashes for each document (known as *certificates*) depend upon a visible chain of actions of other similar parties such that tampering cannot occur without being immediately evident to an observer.

Digital Time-Stamping in Operation

In practice, digital time-stamping requires the existence of time-stamping server software. Client software on a networked computer is also required–to create the hash of a document, to communicate with the server, and (at a later time) to perform authentication.[8] None of the software need be computationally complex, large, or time-consuming.

The user at a client workstation, perhaps a PC, creates the hash of a document (this can be very quickly done at the click of a software button). He or she sends the hash over the network to a time-stamping server, which combines the hash with a hash previously received.[9] The resulting number is called the certificate for the present hash and is sent back to the user's workstation. This certificate becomes part of the authentication means for the original document whether used in the next half hour or the next half century. Note that the certificate is inextricably intertwined with those previously created for hashes received in unpredictable order from unknown (and unpredictable and uninfluenceable) users. The time-stamping server might easily be constructed to serve a region as large as the United States.

The time-stamping server creates a root certificate which is widely published at regular intervals. As a demonstration, the technique's authors for several years have published a root certificate once a week in the personals column of the *New York Times*.[10] Such a widely witnessed event, available for centuries on microfilm or other means, is a tamper-proof tool of authentication. In real-world practice, the intervals would be much shorter, say perhaps one minute.

Real-World Implementation. DTS is one solution being offered to the electronically novel problem of intellectual preservation.[11] There are likely to be others, each with their own assets and liabilities. The preservation community must keep aware of potential solutions and urge implementation of ones most broadly suitable; most of all, preservationists must be aware that the problem exists and requires a solution beyond the important preservation of the media and the technologies.

DTS is being presented as a solution of value to a number of information communities, for example, banking, law, pharmaceutical companies, and government. Its proposers have been intrigued by unique library requirements including long functional life on the human scale. But if DTS were to be used in research librarianship, several practical matters would have to be worked out.[12] These include:

- Means and forms of bibliographic citations using DTS.
- Means of associating certificates with documents.
- Long-term accessibility of roots.
- Utility and practicality of time-stamping servers or repositories dedicated to library needs.
- Financial implications and effect on desirability if DTS is marketed as a proprietary service.

Digital time-stamping may provide for many of the needs of the library (and archival) communities for long-term authentication of electronic information. If this approach turns out not to be suitable, however, it is likely that one relying on similar techniques will be found. In any case, it is important that libraries identify some solution that allows scholars, students, readers, publishers, and information users to have confidence that their electronic resources are authentic.

THE DIGITAL RESEARCH COLLECTION[13]

Intellectual preservation is only one aspect of the larger challenge of providing and maintaining digital research collections, collections that will continue the mission of research libraries to acquire information, organize it, make it available, and preserve it.[14] This has been the significant, distinctive, and successful mission of research libraries with print and other artifactual materials for the past several hundred years.[15]

I can informally put the new problem in the following way (and this audience will know how oversimplified this is): roughly speaking, if I put a book in a room and close the door, when I open the door in 500 years the information contained in the book will still be available. If I do that for any electronic storage device we now know about, the same will not be true, not even perhaps in ten years. The information may still exist in electronic form but we are unlikely to be able to read it with our newer technology. Different requirements arise out of the contrast between the artifactual nature of recorded information to this day and the evanescent instantiations of electronic information.

In this decade, the increasing volume of scholarly electronic information has brought many research libraries to attempt ways of providing it to their clienteles. As yet, however, no research library has taken on the expensive, uncharted, and difficult task of providing an electronic repository that organizes, provides, and preserves information at the levels of long-term commitment established for print materials.

Here I would like to set out some of what is likely to be required for a digital repository to be successful. Such a repository, a digital research collection (DRC), will from the start be committed to organizing, storing, and providing electronic information for periods of time longer than human lives. The information will be accessible through present and emerging access and retrieval technologies. A DRC will benefit from the experience of libraries in providing standardized cataloging techniques and other means of organization. A DRC will be preserved over long periods through several technological means—by protection of the media on which it resides, by regular transfer of data to new technological media, and by migration of information through software technologies.[16] The repository will guarantee the integrity of the information against accident, thoughtlessness, and fraud by providing authentication techniques that combine mathematical security with ease of use, credibility, and privacy protection.[17]

Implementation of the DRC will require two kinds of products, the repository itself and the tools for use with it, and will require commitments of several new kinds. In what follows, the technical requirements are given the most space, yet they probably present the easiest problems to solve; they just cost money. The final section on organizational commitments comprises by far the most difficult set of tasks. The issues are described here in cursory form. Each could be developed in great detail (and I am glad to see that Don Waters is also addressing them at this symposium), but, at the moment, the outline and overall program need most to be defined. Work needs to begin.

The Electronic Storage Repository

Megadocument Contents. An initial repository will comprise many gigabytes of information. The medium itself (disk storage) is cheap and the possible resources are plentiful.

Sources and Potential Participants. It is easy to cite numbers of electronic scholarly resources that now exist. A few are noted here only as examples (some being developed by participants in this audience):

- Johns Hopkins Medical Library medical image database and its e-Journal of Medical Imaging.
- Texts maintained by the Center for Electronic Texts in the Humanities at Rutgers/Princeton (for example, those of the Women Writers' Project).
- Preservation images from projects proposed and in development at the libraries of Yale, Stanford, and Cornell universities.
- Texts at the Georgetown University electronic text center, such as those of C.S. Peirce, Hegel, and Feuerbach, under varying licensing arrangements.
- Survey research data from the Interuniversity Consortium for Political and Social Research (ICPSR).
- AVIADOR, the Columbia University Libraries architecture image resource.
- Commercial publishers, either profit or nonprofit (for example, a university press, publications of a scholarly society, such as IEEE, a partnership with a commercial press); the proposition might be to test the use of the repository as a commercial alternative to local storage or no storage.
- Los Alamos National Laboratories Physics Preprint Data Base (now available on the World Wide Web—but for how long?).
- National Archives and Record Administration materials.
- e-journals now established on networks, especially if peer reviewed, for example, Psycoloquy, Bryn Mawr Classical Review, Journal of Fluids Engineering, Modal Analysis, OCLC Journal of Online Critical Trials (with attendant copyright issues), Scientist, Solstice.[18]
- Early network activity as examples of ephemera, for example, alternate (alt.x) newsgroups, information located at temporary FTP sites, samples of early advertisements, etc.
- Listserv and news group electronic archives.
- Commercial information databases that will not be made widely available, for example, Chadwyck-Healey's English Poetry, where it can be recognized that long-term preservation is necessary even though access might be licensed or otherwise constrained.

All these are only examples. None, of course, should automatically be selected; collection development policies should be adapted and followed. The continuing substantial costs of providing electronic information will require that electronic collection decisions be made even more carefully and parsimoniously than for print.

Staged Access. Alternatives for providing immediate online access to a great volume of electronic information need to be examined. Does it all need to be immediately available? What can be offline, and how would it be retrieved? Present alternatives include magnetic disk, optical disks and jukeboxes, optical disks shelved, and remote storage; perhaps even magnetic tape.

Backup Mechanisms. Backup/restore procedures must be in place and must be automated and economical, for libraries are never likely to have expensive labor available in quantity. Backups must be multigenerational with regular disaster simulations and tests.

Data Structure Standards. In a repository, does information simply exist as is or is complementary information associated with it (widely differing examples might include SGML [Standard Generalized Markup Language] headers, ICPSR code books, picture captions, hypertext links, and early software versions for use with data files)? If there is an association, is it through use of header portions of a file or supplemental files? How are they indicated and connected?

Refreshing Mechanisms. Refreshing will be necessary for long-term preservation across both media and software. There will be organizational and bureaucratic issues in addition to the simply technical: for example, copyright (if information is copied from magnetic to optical disk through an upgraded software version, copyright issues must be recognized), automation to reduce labor costs, work flow and recordkeeping, migration techniques, and standards and techniques that will apply independently of technology. It might be possible to link refreshing to backup techniques for expedience and economy.

Fees and Freedom (which in practice are often linked issues). Standards and techniques will be necessary to solve a knot of interconnected problems surrounding access and ownership, including

- Privacy preservation for users, while also ensuring
- Copyright protection for intellectual property holders, while also protecting
- Fair use mechanisms, and also providing
- Fee-charging techniques, including billing where relevant.

Authentication and Integrity. Intellectual preservation, as discussed above. Using the DTS technique or one like it, the DRC would establish a satellite DTS server and certificate validator, implement DTS on multiple formats, publish root certificates to make authentication practicable, and establish standards and conventions for use and citation.

Redundancy. It will be important to establish standards for the number of redundant repository locations necessary to assure long-term existence of specific electronic information and access to it. One location will not do for a particular major electronic document or set; will two or three? How many? Major institutions may separately or consortially establish repositories. It is not yet clear how much redundancy of their components will be desirable among them.

Aside from assuring longevity, other issues come to bear on decisions to provide multiple permanent copies of electronic information. Geographic location will still play a role (at least transoceanically and probably transcontinentally). The historical interplay between costs of network bandwidth and response time and costs of storage will require informed decisions that will require change from time to time.

Over time, we will learn how collection development plays out in an access environment as well as in an ownership environment. It is sometimes loosely proposed that libraries need not acquire electronic information for it will be available somewhere on the network. Such proposers ignore the obvious truth that some institution must still, in the end, take responsibility for the information–that is, in some way must own it. That has always been a library responsibility.[19]

Access Tools

Usage and Retrieval Mechanisms. The full panoply of present access tools must be supported–FTP, Gopher, World Wide Web (WWW), and clients such as Mosaic–with provision for new access tools likely to be developed regularly for some time. The "granularity" of documents needs to be addressed: how can one retrieve only part of a document when the full document may be of substantial size (for example, a chapter of *Moby Dick* or of a legal code or a particular chart from a numerical presentation)? Must documents be precoded to allow such granular access, or can access-time mechanisms be made available?[20] Techniques for document update and consequent archiving and labeling need to be developed, as well as flags indicating obsolescence or supersession (or, conversely, indicating status as an authorized version), for example, for ANSI standards, monthly statistical reports, or draft versions. A form of SGML is likely to be appropriate in many cases, particularly the format proposed by the Text Encoding Initiative (TEI).[21]

Cataloging. Providing access to voluminous information is an intellectual problem that has historically been solved in the print environment by cataloging, with its attendant rules and procedures to ensure consistency and accuracy. These tools, adapted to suit new needs, will work for electronic information as well.[22] They should be linked to the new retrieval mechanisms so that users can smoothly navigate from having located information to retrieving it without having to shift their mode of use. Early mechanisms will probably link catalog records to documents using tools such as the newly proposed MARC 856 field working with the representation of virtual locations through the Uniform Resource Characteristics, Locator, and Name (URI, URL, and URN).[23] SGML techniques may also offer possibilities for location and linking of documents through its document description techniques.[24]

If the DRC's catalog system works well, users will be able to search for information, locate bibliographic records for *desiderata*, and use those records directly to draw the desired information to their workstation.[25] If the digital time-stamping technique is used, means for including and testing the DTS certificate must be provided. Standards for such cataloging and remote access still need to be developed, particularly for providing catalog access to nonowned materials. The present review of AACR2 Chapter 9 is to be applauded, as is the recent OCLC study on the cataloging of nonbook materials.[26]

Remote Access. A DRC should from the outset be intended for access from multiple remote locations. Procedures for dissemination of such catalog records will be needed; it will be not only a technical matter but a policy matter for libraries associated with the DRC to provide nonlocal access to their local patrons. Presumably the existing bibliographic utilities will play their accustomed role.

The Necessary Commitments

Much of what has been described so far is merely technical, and the outlines of solutions are clear even if the details remain to be worked out in practice (they will only cost money). More difficult will be the social compacts also described, that is, the agreements on standards, intellectual property, and access modes. Most difficult of all to achieve, if electronic preservation and access are to be accomplished on any significant scale, will be the long-term commitments to these goals by institutions. Nothing makes clearer that a library is an organization, rather than a building or a collection, than the requirement for institutional commitment to assure more than a fleeting existence for electronic information.

Institutional commitments will be of at least two kinds: organizational and fiscal.

Organizational Commitment. The organization of libraries is already changing as electronic information increasingly becomes part of their charge. Most research libraries now have substantial systems departments. Some libraries separate the responsibility for electronic information distinctly from that for print. Other libraries see the forms as inseparable and include electronic responsibilities along with artifactual responsibilities in assignments for collection development, cataloging, and public service.

What is new will be the permanent assignment of staff responsibility for the long-term maintenance of electronic information within a library. There is no obvious artifactual parallel for this responsibility. For print, the long-term responsibility is now shared among the departments of circulation, stack maintenance, preservation, and physical plant. Nor are there present preservation parallels in academic computing centers, where staffs focus on technological advance and leave data to the users. The electronic preservation responsibility will be focused as it will require technical expertise likely to be located in a single functional area. We can see possible beginnings of such responsibilities in the electronic text personnel recently established at Iowa State University, Georgetown University, University of California at Berkeley and University of Virginia.

It is by no means clear that this functional area will be what we have called the library's systems department. As libraries move more into the electronic environment the historic tripartite division of libraries into public services, technical services, and collection development continues, but in more fluid arrangements. People who combine bibliographic understanding, problem-solving abilities, and process orientation have often been found in technical services. Similar librarians will take on the demanding new technical, collection, and service responsibilities for long-term support of digital collections.

Fiscal Commitment. The permanent existence of a digital research collection will require assured continuity in operational funding. Almost any other library activity can survive a funding hiatus of a year or more. Acquisitions, building maintenance, and preservation can be suspended, or an entire staff can be dispersed and a library shut down for several years, and the artifactual collections will more or less survive. Digital collections, like the online catalog, require continual maintenance if they are to survive more than a very brief interruption of power, environmental control, back up, migration, and related technical care.

Online catalogs offer a partial parallel. Their maintenance costs have reached a roughly steady state, and the capital costs are decreasing relative to the capabilities provided. The catalog size will continue to increase, but catalog records are small relative to the information to which they refer. However, DRCs, as a proportion of the library's supply of information, will grow for the foreseeable future, and the quantity of information requiring care will become considerable (and much larger than the catalog). Storage costs are likely to continue to drop substantially for some time, which may make the financial burden manageable. (Staffing costs are not expected to increase, as most libraries now recognize that overall staff growth for any reason will not be allowed for some time; reassignments, however, are likely.)

Long-term funding will be required to assure long-term care. Libraries and their parent institutions will need to develop new fiscal tools and use familiar fiscal tools for new purposes. Public institutions with their constraints to annual funding will have particular difficulties; existing procedures for capital or plant funding may provide precedents. One familiar technique is the endowment. It has been difficult to obtain private funding for endowments of concepts and services rather than books and mortar, but it is possible, and institutions might also build endowments out of operating funds over periods of time.

Some revenue streams associated with DRCs may be practical. Consortial arrangements may allow for lease or purchase of shares in a DRC. Shorter-term access might be provided to other institutions on a usage basis. Access could be sold to certain classes of users, for example, businesses, nonlocal clienteles, or specific information projects. Relations with publishers, presently difficult to perceive through the mists of intellectual property, might result in fee income for storage of electronically published materials during the copyright lifetime in which publishers collect usage fees. With commitment and imagination, long-term fiscal tools will be found.

Institutional Commitment. All these are instrumental means of accomplishing the greatest requirement, that of conscious, planned institutional commitment to preserve that part of the human record and human culture which will flower in electronic form. Where museums have preserved artifacts, libraries have preserved information (until now, in artifactual form). For the past century most research libraries have been associated with universities, and this connection seems likely to continue in the immediate future.[27] Whatever the governance structure, the institution will have to make a conscious decision that commits itself to providing resources.

For scholars and other libraries to have confidence that a given DRC is indeed likely to exist for the long term, the commitment will have to be clearly and publicly made. It will probably be desirable for guidelines or standards to be established defining what is meant by a long-term commitment and defining what electronic databases can qualify to be called a digital research collection. Just as donors of books, manuscripts, and archives look for demonstration of long-term care and commitment, so too will scholars and publishers as electronic information is created and requires a home.

CONTINUATION OF THE RESEARCH LIBRARY MISSION

The digital research collection, both for digital images and digital information generally, must guarantee the longevity and authenticity of information held in trust for present and future generations. Establishing a digital research collection continues the research library mission. To do so should be considered as natural as acquiring the next book or cataloging the next journal. Not to do so would be an abdication of that mission. The task calls not so much on new knowledge nor on new techniques, but upon informed commitment, that is, upon will. For librarians wondering what is to come of their profession in the electronic age, here is their challenge.

NOTES

1. Portions of this talk were derived from two publications of mine, *Intellectual Preservation: Electronic Preservation of the Third Kind* (Washington, DC: Commission on Preservation and Access, March 1994) and "Requirements of the Digital Research Collection" (submitted for publication to *College & Research Libraries*, January 1994; accepted, pending revisions, August 1994).

2. For one concise summary of the implications of the "sharp distinction between the carrier and the intellectual knowledge it contains," see Patricia Battin, "From Preservation to Access—Paradigm for the Future," *Annual Report July 1, 1992-June 30, 1993* (Washington, DC: Commission on Preservation and Access, 1993), 1-4.

3. See especially Lesk (below), but also Janice Mohlhenrich, ed., *Preservation of Electronic Formats: Electronic Formats for Preservation* (Fort Atkinson, WI: Highsmith, 1993), the proceedings of the 1992 WISPPR preservation conference. In it, Karen L. Hanus provides an extensive "Annotated Bibliography on Electronic Preservation" (121-136). See also "Implications of Electronic Formats for Preservation Administrators," Newsletter Insert: *Newsletter*, Commission on Preservation and Access, No. 62 (Nov.-Dec. 1993), 1-2.

4. Michael Lesk, *Preservation of New Technology: A Report of the Technology Assessment Advisory Committee to the Commission on Preservation and Access* (Washington, DC: CPA, 1992: available from the Commission at $5: 1400 16th S. NW, Suite 740, Washington, DC 20036-2217).

5. The archive community speaks of the importance of provenance in establishing that a piece of information is in fact a record. Electronic information by itself can have no demonstrable provenance; the authentication solution hereinafter described may be able to provide the equivalent.

6. Stuart Haber and W. Scott Stornetta, "How to Time-Stamp a Digital Document," *Journal of Cryptology* (1991) 3, 99-111; also, under the same title, as DIMACS Technical Report 90-80 ([Morristown,] New Jersey: December 1990). See also D. Bayer, S. Haber, and W.S. Stornetta, "Improving the Efficiency and Reliability of Digital Time-Stamping," *Sequences II: Methods in Communication, Security, and Computer Science*, ed. R. M. Capocelli et al (New York: Springer-Verlag. 1993), 329-334. A useful brief account is in Barry Cipra, "Electronic Time-Stamping: The Notary Public Goes Digital," *Science*, Vol. 261 (July 9, 1993), 162-163.

7. This is consonant with what Battin notes as in the future for librarians: "For analog information, we must develop triage strategies for the past: for digital, prospective triage strategies at the point of acquisition or *creation*" (my emphasis); Battin, 3-4.

8. Client/server software assumes a planned, cooperative relationship between two computers. The server typically provides a generalized source of information or a generalized service to a wide clientele, while the client provides computing intelligence physically close to the user and tailored to the user's specific machine and needs.

9. *Intellectual Preservation* (see note 1) contains further text and figures which amplify the discussion here of hashing and, below, of time-stamping. See also Peter S. Graham, "Preserving the Intellectual Record and the Electronic Environment," *Scholarly Communication and the Electronic Environment: Issues for Research Libraries*, ed. Robert Sidney Martin (Chicago: ALA, 1993), 71-101. Also published as "Intellectual Preservation and the Electronic Environment," *After the Electronic Revolution, . . . : Proceedings of the 1992 Association for Library Collections and Technical Services President's Program*, ed. Arnold Hirshon (Chicago: ALA, 1993), 18-38.

10. Stornetta reports that the newspaper was initially reluctant to accept the advertisement, fearing that a numbers scam or a drug connection was involved (informal communication).

11. Bellcore in 1994 spun off a small startup company, named Surety Technologies, Inc., which intends to market Digital Notary based on this concept.

12. The Research Libraries Group has determined to embark on a pilot project to develop a repository of electronic research collections. Identifying authentication requirements and solutions is seen as one task of such a project, and the Haber/Stornetta technique is under consideration.

13. Preliminary forms of what follows were presented at the ALCTS Institute: The Electronic Library (October 1993) and at a task force meeting of the Coalition for Networked Information (November 1993).

14. I have chosen the term *digital research collection* in preference to *digital library*. The latter term, preempted and given currency by Vice President Albert Gore and by the National Science Foundation, has become used typically to define merely a quantity of databases available for use at a given time. A library, however, is an organization, not a building full of books nor a network full of

databases. In library terms, therefore, a DRC is a set of electronic information organized for the long term.

15. Artificial materials include books, journals, manuscripts, recordings, and other information resources which are inseparably linked to the objects that are their medium, and therefore exist in space and require specific physical handling to use. In contrast with such materials, where to preserve the artifact is to preserve the information contained in it, electronic information is easily transferred from one medium to another with no loss.

16. See above and Lesk, as cited in note 4.

17. See above and Graham, as cited in notes 1 and 9.

18. Others will be found listed in *Directory of Electronic Journals, Newsletters and Academic Discussion Lists*, ed. Ann Okerson (Washington, DC: Association of Research Libraries, 1994, and earlier editions).

19. I take note of Stuart Lynn's comment in his initial presentation that there is much information out there on the network that is not dreamt of in our libraries and will never be maintained by us; yet the nature of what we select as libraries does force us to consider long-term implications. There are interesting print analogies with ephemera, gray literature, popular culture (such as ballads and now comic books), and libraries' dependence on the zealous initiative of collectors (for example, Pepys) as we eventually build great collections.

20. Clifford Lynch, *A Framework for Identifying, Locating, and Describing Networked Information Resources* (March 24, 1993; electronic "Draft for Discussion at March-April 1993 IETF Meeting"), n.p., section "Referencing Parts of Objects" (my citation in this form exemplifies the problem).

21. L. Burnard, *What Is SGML and How Does It Help?* TEI document TEI ED W25, October 1991, available from TEI fileserver (listserv@uicvm.uic.edu; send the line "get tei-L filelist"); International Organization for Standards, *ISO 8879: Information Processing–Text and Office Systems–Standard Generalized Markup Language (SGML)*, ISO, 1986; C.M. Sperberg-McQueen and L. Burnard (eds), *ACH-ACL-ALLC Guidelines for the Encoding and Interchange of Machine-Readable Texts [TEI]*, Draft version 1.1 (Chicago and Oxford, 1990; Draft version 2 to appear in 1994).

22. Lynch, in *Framework*, proposes "that the emphasis be on describing content . . . rather than access mechanisms" (§"Cataloging Networked Information Resources").

23. T. Berners-Lee et al, *Uniform Resource Locators (URL)*, August 13, 1994, available at <URL:ftp://ds.internic.net/internet-drafts/draft-ietf-uri-url-06.txt>; Michael Mealling, *Encoding and Use of Uniform Resource Characteristics*, July 8, 1994, available at <URL:ftp://ds.internic.net/internet-drafts/draft-ietf-uri-urc-spec-00.txt>; and K. Sollins and L. Masinter, *Requirments of Uniform Resource Names*, March 26, 1994, available at <URL:ftp://cnri.reston.va.us/internet-drafts/draft-sollins-urn.00. txt>. See also MARBI Proposal 93-4 (Nov. 20, 1992), p. 5 ff, for comments on the possible relations between the URL and the proposed MARC Jfield 856 (Electronic Location and Access); and MARBI Proposal 94-3 (Dec. 6, 1993), which specifically proposes adding a subfield $u to field 856 to accommodate a URL.

24. Lisa Horowitz, ed., "CETH Workshop on Documenting Electronic Texts: Technical Report #2" (Center for Electronic Texts in the Humanities, Rutgers/ Princeton, in press; the proceedings of a workshop held at Somerset, New Jersey, May 16-18, 1994).

25. For a further description of this potential for integration, see Peter S. Graham, "The Mid-Decade Catalog," in *ALCTS Newsletter* (January 1994), A-D.

26. Martin Dillon, et al, *Assessing Information on the Internet* (Dublin, Ohio: OCLC, 1993).

27. The national libraries are the great exceptions, such as those of Britain, Russia, France, Canada, and the United States. Exceptions in this country include the handful of independent research libraries such as the Folger, the Huntington, and the American Antiquarian Society, and some of the great civic institutions such as the Boston and New York Public Libraries.

For the possibility of the link between research libraries and universities being lost, see the 1991 Malkin Lecture of Terry Belanger, *The Future of Rare Book Libraries* (Charlottesville: Book Arts Press, in preparation; text available from Dec. 16, 1991 archive of ExLibris, a listserv at rutvm1.rutgers.edu, message from: terry@cunixa.cc.columbia.edu, subject: Malkin Lecture).

Transforming Libraries
Through Digital Preservation

Donald J. Waters

I would like to step back from the close technical detail of the various and excellent tutorials that have been presented and to fill in some details of other important dimensions of digital preservation. I want to put digital preservation in the larger context of changes in scholarly communication and to argue that preservation is at the center of those changes and that preservationists should not shrink from but rather aspire to the high purpose of that central transforming role. Then I want to turn to some of the economic and political aspects of this emerging transformation.

PRESERVATION AS AN AGENCY OF TRANSFORMATION

Jaroslav Pelikan, the renowned religious historian at Yale, tells a story which, he says, is no doubt apocryphal. In his book *The Idea of the University*, he recounts "that at the outbreak of the first World War a group of patriotic Englishwomen who were going about the countryside recruiting soldiers swept into Oxford. On the High Street one of them confronted a don in his Oxonian master's gown who was reading the Greek text of Thucydides. 'And what are you doing to save Western civilization, young man?' she demanded. Bringing himself up to his full height, the don looked down his nose and replied, 'Madam, I am Western civilization!' "[1]

I think of the role of the preservationist in today's research libraries in

---

Donald J. Waters is Director, Digital Library Federation, Council on Library and Information Resources, formerly Associate University Librarian at Yale University.

[Haworth co-indexing entry note]: "Transforming Libraries Through Digital Preservation." Waters, Donald J. Co-published simultaneously in *Collection Management* (The Haworth Press, Inc.) Vol. 22, No. 3/4, 1998, pp. 99-111; and: *Going Digital: Strategies for Access, Preservation, and Conversion of Collections to a Digital Format* (ed: Donald L. DeWitt) The Haworth Press, Inc., 1998, pp. 99-111.

much the same way as that Oxford don thought of his job, as personally discharging in his or her daily work the central mission of the university in the wider society. I would assert that the mission of the university and the library is to produce a literate citizenry. The broader functions of the university in support of that mission, including the preservation of knowledge, are enduring, but the means of scholarly communication by which the university discharges these various functions are today in flux. The university community must adjust to the changing means of communication, and because preservation programs are by definition a principal mechanism for renewing the assets of the university and the library, they can and should help drive the necessary adjustments. Let me develop this argument.

The Changing World of Scholarly Communication

Literacy, which is the business of the university and the library, is a critical faculty that enables citizens in a democratic society to engage sensibly and productively in the discourse of the world in which they live. Literate citizens are smart about information and its uses. The special functions of scholarly communication that contribute to literacy include enlarging and disseminating knowledge through teaching, research, and publication and through the preservation of access to the scholarly record in libraries.

These various scholarly functions that contribute to literacy will no doubt endure, but the means of scholarly communication are changing before our eyes. Today, computers can read to us. They can listen and obey, help compose and transform text, visualize complex processes, and create, store, and manipulate images, including photos, animation, and moving pictures. Through networks and digitization, scholarly communities now increasingly have a wide range of resources readily at hand, all creating needs for new kinds of literacy. The technology has improved access to people both near and far with vast arrays of personalities, skills, propensities, and special interests, and to knowledge of all types and in various media, from theories to raw data, from commentary to research proposals.

The pace and extent of change in these various means of communication differ by discipline, but scholars today exercise a growing ability to generate, transmit, and gain access to information when and where they need it. Moreover, the students they now face in the classroom belong to the Nintendo generation, the first generation of students who take highly interactive information technology for granted. There are negative elements about the video games that our children play. However, there are positive aspects that we should not overlook. For example, through interactive media, this generation is the first to have learned sophisticated problem solving in the company of artificial intelligence, rudimentary though that intelligence may be.[2]

Resources of the Past Enter the Electronic Future

In the face of changes in the means of scholarly communication and in the expectations of both faculty and students, the university community must adjust. Preservation programs can and should play a significant role in facilitating the needed adjustments. Preservation must be taken largely to include collection care, conservation, and reformatting. These processes all serve to recreate the printed record of knowledge in the technologies of the present and the future. Digital preservation or, more precisely, in the sense of this conference, digital reformatting, is an opportunity to bring paper-based or analog resources of the past into the electronic future. It can thereby serve to renew the scholarly record and, with it, the economic and political foundations of the larger library and university institutions.

THE POLITICAL ECONOMY
OF INSTITUTIONAL TRANSFORMATION

I turn now to some of the dimensions of digital preservation that we have not yet fully addressed in this conference–to what I would call the political economy of institutional transformation. Other speakers in this conference have asserted that we need new capacities to accommodate digital information in addition to the existing capacities required to support analog information. I want us here to focus on the economies of adding such new services and turn then to some of the accompanying organizational issues.

Economic Issues

With respect to the economic issues, the central questions that we have to address are these: what is the business case for adding new digital capacities and services to the library? And what are the scarce resources that need to be economized in order to pave the way for adding these new capacities and services? To help answer these questions, I want to introduce the broad distinction between just-in-time and just-in-case service.

In making a business case for additional digital capacities and services, it is not enough for us to assert that there is a need for them. There are simply too many worthy and competing needs in our institutions–for teaching and research programs, for information resources, for facilities, and for staff to manage them all. As responsible administrators in higher education today, we have to persuade ourselves and our colleagues that the need for digital information services is sufficiently compelling that we and they can and must allocate limited, if not shrinking, resources to the effort. There are several lines of argument that one can follow to make a persuasive case.

Reallocation of Resources. One can assert, for example, that existing services be routinized, streamlined, and automated to allow current resources to be reallocated to new and anticipated services. Despite the pain of cuts in library budgets, which all of us have recently endured, we are still looking for more ways to trim expenses, and there seems to be room for more. Many of us are developing methods of automated or outsourced cataloging, authority control, and acquisitions, and we are all investing in work-stations that will enable staff to streamline their flow of work. We intend all these efforts to drive the cost of existing processes down. The larger question, as we work on those efforts, is whether or not we can reallocate those savings in the library.

New Technologies and the Possibility of Real Savings. Another argument is that investment in these new services will produce savings over the old–that is, new digital resources and services will transform and replace the paper-based services that libraries traditionally provide. In the rhetoric about new technologies and the emergence of the so-called virtual library, one frequently encounters the assertion that digital services will not produce savings but will instead require huge incremental investments of resources over what we are currently spending. At Yale, we decided to challenge the perceived wisdom about the need for incremental spending and explore whether the adoption of digital technologies and services might not eventually reduce our investment in traditional services. In the following remarks, I present some of our preliminary findings.

As we pursue the question of generating real savings in our current library operations through investment in digital technologies and services, we must ask a further question: what are the scarce resources that need to be economized to produce the savings? Information most definitely is not the scarce resource here. The effects in libraries of rising journal prices notwithstanding, we are choking on information. And there are many images in the popular media that immediately come to mind to illustrate the information glut.

One popular image is the information spigot. You probably all have seen the cartoon: the huge pipe pouring out its contents into the open mouth of an individual who cannot swallow it all and is choking on the volume. Another image with a similar message is the house on the prairie where the massive cables constituting the information highway overload the house. From inside, a voice asks, "Now, how do I order pizza?"

Indeed, the scarce commodity in the present environment, as depicted more or less clearly in these popular images, is the human attention required to make sense of the information. Richard Lanham refers to the scarce commodity as an *attention-structure*.[3] I particularly like his characterization because it is service-oriented and applies directly to the value we add in libraries as we preserve access to the scholarly record. We organize it in meaningful ways so that relevant material comes to the attention of scholars and students as they need it.

Just-in-Time vs. Just-in-Case. On the demand side of the library attention-structures, there are, as we have already discussed, sophisticated applications of digital technology that now make it possible for scholars to gain access to widely dispersed materials whenever and wherever they want. On the supply side, one can broadly distinguish just-in-time accessibility from just-in-case service. To help analyze the differences between these two approaches, one can develop a model of comparative costs. Table 1 contains a summary of such a model, which we have developed at Yale. I want to highlight several features of the model and suggest some conclusions we might draw from it.

As we have seen in this conference and in other forums, digital preservation is a very complex business involving a multitude of interacting components. For planning purposes, the assumptions we make about the interactions need to be explicit. A model like the one we have developed at Yale, and which you see summarized here, is a way of making those assumptions explicit so that we can rigorously test, explore, and reason from them to plausible conclusions about our digital future.

As we created this particular model, we recognized that the organizational, social, and physical differences between the just-in-case and just-in-time approaches are numerous and that for each library function we could analyze the differences in detail. However, we have assumed that the central distinction between the two approaches rests in two components: storage and access. For simplicity, we have factored out the other variables.

We have projected the costs of the storage and access components over ten years, and the model here shows only the cost of storing and providing access to new materials for the year in which they are first brought into the library; it does not show the continuing costs for carrying those items in the library. Nor does this model account for the costs of conversion; we

TABLE 1. Summary Model of Just-in-Case vs. Just-in-Time Library Service

	Year 1	Year 4	Year 7	Year 10
New Volumes	180,000	180,000	180,000	180,000
"Just-in-case" Storage and Access–Paper Depository Model **(volumes stored = new volumes)**				
Estimated Annual Use (13% of volumes)	24,051	24,051	24,051	24,051
Depository Storage Costs Per Volume	$0.24	$0.27	$0.30	$0.34
Total Depository Storage Costs	*$43,200*	*$48,594*	*$54,662*	*$61,487*
Depository Access Costs Per Volume Used	$4.04	$4.54	$5.11	$5.74
Total Depository Access Costs	*$97,075*	*$109,196*	*$122,831*	*$138,168*
Total Depository Storage and Access Costs	**$140,275**	**$157,790**	**$177,493**	**$199,655**
"Just-in-Time" Storage and Access–Digital Model **(volumes stored = volumes used)**				
Estimated Annual Use (18% of volumes)	33,051	33,051	33,051	33,051
Digital Storage Costs Per Volume	$3.32	$1.00	$0.30	$0.09
Total Digital Storage Costs	*$109,684*	*$32,989*	*$9,922*	*$2,984*
Total Access Costs Per Volume Used	$8.28	$3.71	$2.08	$1.46
Total Digital Access Costs	*$273,628*	*$122,588*	*$68,609*	*$48,187*
Total Digital Storage and Access Costs	**$383,312**	**$155,577**	**$78,531**	**$51,171**
Difference	*($243,036)*	*$2,214*	*$98,962*	*$148,484*

have assumed that publishers can generate volumes for purchase in either paper or digital image form. Finally, we made some assumptions about the quantity of information that comes into the library and that readers use each year. On the just-in-case side–the traditional way of doing business in research libraries–we have used actual circulation statistics to project the portion of newly acquired material that actually gets used in any one year. For the just-in-time approach–the digital library–we have assumed that the material is more accessible and it will see a slightly higher rate of use.

The High Costs of Storage and Access. Research libraries have traditionally mediated teaching and research by selecting substantial and intellectually coherent portions of the published record to store locally just in case the scholar or student needs them. However, the ideal mode of storing this material, the browsable stack, is difficult if not impossible these days to justify for new construction. Increasingly, our institutions are concluding that remote depository libraries are an acceptable and more economical alternative to the browsable stack.

A depository library can store large amounts of material very efficiently. The published price at the Harvard depository, for example, is $2.40 per linear foot per year. A linear foot consists, on average, of 11 books. This is an extremely cheap mode of storage.

However, to gain access to the materials, scholars must page needed items from those depositories and wait for them to be delivered. Document delivery in the depository version of the just-in-case approach is highly labor dependent and subject to increasing inflationary costs. The high and rising unit cost for access in this approach, which is apparent in Table 1, captures the biggest weakness of this approach. It puts needed material out of reach just when scholars are motivated otherwise to look for it just in time.

On the other hand, the just-in-time approach provides for the digital storage of image texts and for access to them over networks just as scholars need them, at least theoretically. Large simplifying assumptions are necessary in this model about the ready availability of material in digital form from publishers and the contractual agreements that can be made. We assume that the library contracts with publishers for the eventual use of materials and then makes these materials accessible on campus only after the first request, that is, just in time. We assume further that hardware and software costs will continue to deflate rapidly over the period projected here. Under these assumptions, access services for the just-in-time approach dominate the model.

Notice that by the fourth year unit access costs are projected to be cheaper than the depository approach; total access costs exceed the depository model only because we have assumed a higher rate of use in this just-in-time library. Digital storage, however, is relatively inefficient over the period. Unit costs do not overtake those projected for depository storage until the seventh year. The total storage costs are less in the just-in-time approach than in a depository approach because volumes are stored only as they are used.

A Time for Research and Development. What kinds of conclusions can we draw from this analysis? If we can accept the underlying assumptions, there is both good news and bad. The good news is that investments in digital technologies and in related just-in-time services appear to provide an opportunity for libraries to realize substantial ongoing savings over the next decade. However, the technology is clearly not economical for operational use today. And no matter how economical digital technology may appear in the immediate future, if scholars do not find it useful, any investment will fail. Unfortunately, we know almost nothing concrete about the usefulness of digital image technology in a scholarly context.

Given the prospect of future savings over a four- to seven-year horizon, I would assert that a business case does exist, and would characterize it in the following way: the time is right for investment not for operational use but for intensive research and development to ensure the use and usability of new technologies and services. If we think clearly of our efforts today not as operational but as developmental, then we must ask ourselves a further question: what actions are necessary today to prepare our organizations for a just-in-time model of library service in the future?

Organizational Issues

Essential to developing an appropriate organization in which we can incorporate both traditional paper-based and digital library services is a conceptual model of the emerging library and information services. As we work to develop such a model in practice, we need to think very carefully about creating organizational structures that effectively sideline existing staff from one or the other kind of service. Furthermore, we need to engage faculty and students systematically in processes to gauge the quality and usability of digital text. Let me develop each of these points in turn.

Figure 1 depicts a model of emerging library and information services. In the foreground is the reader, who uses the workstation at his or her desktop and traverses a network to gain access to a variety of information sources. The sources range from online catalogs to various kinds of hypermedia and include abstracts and indexes, finding aids, full-text documents, numeric data, images of various kinds, maps, sound and video, and multimedia. These various kinds of sources presumably exist at one's local institution and are all mirrored at other places that are accessible, at least theoretically, over the network. To gain access to these sources—and this is the point that I want to emphasize—the reader has to penetrate a variety of services: the network, what I call retrieval services, data and document

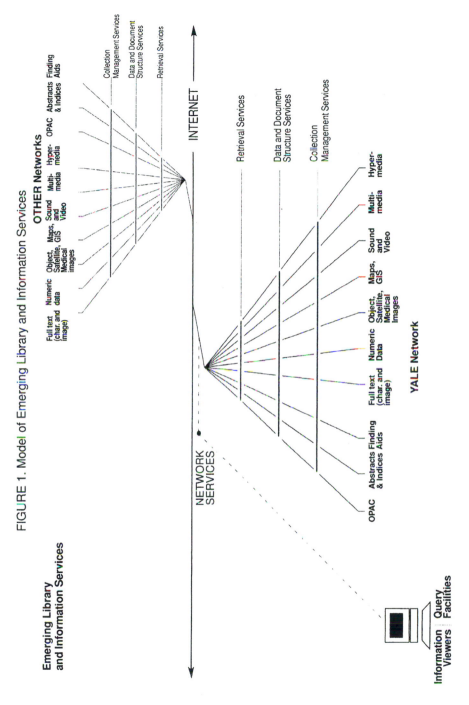

FIGURE 1. Model of Emerging Library and Information Services

structure services, and collection management services. The structure required to bring relevant information to the attention of the reader is, I would argue, complex, layered, and similar to, if not isomorphic with, the layered structures libraries have long developed to provide paper-based information services.

Networked Digital Information. In developing this model one has to assume that readers have access to workstations and are skilled in their use. Of course, in many of our institutions today, this assumption is not necessarily valid. Use of the workstation requires, moreover, navigation tools to locate, query, and view network-based information sources. Those services are represented at the terminal.

With respect to the network, digital information services require the development of a dependable, high-speed, high-bandwidth network to support the use of digital information. We must also provide reliable authentication and security services, a point that Peter Graham emphasized in his talk and that Clifford Lynch developed at length in a recent paper for the Office of Technology Assessment. Authentication and security services are desperately needed to foster the development of vigorous and competitive markets and network-based digital information. Large competitive markets for networked digital information will help drive down the costs of digital technology. Commerce in those markets will develop, however, only if transactions are secure and confidential, only if there is some form of electronic rights clearance and protection, and only if users can readily verify that the attribution of authorship in a document is true, and that the copy they are looking at has the same content as the version the author originally published.[4]

Retrieval Services. Retrieval services link queries initiated at the desktop with relevant information, and they deliver the information for display to the user. We need to anticipate and prepare for a generation of integrated library systems that link catalog records with electronic text and other electronic sources. We also need to select and support servers for marked-up text, compound text, and graphic documents, and we need to ask how our retrieval systems interact with the query facilities through such protocols as Z39.50, Gopher, and World Wide Web on the workstation side and, on the other side, with the automated facilities for the other underlying services.

Data and Document Structure Services. Work at the data and document structure services level consists of the ordering and shaping activity that generates the core of any effective attention-structure. In a networked environment where movement through gopher tunnels or world wide webs can rapidly leave one lost in cyberspace, there is a continuing need for catalogs, abstracts, indices, and other kinds of finding aids. There is also an increasing need for new and higher-order kinds of representations of knowledge and information. Examples of such products that would support network navigation include the development of catalogs of catalogs, the representations of the internal document structures via mark-up languages and other methods, and the representations of visual, video, and sound materials as well as hyperlinkages among these various documents and sources.

Selection, Storage, and System Management Services. Finally, there is a variety of collection, storage, and system management services to which we need to pay attention. What materials are going to comprise the digital collection? We have barely scratched the surface of the selection issue, which promises no fewer challenges in the digital than in the analog world. How are digital materials most effectively and efficiently stored and staged for delivery? We have a lot to learn here technically and organizationally about the nature of electronically distributed information systems. What are the policies and procedures for backing up a digital library and refreshing or converting it to accommodate new media and encoding techniques? This is the problem of refreshment. And then, perhaps at the lowest level, is the facilities question: what operating systems and computer platforms will we support?

The Isomorphic Model. Given this model, what kinds of organizations do we need to institute the emerging services effectively and efficiently? The temptation, of course, as we begin to introduce digital services is to stress the different qualities of those services and to set up a separate organization that exists alongside our existing organizations for paper-based services. I would suggest that we need to think cautiously about such parallel organizations. They are very easy to fabricate, but often difficult to dismantle or to integrate, as they eventually must be, with the existing organization. Instead, the model that I have advanced here emphasizes the similarity–the isomorphism, if you will–of the traditional and emerging services.

The retrieval services that I have outlined are isomorphic with traditional public services, the data and document structure services are isomorphic with cataloging, the collection management services with acquisitions, and the collection development and network services isomorphic with circulation. The isomorphism suggests, I would argue, a strategy for organizational and political transformation from within our institutions. It suggests where the resource trade-offs need to occur and what kind of skills we need to develop in our staff. As a practical application of the principle of isomorphism in organizational change, consider the strategy we adopted in Project Open Book to define the staff positions we need to operate the conversion process. Rather than create a new position for digital reformatting alongside the microfilm operator, we worked with the local union and the human resources department to create a series of positions called reformatting technicians, which encompasses both activities.

User-Centered Design. Finally, as we move to create organizations capable of delivering traditional and emerging digital information services, we need to engage faculty and students systematically and develop processes to gauge the quality and usability of digital text. Each layer of service that I have outlined affects usability and needs a user-centered design. The design point is that the use of digital text should measurably improve scholarly communication, and we must be rigorous in holding to this standard. We need to assume that users will want to transfer to a digital environment well-known and documented information-seeking strategies for research and teaching, such as footnote chasing, citation searching, and so on.[5] We need to measure the appropriateness of those emerging digital-based services by their ability to facilitate these kinds of strategies. Periodically we then need to confirm that teaching and research in a digital environment still depends on the strategies transferred from an analog or paper-based environment, and we must monitor, adjust to, and incorporate the transformed means of scholarly communication that will almost certainly develop and that will be especially adapted to forms of digital information.

A REVOLUTION IS LIKE A COCKTAIL

Will Rogers once said that a revolution is like a cocktail–it just gets you organized for the next. The information revolution that appears to be underway is not the first revolution in the organization of knowledge. The question is, how well did those earlier cocktails organize us for this one, or are we again just drunk with hype? And let me read to you some hype.

We are very much concerned with the user's access to information at the desktop. Here is a description of a desktop.

> With this desk a man absolutely has no excuse for slovenly habits in the disposal of his numerous papers, and the man of method may here realize that pleasure and comfort which is only to be attained in the verification of the maxim: a place for everything and everything in its place. The operator having arranged and classified his books, papers, et cetera, seats himself for business at the writing table and

realizes at once that he is master of the situation. Every portion of his desk is accessible without change of position and all immediately before the eye. Here he discovers that perfect system and order can be attained; confusion avoided; time saved and [I love this] vexation spared; dispatch in the transaction of business facilitated and peace of mind promoted in the daily routine of business.[6]

Don't you want one of these? This advertisement appeared in 1880 and describes the Wooton Patent Desk. The desk is a lovely piece of furniture, but, as Donald Norman points out in *Things That Make Us Smart*, it proved for a variety of design reasons to be relatively useless.[7] It did not spare vexations. It created more and worse ones.

As we as preservationists aspire to the high purpose of renewing the record of knowledge using digital technologies, and as our political, economic, and technical strategies for doing so lead us to transform our institutions, let us resolve at least to learn from one past drunken mistake and avoid the fabrication of another Wooton Patent Desk.

NOTES

1. Jaroslav Pelikan, *The Idea of the University—A Reexamination* (New Haven: Yale University Press, 1992), 137.

2. Paul Evan Peters, "What Networking Means for Higher Education." Talk presented to the staff of the Yale University Library, New Haven, Connecticut, February 15, 1994.

3. Richard Lanham, *The Electronic Word: Democracy, Technology and the Arts* (Chicago: The University of Chicago Press, 1993), 227-228.

4. Clifford Lynch, *Accessibility and Integrity of Networked Information Collections* (contractor report prepared for the Office of Technology Assessment, Telecommunications and Computing Technologies Program, July 5, 1993), 69.

5. See, for example, Marcia Bates, "The Design of Browsing and Berrypicking Techniques for the Online Search Interface," *Online Review* (1989) 13:5, 412-414.

6. Quoted in Deborah Cooper, "Evolution of Wooton Patent Desks," in *Wooton Patent Desks: A Place for Everything and Everything in its Place*, J. Camille Showalter and Janice Driesbach, eds. (Indianapolis and Oakland: Indiana State Museum and The Oakland Museum, 1983).

7. Donald Norman, *Things That Make Us Smart: Defending Human Attributes in the Age of the Machine* (Reading, Massachusetts: Addison-Wesley Publishing Co., 1993), 158-159.

PART 2.
STRATEGIES FOR SELECTING COLLECTIONS FOR CONVERSION TO A DIGITAL FORMAT

Why Make Images Available Online: User Perspectives

Hinda F. Sklar

THE USERS' POINT OF VIEW

Imagine you are an architectural historian located in New York City doing research on the Empire State Building. You are particularly interested in finding pictures of the building and its immediate surroundings in the early part of the 20th century. You decide to visit your favorite research institution, the New York Public Library, to investigate possible sources of information. A librarian sends you to the Division of Art, Prints, and Photographs, where you begin your search for images. Your research indicates that the Avery Library at Columbia University has an Empire State Building archive and that the photographer Karl Struss, whose collection is at the Amon Carter Museum, also photographed New York

Hinda F. Sklar is Associate Dean for Information Services and Librarian at the Frances Loeb Library, Harvard Graduate School of Design.

[Haworth co-indexing entry note]: "Why Make Images Available Online: User Perspectives." Sklar, Hinda F. Co-published simultaneously in *Collection Management* (The Haworth Press, Inc.) Vol. 22, No. 3/4, 1998, pp. 113-122; and: *Going Digital: Strategies for Access, Preservation, and Conversion of Collections to a Digital Format* (ed: Donald L. DeWitt) The Haworth Press, Inc., 1998, pp. 113-122.

City between 1908 and 1917, and therefore might be a resource for pertinent images for your study.

Discussion with the division librarian leads you to an online resource located in the department, the Digital Image Access Project online database, containing the images and records from photographic collections from nine institutions across the country. You sit down at the designated terminal and, after searching simultaneously across all nine databases using the term "Empire State Building," you cull a series of small images which display together on your screen. You select six of these images to enlarge and further study on the screen before you decide to request photographic copies of three images: two from the Avery Library collection and one from the Struss collection. You decide to download the three images to some floppy disks so that you can study them further at home, noting as you do the copyright restrictions on the images. You then speak to the librarian about contacting the two institutions to arrange for $8'' \times 10''$ photographs to be made. Your work complete, you gather up your things and prepare to leave. The entire process has taken you about an hour and a half.

The Research Libraries Group Digital Image Access Project (DIAP), which has been the focus of our efforts over the past year and a half, had as its central goal the exploration of "the capabilities of digital image technology for providing effective access to photographic materials."[1] Photographic materials, which are a subset of a broader class of visual materials that includes slides, drawings, paintings, maps, plans, posters, and all manner of two-dimensional visual works, can be scattered within any given collection or across collections, may be voluminous in size, fragile in form, and are generally difficult to manage and handle. Digitization of these unique visual resources can provide users of our collections unprecedented access to these materials in an effective, efficient manner while preserving the artifactual integrity of the individual items. I will talk today about the user perspective on digitizing visual materials: what are the benefits for the users of our collections, and how does digitization enrich the scholarly and nonscholarly community of users?

THE USE OF IMAGES

Images—photographs, paintings, drawings, and such—are unique resources. Why do people want images? Images serve a variety of functions in a research or information environment. They can visually illustrate an idea or concept, such as an illustration of the concept of perspective or how light refracts into a range of colors when passed through a prism.

Images can be used to develop a theory or idea further. For example, Wassily Kandinsky, a prominent member of the Bauhaus, developed creative theories about color which formed one of the core principles of the Bauhaus approach to color; his students used a variety of images to illustrate his color theories. Images also allow people to understand the visual environment that might serve as the context of a philosophical idea, a built environment, or a period in social history. For example, what does the area look like around the National Gallery in London, and how did that affect or influence the architects' design of the new wing of that museum? Or what were the social conditions in 1919 that gave rise to the Bauhaus movement in Weimar, Germany? And finally, images can be used simply to provide a visual hook upon which to hang a hat: an image of the Empire State Building used to represent New York City, for example, or the famous photograph of Jackson Pollack painting in his studio used to exemplify modern artists and techniques.

Once people determine what images they might need, they then are faced with the task of locating them–no easy feat these days with the variety of periodicals, books, and special collections in our public libraries, museums, and academic institutions around the country and the world. Most users find themselves consulting card catalogs, printed finding aids, or other research tools to locate the images they need. Using a variety of controlled vocabularies, familiar and unfamiliar, and a host of different systems, local and national, they comb these resources to locate appropriate images. Often, however, they find the easiest way to locate images is to search through books on their particular topic to look for visual clues.

When users have located images, the images are then physically handled in a variety of ways. Users look at the images to ensure their suitability for the intended purpose, often comparing several images with each other and then sorting and arranging them by personal criteria. Once researchers have sorted them into categories for use in a particular context, they may choose a specific image, or two or three, for which they want copies. The copies may take the form of photocopies, or users may ask for photographs. Depending on the intended use for the image, users might, during the course of their work, need to modify a specific image or manipulate it and change it in some way. Images, then, are used in different ways by researchers, historians, publishers, or designers; the intended use of the images helps determine the nature of the particular chosen image or series of images.

IMAGES IN DESIGN EDUCATION

I will illustrate some of what I have been discussing by describing how images play a role in the educational process at the Graduate School of Design (GSD) at Harvard. The GSD focuses on teaching architecture, landscape architecture, and urban design to future design professionals. Our users are primarily visually oriented; they read, of course, but the printed word ranks far down their list of primary resources! Certainly their first frame of reference is visual, and they use a healthy proportion of the library's resources almost exclusively for their visual content.

What do they look for when they go through our materials? For architects, landscape architects, and urban designers, the products of spatial design are buildings, landscapes, or urban contexts. The designer's art relies in large part on the ability to represent the abstract spatial concepts which form the basis of the designed environment. The design process involves the statement of a problem, the subsequent definition of a series of possible solutions, and the selection of a final design solution that, in the eyes of the designer or design team, best solves the stated problem and also meets a set of criteria that emerged during the process of defining potential solutions. The designer may arrive at design solutions using an array of design methodologies ranging from the study of historical and contemporary precedents in building or landscape types to the analysis of work produced over a specific time period by a single designer or by a design movement.

The design process itself draws on a wide range of material: site plans, soil surveys, census data, zoning codes and other regulatory statutes, maps, drawings, and sketches. Of necessity the designer amasses a large amount of data which is consulted throughout the design process. The design student or professional architect also depends heavily on images (for example, photographs and three-dimensional models) which are copied, disassembled and reassembled, or reconstructed in other ways to stimulate his/her design thinking. The result, regardless of the designer's methodology, is a design that fulfills both the spatial needs of the problem and the social and contextual criteria that are developed during the design process.

At the GSD, the search for visual materials leads our users to a variety of resources: periodicals, books, videos, planning reports, maps, drawings, plans, and sketches. Our students go through quantities of material very rapidly, often using them where they find them—on the floor, between stack ranges, on shelving trucks in the photocopying room. They photocopy materials heavily, sometimes to actually read something, but more often to further play around with or manipulate and analyze images. And they scan images from books and periodicals as well, using a flatbed scanner that produces digital images that can be manipulated or deconstructed, using a computer, to understand the underlying design principles.

ONLINE IMAGES: ADVANTAGES TO USERS

As you can see, at the GSD images are paramount to our students–and in an environment where constant pressure is the rule and time is a precious commodity. How then can an online environment benefit those who need illustrative materials, such as GSD students or users of the New York Public Library, who range from publishing industry to academic to private researchers?

First, users can perform a range of searches in a variety of contexts in one location through one tool–the computer. In addition, computerized access allows users enormous flexibility in how they formulate and manage searching. Users can search using specific subject terms through controlled vocabularies, using keywords, or using form and genre terms. Computers also provide browsing options to users, for example, from the "top down" (the traditional archival system of cataloging) or other logical ways across hierarchies and subject headings and indexing terms.

Second, computerized access also allows searching many collections in many different locations–either in one search or in multiple searches in one system. This means that users do not have to travel to far-flung sites or search individually through a multiplicity of finding aids to get information–and visual information–on widespread collections and resources.

Third, when computerized searching provides access to the images themselves, users have instant direct access to surrogates of the material. And electronic access provides new ways of using visual resources. A number of images can display on the screen at once and be compared easily and rapidly. Movement between images is simple, and selection of possible images for use can be done in a relatively short period of time. Studies have shown that users can make decisions based on electronic visual stimuli much more quickly than when examining slides individually on a light table, for example. The images that have been selected can be enlarged and studied in detail with a simple click of the mouse, and images can be downloaded for further study and use (providing existing copyright restrictions are followed). Downloading onto a floppy or the hard drive offers users the ability to import images into photo-rendering software and to then manipulate and edit the images and create new images. Downloading also offers the possibility of transferring images directly onto slides or of projecting the images from the computer through an overhead digital projector onto a large-sized screen, thus allowing presentations to be done easily and directly from the computer.

Fourth, as more and more of our images in collections are digitized, users can find materials that span collections and institutions that might otherwise not he known or available. Broad access can be offered to a unique set of resources, fostering new intellectual depth and breadth in research.

Fifth, in today's networked environment, resources can be found and examined from almost anywhere without time constraints, as long as one has access to a computer with a modem and communications software. The students at the GSD, for example, are interested in any form of access to resources that will free up time and allow them to work whenever they want from wherever they are–which is often at their studio desk at 3 a.m. in the morning! Online access to a database of digital images will enable them to do what is currently considered library research whenever they want, whether the library is open or not.

And, finally, in our familiar library/museum context, there is a "one user/one image" limitation on access to materials. Each piece of visual material is available to only one user at a time–that is, there are not necessarily multiple copies of books or images, so that when one slide or book or photograph is in use by one user, generally no one else can use it. This principle constricts users' ability to use all the resources that might exist on a topic. Digital networked images can be used simultaneously by a number of users, thus broadening the range of resources available at a given time.

ONLINE IMAGES: ADVANTAGES FOR SERVICE PROVIDERS

What are the advantages of online access to images for those who provide access to users–the librarians and archivists of our world? If we look at the list of advantages for users, we see that the same advantages hold true for service providers.

First, computers offer access via a variety of vocabularies to resources within and outside our immediate collections. Users can look for things using familiar terms or, with a bit of guidance, they can string together creative searches to more narrowly–or broadly–come up with a range of possible solutions. The fact that multiple vocabularies and searching techniques are possible allows users to use terminology and methods with which they feel comfortable with a minimum of guidance. As the caretakers of images and collections, it is to our benefit to lead our users to as rich an array of resources as possible, and giving our users the capability to do so on their own is an important benefit.

Second, through the effective online cataloging and digitization of related images, we can provide broad access across subjects and collections to a disparate set of materials without having to locate images through a multitude of separate finding aids or catalogs, and then retrieve each image. As collection managers, this means that we will no longer need to keep the variety of physical finding aids at hand that we currently do and work with our users to understand how to use the sometimes bewildering array of material. Neither will we need to pull out and refile boxes of photographs or dozens of slides for users who are searching for the perfect illustration, or indeed, provide so many large, flat work spaces for users to spread out those numbers of photographs and drawings to study.

Third, by providing direct access to digital surrogates of images (which can be used in so many ways), we can defray the wear and tear on our originals, thus preserving those originals for more intensive scholarship and study needs. The preservation community has long recommended the creation of surrogates as a preservation tool, and microfilm has been the recommended format. However, as standards are established for digital reproductions, I believe that digital formats will become an accepted standard, particularly since the quality of the image is far superior to that on microfilm for certain kinds of material, particularly visual materials. Additionally, because digital imagery offers the possibility of saving a single image in a number of different resolutions (that is, in a variety of dots per inch), which affect the quality of the image as well as the amount of storage per image, we can give users lower-resolution images for study purposes, while higher-resolution images can be reserved for approved, licensed, copyright-acknowledged-and-paid-for reproductions. The Getty Art History Information Program (AHIP) Imaging Initiative is currently pursuing a project that is investigating the acceptable quality levels for images needed by users for particular classes of use. As collection managers it is a wonderful benefit to be able to provide access to large amounts of material without having to deal directly with the physical images themselves.

Fourth, much as computerization provides access to information that might be spread out across collections, institutions, or countries, digital images can be distributed among a variety of locations and accessed over a network from any properly equipped terminal. This capability for distributed location and networked access will allow librarians and archivists to manage their digital resources locally while providing widespread access to these resources to as broad a community of users as they wish.

Fifth, access to resources which are delivered electronically and can occur without regard to date or time of day—when the researcher needs information, research can take place—can only benefit us as service providers at a time when fiscal constraints have already shortened open hours in many collections.

And, finally, as I said earlier, multiple users can access the same material, thus providing a broader accessibility to limited resources. This network access capability is the first step in the development of the true library without walls open to all, at any time, from anywhere, to provide information needs to a community of users.

COPYRIGHT ISSUES

The question of copyright is always raised when people talk about a digital environment. How do we handle copyright? Are these image databases violating copyright? What are we doing to protect the copyright owners?

Copyright is a major issue in the development of any widely available networked resource. Indeed, it has become one of the biggest stumbling blocks in the move towards the notion of a digital library of the future. In the United States, the copyright laws protect material from being widely copied and distributed without permission from the copyright holder except as defined under the "fair use" provision, which allows one-time copying for a class or for personal use, following defined guidelines.[2] How do these laws translate to the electronic world, where digital technology empowers people to manipulate and modify information they receive from other sources? Although no definitive legal statement has been made about image databases, there is a growing body of research and writing in that area.

Perhaps the clearest positive statement on copyright related to electronic resources that I have read comes from an article by Mary Kay Duggan, a library science faculty member at the University of California at Berkeley. She explains that the fair use principle allows single copies of pieces of information—sound, text, image—to be used for educational database creation by direct downloading, OCR scanning, optical scanning, or sound recording.[3]

However, copyright is being hotly debated by publishers and vendors even as we meet here, and the concept of fair use as it applies to digital environments is coming under close scrutiny. The publishers believe that digitization offers unheard of (and irresistible) opportunities for violation of copyright, and are currently pursuing a path that would disallow the concept of fair use for the digital world. In the meantime, what can we do?

We can build in features specifically to manage copyright and reproduction issues, for example, by providing fields in each record associated with the image that cite the source of that image and the copyright owner. We can provide a copyright "stamp" below each image. As I stated earlier, by providing lower-resolution images for certain levels of study we can prevent the downloading or copying of images that would be usable for other purposes, particularly publication. We can also prevent downloading or copying of images based on user ID or IP address; in other words, where we know we own the copyright and wish to provide our own users with copying capabilities, we can do so more easily in an online environment. We can also track image use and copying and build in charging mechanisms such as commercial services do; at the same time, we can provide far better records than we currently do in an age where everything gets tossed onto a photocopier by users.

For the RLG Digital Image Access Project, the nine institutions involved used images for which they owned the copyright or for which there were no copyright issues. At the GSD, where we are currently developing an image database called DOORS (Design Oriented Online Resource System), we have been careful to include only images that we know are either out of copyright or from known, relatively "safe" sources. We are not scanning slide sets or illustrations from books or periodicals. When students begin to put in their own material, we will provide copyright guidelines and request they indicate the source of their images. But we cannot guarantee that something copyrighted will not get into the database, and so we have said clearly that this is an educational tool to be used in the study and teaching of design and is not a commercial product. We also will not provide access to outside users until we can have in place the security needed to allow look-but-can't-touch access to users outside the GSD community. In this way we feel we are protecting our interests and those of possible copyright owners while developing an important schoolwide resource.

OBSTACLES, CHALLENGES, AND NEW PARADIGMS

Any new technology brings with it certain obstacles that must be overcome. Copyright is and will remain a thorny issue for some time. There is still a certain amount of computer phobia in libraries, although it is rapidly disappearing as younger generations seem to become computer-literate in kindergarten. The process of creating and maintaining digital online resources is certainly expensive, not only in terms of equipment and technological resources but also in manpower–the human resources needed to design, develop, enrich, and maintain these networked resources. And the technology is constantly changing; you can be guaranteed that nothing will be fixed for more than a few years at best.

However, digital technology can open our collections and inspire our users in ways we may never have imagined. At the same time, it can preserve and protect our most precious resources for generations of users to come. It is a difficult challenge, but well worth the effort. New ways of looking (literally) for or at images may create new paradigms for using images. And, after all, isn't that what libraries and museums are for–helping users find new ways of thinking and looking at the world around them?

NOTES

1. Patricia McClung, "RFP for RLG Digital Image Access Project," letter addressed to RLG member representatives, dated March 23, 1993.

2. T.M.J. Hemnes and A.H. Pyle, *A Guide to Copyright Issues in Higher Education.* Washington, DC.: National Association of College and University Attorneys, 1992.

3. Mary Kay Duggan, "Copyright of Electronic Information: Issues and Questions," *Online* (1991) 15(3), 21.

Options for Digitizing Visual Materials

Ricky L. Erway

Digital-imaging projects are expensive and should not at this time be considered a cost-saving endeavor. They can, however, be an efficient way to reach new audiences, expand access to collections, provide surrogates or preserve originals, or make previously unavailable materials available.

Digitizing visual materials is a complex process that involves selecting collections for conversion, conserving individual items to optimize capture and minimize damage, organizing the collection, cataloging or preparing a finding aid, choosing quality levels and standards, archiving the files, and finding the best ways to make them accessible. In this time of increasing demand for library services and decreasing financial support, it is especially important that we are aware of all the options and make the right decisions to optimize our efforts.

Typically, there are two approaches to embarking on a digitizing project. The more rational approach is the identification of a need or problem and the consideration of digitizing as a solution. More prevalent today, however, is the desire to create a digitizing project followed by the decisions of what to digitize and why. This cart-before-the-horse approach can at least be done rationally.

WHY ARE WE DIGITIZING?

The first thing to understand is why digitizing is being considered for a particular project. Is it for preservation, for reference access, or to be able

Ricky L. Erway is Member Services Officer for Digital Initiatives at the Research Libraries Group; at the time of the symposium, she was Associate Coordinator of the Library of Congress's American Memory Program.

[Haworth co-indexing entry note]: "Options for Digitizing Visual Materials." Erway, Ricky L. Co-published simultaneously in *Collection Management* (The Haworth Press, Inc.) Vol. 22, No. 3/4, 1998, pp. 123-132; and: *Going Digital: Strategies for Access, Preservation, and Conversion of Collections to a Digital Format* (ed: Donald L. DeWitt) The Haworth Press, Inc., 1998, pp. 123-132.

to reach broader audiences? The answer will guide many subsequent decisions, such as whether a film intermediate will be created, which standards will be chosen, and what the level of image quality will be. The answer will also affect storage needs, transmission speeds, rights issues, and cost factors.

Preservation. There are two primary ways to realize preservation objectives through digitization: creation of a surrogate to preserve the original or creation of a high-quality reproduction to replace the original. The first is easier to achieve through digitizing than the second.

Reference Access. There are two possible reference access gains: Provision of new access or provision of improved access. New access can mean access to materials so fragile they cannot be used in their original form. Improved access can mean providing more immediate access and more efficient browsing of large numbers of materials. Either way, this improved access saves time that researchers can instead put to use on thought and discovery.

As an example, a few years ago at the Library of Congress, a regular out-of-town researcher sized up his task based on his past experience using a particular collection of photographs and made his airline and hotel reservations to accommodate a week of research. When he arrived, he found that the collection had been made electronically available. No longer did he have to have material fetched in small batches from storage and handle the materials very carefully with white gloves and under curatorial supervision. This time he was able to search for specific things and view them immediately on the screen, and for the first time he could actually browse through thousands of photographs without using any finding aid at all. He reported that he accomplished more in a single day than he had hoped to in a week.

Remote Access. Remote access can mean reaching researchers beyond the walls of the institution. They can now do the research, find what they need, make reference copies, and order reproductions right from their own desks. And remote access can mean providing internal users with access to collections beyond the walls of your institution.

It is difficult and expensive, though not impossible, to achieve all these goals. However, if one is digitizing to achieve any one of these goals, it is wise to consider whether any other of these goals can be accomplished at the same time. With all the effort and expense, we want to maximize the benefits received.

Some combinations of goals can be more easily achieved. While improved reference access obviously helps the researcher, it also helps the library preserve its collections and, through decreased handling, secure them from theft or damage. Providing remote access can mean the over-crowded reading room has more readers, but fewer bodies.

IS DIGITIZING THE RIGHT SOLUTION?

After determining what our motivations are, we should also consider other means of achieving our ends. Could improved cataloging or finding aids alone allow us to realize the improved access or decreased handling we desire? Might capturing the images on film or analog videodisc or some other means be easier, cheaper, higher capacity, quicker to prepare, quicker to access, and easier to distribute to the intended audience?

It is wise to consider whether, when the primary objective is achieved, other objectives might emerge. If it is certain that the images will be only accessed internally, many different approaches can be considered. But it is far better to know ahead of time if we intend to allow other institutions to access the digitized resources. Digital images prepared for access purposes may increase the demand for access to the originals, thereby generating preservation concerns.

WHAT ARE WE DIGITIZING?

After we know *why* we are digitizing, the next decision is *what* to digitize. Again there are a number of approaches.

We can select a collection that is in need of preservation or is in high demand by researchers. We can review past use of our materials and select the most accessed images–the greatest hits approach. We can digitize individual items on demand and add them to our archive. As materials are selected for other reasons, such as conservation, photographic reproduction for researchers, or publication in traditional forms, we can also digitize them. We can identify a new audience and select items or a collection to meet their needs. We can start with items or collections in which there is private sector interest–private sector companies may be willing to do or fund the digitizing, or even pay the institution royalties based on usage or sales.

Other factors will influence our selection. What are the rights issues? Do the materials lend themselves to the technology? Is there uniformity in size, type, condition, and readiness? Do we have finding aids to access the digital files?

WHAT ARE THE REQUIREMENTS?

Once the materials are identified, we can assess the quality and formatting requirements.

The level of quality will affect cost, storage requirements, and transmission time. One approach is to provide lower-resolution reference images and continue to use photographic reproductions to satisfy user needs not met by the reference images. The intended use of the images or the need to capture text or other fine details in the originals will affect the degree of resolution required.

Resolution. Very-high-resolution images will typically necessitate decisions about how they will be displayed. It can be disconcerting for the user to display an image and see only a piece of sky in a landscape scene–or a nostril in a portrait. Will the images be scaled at display time? Are lower-resolution images needed for quicker transmission and meaningful display?

We typically talk about resolution for document scanning in terms of dots per inch (as in 300 dpi). But for photographic materials, we more often refer to resolution in terms of the total number of dots vertically and horizontally (as in 480×640, which for an $8'' \times 10''$ original photograph means about 60 dpi).

In addition to determining spatial resolution, we need to identify the required pixel depth. Line art is typically captured as 300 dpi bitonal images. Pixel depth can increase the apparent resolution of the image, allowing for lower spatial resolution. Grayscale photos can usually be adequately represented by 8 bits per pixel, allowing for up to 256 shades of gray. We should consider if we wish to retain sepia or some other nongray value. If photos are in color, they are often captured at 24 bits per pixel, allowing for millions of colors. For color graphic originals, such as posters or watercolors, 8 bits per pixel may suffice. Sixteen bits per pixel, allowing for 65,000 colors, is a middle ground. Thirty-two bits per pixel is typically the highest pixel depth captured. Increases in pixel depth will affect file size more than increases in spatial resolution.

Low-resolution thumbnail images are often captured at 8 bits per pixel to minimize file size. While 8 bits per pixel is usually adequate for a single image, if the same color palette is to be used for a vast range of subject matter, the colors become quite limited. An alternative is to use adaptive optimized palettes (each image selects its own 256 colors). But if the thumbnail images with adaptive palettes are to be displayed proofsheet style on Super VGA displays, the active image will temporarily impose its palette on the other images.

Another consideration is the effect of the colors used in the end-user environment. For example, in Windows™, a few colors are reserved for menu bars, highlighting, and so forth; these colors can affect the display of the thumbnail colors. This can even affect black-and-white images, for instance, adding a moldy-green cast. A solution is to capture black-and-white originals as 8-bit color images with adaptive palettes that reserve eight colors for local use.

High spatial resolution and increased pixel depth make compression necessary rather than optional. For each type of original, we should experiment with varying degrees of resolution, depth, and compression. Lossless and lossy compression should be evaluated. If an uncompressed version is to be retained, we can take advantage of significant compression to minimize file size.

A 3 K × 3 K image at 24 bits per pixel results in a 27 MB file–only 24 of them will fit on a CD-ROM. It becomes impractical to consider retaining uncompressed images for large collections. If an average of 30:1 compression is applied, the resulting files will average under 1 MB, and over 700 will fit on a CD-ROM. The risk, however, is that when improved compression algorithms are developed, recompressing a decompressed image may result in deleterious artifacts.

Other decisions to be made include whether edges of the original are to be included in the image, whether masking is wanted, whether enhancement, such as sharpening, is desired, and whether color bars should be captured to allow users to adjust the color on their monitors to get an accurate rendition of the original colors.

Formats and Standards. Decisions on formats will be largely determined by intended use but should take into account longevity issues. Even if the images will be made available only in a local closed system, possible future systems should be considered. The planned-for hardware and software may not always be supported or maintainable. Choosing standard data formats and media will allow for future reformatting so that the digital resources will always be accessible.

Collaboration on standards among libraries, educational institutions, government, and the private sector will be critical to ensure that information digitized by one can be accessed by another. It will also allow for cross-collection retrieval on collections from multiple institutions.

The standards and tools for photographic images are perhaps the best-defined and accepted of all those involved in conversion of archival materials. There are very few large-scale photo-imaging projects I know of that do not use the TIFF image format and JPEG compression.

TIFF is in such common use that it has become a de facto industry standard. It is possible for an image to become separated from its cataloging or other descriptive information; the TIFF format allows storage of a significant amount of information in the TIFF header, such as capture resolution and date, source of the image, file name, version information, or even copyright restrictions. JPEG images can have JFIF (JPEG file interchange format) headers that can include similar data.

The most common alternative to the TIFF format and JPEG compression is Kodak's PhotoCD system. This system allows for a range of resolutions–from 200 × 100 dots to 3 K × 2 K. Compatible hardware and software are now widespread. Disadvantages include the use of a proprietary format, imposed file-naming schemes, lack of header information, and the need to digitize from negatives or slides–which, for archival collections, often requires an intermediate capture step. The sets of five derivative-resolution images together amount to about 60 MB of data–100 per CD-ROM. The ProPhotoCD allows for more flexibility.

Accepted standards should also be used for descriptive information. MARC and SGML are obvious choices for catalog records and finding aids. Sometimes we are tempted to choose solutions based on today's software tools, but these are not long-term solutions. It is better to adopt accepted standards (for example, TIFF and SGML) and convert them for short-term needs (for example, GIF [Graphical Interchange Format] and HTML [Hypertext Markup Language] for World Wide Web servers).

A third area where standards should be considered is retrieval systems. A Z39.50 server may be the best choice if access is likely to be made available to multiple libraries. For stand-alone systems, the operating system, retrieval engine, storage medium, and user interface will be chosen to best suit local needs.

In determining data formats and quality levels, we should consider end-user requirements. Will the users have readily available playback equipment? Can they use the files in readily available software? High-resolution, 24-bit-per-pixel images will best be viewed on computers with fast processors and high-resolution, large-sized monitors with special video display cards and additional video memory. The speed of modems, network connections, and disk drives will affect access times. Printers should have extra memory and, unless our beautiful 24-bit images are to be halftoned on a standard laser printer, a special printer may be desirable.

File Naming. Another requirement to be considered is how the files are to be named. If unique numbers are already associated with the images, it makes sense to incorporate them into the file names. It is advantageous if, even in a UNIX environment, the file names conform to DOS file-naming requirements. The three-character extension should identify the format of the image. If there are multiple versions of each image, a character should be reserved to differentiate between a thumbnail, a compressed, a higher-resolution, or an uncompressed image. If a group of images relates to a single record or a hierarchical level in a finding aid, the file names should left-match to that degree. Sometimes a file-naming system is worked out ahead of time; in other cases, the file names are created at the time of scanning. In either case, there must be a way to maintain the relationship from the image to its descriptive information.

Directories and Links. Each collection of images should be in its own directory. A system for placing images in subdirectories will also need to be determined; a thousand images in one directory is unmanageable. If the directory-naming scheme is derived from the file names, it will not be necessary to provide the entire path name in the links. If the link provides both the collection name and the file name, a locator file can reference the collection name to the location on a storage device and the file can then be automatically located. In this way, when a storage device is replaced or reorganized, only the locator file need be updated, not each link. At a metalevel, the same approach can be used for institutions and their collections, using a handle server to maintain those links. The evolving use of uniform resource numbers (URNs), uniform resource locators (URLs), and uniform resource identifiers (URIs) may make these accommodations.

While at first a relatively small number of images linked to a large existing catalog will get lost, as more images are made available, it may make sense to maintain a single system to best serve the researcher.

WHO WILL DO THE DIGITIZING?

Once the why, the what, and the how have been addressed, the next question is, who will do it? Will the digital capture be done in-house or on contract?

Since most libraries are finding it difficult to get funding to hire enough staff for traditional acquisitions, cataloging, and reference work, it is unlikely they will be able to develop the technical skills to handle the digitizing in-house. Especially if many digitizing projects are planned, the types and sizes of materials to be digitized may vary tremendously, requiring multiple specialty firms with the range of equipment and skills to handle, for instance, posters, architectural drawings, and an array of different photographic formats.

Contracting requires significant resources, both in contracting dollars and in staff time to prepare and monitor the contracts. Archival collections may require onsite scanning under curatorial supervision. The materials challenge a production-line approach.

En route to digital images, it may be prudent to create a film intermediate. The originals can be captured on film onsite, creating a high-quality preservation copy that can be digitized offsite. Later, if higher-resolution digital images are desired, the film can be rescanned without further handling of the originals.

Contracting out still places significant demands on library staff to prepare the materials for scanning and to perform quality verification on the reproductions. The quality review process requires adequate equipment and significant staff time to assess the level of quality and track any rescanning that may need to be done. The effect of wrong, poor, or missing images should be evaluated to determine the degree of quality control.

Another decision is, what activities are best done before or after digitizing? One approach is to organize and catalog the photos before scanning. In this way, targets can be prepared to help the scanning proceed smoothly. Another approach is to use the digital versions to sequence and catalog the images. This is especially helpful when the originals are large, fragile, or in poor condition. A by-product of this approach is 100% quality control of the images, although missing images may not be identified.

HOW SHALL WE MANAGE THE DIGITAL FILES?

Will the images be delivered in the form in which they will be accessed? Will the delivery medium be the medium from which the images will be accessed? Or will the images be transferred to another medium? How will they be backed up? Will they need to be refreshed, reformatted, or migrated?

Archiving these digitized materials will require storage devices, staff, and maintenance and security software systems beyond those already in place in most libraries. We need to determine which data should reside online, near-line, or offline. Can we keep lower-resolution thumbnail images online and higher-quality images near-line? Should uncompressed versions of the files also be retained? Tracking the movement or renaming of files must be managed so that users do not reach data dead ends.

High-demand digital resources may be replicated at other locations. There must be a way to update those sites when defective images are replaced or errors in records are corrected. We may need to be able to detect alteration or identify an official version to serve as the authority for the integrity of the original.

NOW THAT WE HAVE THEM,
HOW WILL USERS ACCESS THEM?

While providing intellectual access to digitized materials raises many of the same issues as providing intellectual access to materials in their original form, the stakes are higher. Uncataloged photographs in a pile or in a drawer can still be viewed. Digital images without any reference to them may be lost forever.

Will the images be made available online or on disk, in-house or beyond? Is appropriate retrieval and display software available? What text should be indexed? How should the text and images be displayed? What sorts of accompanying information will be provided: photographer biographies, time lines, bibliographies?

Searching at a single workstation across multiple collections from multiple libraries requires use of standards, both in the digital formats as well as in the means of describing and linking to the digital resources. The recent adoption of the 856 MARC field is a significant step in that direction.

World Wide Web servers have rapidly been adopted as an appropriate means of making collections available to others. The user software is easily and inexpensively available. Powerful searching tools are becoming available. Web browsers can effectively accommodate multimedia content.

SHOULD WE COLLABORATE WITH THE PRIVATE SECTOR?

As the Internet approaches ubiquity, more and more companies are seeking more and more content. This often brings them to libraries, museums, and archives—with a variety of propositions.

We must be somewhat wary of these offers. Many corporations appear eager to help, but we must evaluate the help they want to give. Often they offer to lend or donate equipment, but we know that the labor has a more significant impact on our budgets than the acquisition of equipment. Some companies will do the digitizing if they can get an exclusive right to distribute it. Or they will offer to do the digitizing, but it will be in their proprietary format, compelling the library to use their hardware or software system.

Where there is commercial collaboration, libraries should attempt to retain the right to make the information freely available. The commercial interests will have to add value to the information or to the means of accessing it to make their profit. Those with the skills, talent, and knowledge of the markets can customize products for various audiences. In this way, the libraries, the companies, and the researchers all benefit.

WHAT ADVANCES CAN WE EXPECT?

While there are many incremental improvements that will make our lot easier–faster capture devices, higher resolution, improved compression, greater storage capacities, and improved archive maintenance software– significant advances at the user end, such as faster transmission speeds and improved display and printing devices, are likely to arrive more quickly.

If the World Wide Web continues to be a dominant means of access, Web software will need to more fully accommodate the needs of libraries. We need software that understands MARC records, can search and display SGML-encoded texts, and can display bitonal images. We need software that accepts current standard file formats rather than, for instance, having to convert our SGML texts to HTML or convert our TIFF images to the GIF format. These changes are likely to come quickly.

We need to render the computer a more hospitable and forthcoming host to the riches within. Navigation to and among the myriad of image databases that will soon be available on the Internet is an area ripe for refinement. Improved tools for access are being developed, though there have been delays in achieving retrieval interoperability. Users and librarians cannot be expected to learn a new search interface for each new resource. Implementation of standardized approaches will better enable cross-collection and cross-institution searching.

The most certain advancement is that costs will decrease as quality and capacity increase. Although that statement may not mark me as a great prognosticator, it is a rather encouraging forecast.

The Role of Digitization
in Building Electronic Collections:
Economic and Programmatic Choices

Clifford A. Lynch

The conversion of materials from printed format to digital representations is no longer experimental. Digitization has been demonstrated and its value has been proved by a series of projects, including work at Cornell University, the National Agriculture Library, Elsevier Science Publishers, Bell Labs, the University of Michigan, and the Library of Congress. The cost per page for scanning materials into digital form continues to drop as the process becomes more automated, at least for those classes of material that have relatively uniform characteristics and have not severely deteriorated. Production digitization of other "print-like" formats, such as microfilm and photographs, remains more experimental (given the great variations in the characteristics of these materials), but some aspects have already been explored through several large-scale pilot projects. The use of digitization technologies to convert analog sound and motion picture recordings to the digital domain is still quite costly and complex. While now used routinely in the entertainment industries (for example, in the production of audio CDs from old master tapes), the process is not yet viewed as a practical method of transforming most library collections.

Clifford A. Lynch is Executive Director, Coalition for Networked Information, formerly Director of the Division of Library Automation, University of California Office of the President.

Note from the author: This paper is based on my presentation at the RLG symposium Selecting Library and Archive Collections for Digital Reformatting held November 5-6, 1995, in Washington, D.C.

[Haworth co-indexing entry note]: "The Role of Digitization in Building Electronic Collections: Economic and Programmatic Choices." Lynch, Clifford A. Co-published simultaneously in *Collection Management* (The Haworth Press, Inc.) Vol. 22, No. 3/4, 1998, pp. 133-141; and: *Going Digital: Strategies for Access, Preservation, and Conversion of Collections to a Digital Format* (ed: Donald L. DeWitt) The Haworth Press, Inc., 1998, pp. 133-141.

But the vast majority of research library holdings are printed materials, microforms, and photographs. The transformation of these collections into digital form is now within reach, although it represents a massive investment. At the same time, a growing proportion of the new material being acquired by libraries is now available in digital formats, though perhaps at a substantial price premium. The costs of developing systems to provide patron access to digital materials of all kinds is clearly a large and ongoing investment, as is the continued management of these digital materials. Libraries face both opportunities and potentially unmanageable budgetary demands from all quarters. The questions now facing libraries arise less from the availability of technology than out of the development of strategies for collection development and management and supporting resource allocation choices.

This paper will outline some possible strategies for approaching the transition to collections that incorporate increasing quantities of digital information, and will offer some perspectives that may help in comparing and evaluating these strategies.

GENERAL ISSUES

Before considering various types of collections specifically, it is worth examining a few general themes that apply across the various types of material.

Library users clearly expect more and more material in digital form, but their reasons vary greatly. Much has been written on the general advantages of digital materials over printed materials, and a number of case studies affirm the impact and value of having certain very specific materials in digital form to support various research and instructional programs. But we really know very little about the cost-benefit tradeoffs that might guide us in selecting one strategy over another. There is a great need for even basic measures such as raw usage data for different types of digital material.

Further, in cases where the intellectual property rights to materials are controlled by organizations outside the library community, cost-benefit considerations are muddled by the marketplace. A publisher, for example, will try to charge a premium for materials in electronic formats that basically discounts the added value that the library and its patrons would gain from having the material in electronic form, thus weakening the justification for migration to the electronic version of the material.

There is clearly a critical mass issue with digital collections, however they may be selected. The availability of small amounts of digital material randomly interspersed through a primarily print collection has been shown again and again to have little value to users beyond a technological proof of concept. Once the novelty wears off, users tend to avoid the extra effort of accessing the occasional digitized works they may encounter in the course of their library use. Any strategy to incorporate substantial amounts of digital content into the "production" library collections and services needs to ensure that at least some subset of the library patrons is quickly offered a critical mass of materials in digital form.

Different strategies for approaching critical mass have been suggested, but with little comparison of results. One strategy might be to build up a base of source materials and secondary commentary structured around instructional programs–an extension of an electronic reserves and class reading approach. In particular the ready availability of source material from special collections for large classes (often impossible or at least impractical with the physical collections) offers exciting new possibilities for approaching some types of instruction. An alternative approach involves much larger-scale bulk digitization of material on a disciplinary basis, perhaps guided by an editorial board of working scholars. Thus, a digital collection would be available from which researchers and teachers could extract what they needed for various purposes with a high expectation that the required materials would be available in digital form.

Finally, there are issues of the organization of digital materials and the construction of access systems. Early digitization projects tended quite naturally to focus on the costs of scanning and storage and the technology infrastructure (network bandwidth and workstations) needed to deliver the materials. We now recognize that the cost of constructing or acquiring abstracting and indexing databases and finding-aid systems to assist users in locating and navigating through digital collections is a substantial part of the cost of the large-scale introduction of digital content, particularly if the standards of quality established for access to print materials are to be retained, and if the user is to be assured of a coherent view of collections that increasingly span print and digital materials.

CANDIDATES FOR DIGITAL COLLECTIONS

I believe that from the perspective of assigning priorities and developing strategies for the transition to digital formats, library collections can be divided roughly into four categories.

Current Published Literature

These are materials that are being acquired from publishers today, including monographs and journals. Here the main question is whether the library wants to acquire the material from the publisher in printed or electronic form (or both). Availability of this class of material in electronic form is largely paced by publisher marketing decisions and the rate at which publishers can convert to electronic systems. Many of the central issues are economic, and the forces defining the marketplace for published materials in electronic form are beyond the scope of this paper. A few specific issues should be noted, however.

Unlike other types of material that libraries may digitize through their own efforts, and which will typically be converted to some kind of bit-mapped format, there is a wide range of formats available from publishers. Each of these formats (bitmap, portable document format, SGML, etc.) raises unique issues about the added value of the electronic version of the material, as well as about the cost and complexity of providing access to the material and managing it over time. Cost-benefit issues become partic-ularly complex in this arena, particularly when the context of the market-place and its effects on pricing, and hence costs to libraries, are consid-ered. There are also some significant conceptual and technical problems in connecting the electronic offerings from various publishers to the existing abstracting and indexing databases that have traditionally provided a coherent view of disciplinary literatures. From the user's perspective, the publisher-by-publisher, uncoordinated migration to electronic formats threatens to fragment the literature.

The range of currently published materials that are available to the users of a given library is likely to become, if anything, more uniform over time as publishers offer acquire-on-demand programs for their products (particularly at the journal-article level). Libraries can offer access to a wide range of materials without having to purchase them in advance. At the same time, the transition from purchase of materials to licensing means that interlibrary loan will become much less of a factor in equalizing access to information from one library to another.

Finally, given the massive cancellation programs that most libraries have implemented in the past decade, the majority of the material currently being purchased is very important to patrons. Its value has been reviewed and justified again and again. There is likely to be a high demand for this material in electronic format. If patrons use the material heavily, having it in electronic form is likely to facilitate its use.

I believe that one large and vocal group of library patrons will argue that currently acquired published literature should receive the majority of funds for digital content, both to increase the utility and accessibility of this material and to extend its scope through acquisition-on-demand pro-grams.

Published Literature Already Owned by Libraries

This base of materials has two parts. The first is the set of materials that remains under copyright, where the owning library does not have the option of converting the material into a digital format without entering into some arrangement with the rights holders. Not much can be said about this type of material. On one hand, there are opportunities for libraries to enter into joint agreements with rights holders where they provide capital and/or labor for digitization in exchange for local licenses to the digital materials. On the other hand, except for preservation considerations, libraries already hold this material in print and may be reluctant to make further investments to obtain it in digital form, except for the few cases where it is very heavily used and having it in digital form would add significant value. Given the continued legislative moves to extend the term of copyright, the amount of material falling into this category may not decrease much over time.

One trend, which should encourage the exploration of joint ventures between libraries and rights holders to fund digitization, is the evidence that many scientific and scholarly publishers do not regard old journals as significant sources of revenue and actually want to see them available to the community in digital form (in part, as a way of enhancing the reputation and perceived value of current issues of the journal). In many cases, the costs of clearing rights for digitization may not be a major problem.

There is a vast body of material that is out of copyright. Because copyright is tied not to the date of publication but to the date of the author's death, identifying the boundaries of this part of the collection is now problematic But it is large, much of the material is in poor condition, and investments are now being made to preserve it using microfilm. In my view, this material calls out for an organized national and international program of digitization. Existing practice in the coordination of preservation microfilming may provide a partial model for such a program, although the goals of a digitization program would encompass not only preservation but also increased access.

It is also important to recognize that while this corpus of material is enormous, it is finite, and, to an extent, digitization can be viewed as a one-time capital expense (though there is, of course, an ongoing cost for managing and preserving the digital versions). Also, the costs for such a digitization program are entirely within the control of the libraries and are likely to diminish slowly as technology improves. There is no marketplace in rights to complicate the economics.

Special Collections

These are typically rare or unique, often unpublished, materials held by individual libraries. In some cases they are in the public domain; in other cases the holding library also controls the rights to the materials. Even if the materials are public domain, the holding library, by controlling access, exercises a great deal of control over the fate of these materials in digital form. These collections often represent scholarly treasures of vast importance, though many collections are of interest only to relatively small groups of scholars. Historically, these collections have not been very accessible to scholars, either nationally or internationally. The items rarely circulate and are often fragile. In addition, they frequently have only the most basic access and navigational tools to support their use. There are a number of major programs currently underway to convert specific collections at various research libraries to digital form, many of which are funded by grants.

Special collections represent one of the most interesting and complex issues in digital collections. In a world of increasingly uniform access to published literature as networked information, special collections are an important part of what makes each great library unique. The issues here are how to provide incentives and support to permit and encourage libraries to convert their special collections to digital form and make them available (along with the appropriate access and navigational apparatus).

It is probably unreasonable to expect major research libraries to find funding and undertake responsibility for making their local special collections available to the world just on the basis of a sense of community and support for the public good (though clearly some progress is already being made on just this basis). The development of such an economic framework, which might include agreements about sharing, reciprocity, and joint investment, will play a major role in defining the scale of the resources that individual libraries are prepared to commit to digitizing special collections.

In the absence of such a framework, decisions will be driven primarily by opportunistic factors (such as the availability of extramural funds to support digitization of specific types of materials) and local priorities (such as the conversion of special collections where that conversion can support and leverage local instructional and research programs). Put perhaps more crudely: Few patron communities will support large-scale investment in the creation of digital content as a "gift" to the global network over investment in the acquisition of content to serve that patron community.

New Genres of Scholarly Communications

It is clear that in many scholarly communities new forms of scholarly communication are developing. In the sciences this includes the development of large community databases in areas such as physics, molecular biology, or crystallography which are intertwined with the more traditional literature, or the evolution of preprints and technical reports as a replacement for many of the roles of the archival published literature. The role of libraries–or, for that matter, professional and scholarly societies, traditional publishers, and academic departments–in the creation, management, dissemination, and preservation of these new genres of scholarly communication is unclear.

Everything is potentially new here and open for reconceptualization: the means of organizing information; the sociology of collaborative "authorship" or management of a community knowledge base; and the interactions between information technology that can provide collaborative environments and record their use, observational data, and interpretation and analysis of this data. Yet this area represents an important priority for investment by libraries, and visions such as Richard Lucier's "knowledge management" point towards an environment in which libraries become an active partner in the evolution of this new discourse.[1]

This area of digital collections is still emerging, and much of the work still relies on small collaborations and individual vision and leadership. The specifics of local institutional environments and funding opportunities also shape developments. It is clear that the parameters will vary greatly, depending on the culture and practices of the individual scientific and scholarly disciplines.

BREAKING AWAY FROM TRADITION

In all areas but the changing modes of acquisition for currently published materials, libraries are likely to be either partners or driving forces in the production of digital content. I believe that the central challenge for libraries, as they plan how to exploit this opportunity, is to break away from a traditional "publishing" mentality and develop models that build on the strengths of the global networked community of scholars and the nature of networked information.

In special collections, there is a tradition of producing books of the treasures of some collection or individually edited comprehensive presentations of specific collections. More recently we have seen these publishing activities move from books to CD-ROMs. These are closed, bounded *artifacts* that do not facilitate–in fact, they inhibit–the redirecting and reuse of content from these collections.

The challenge is how to convert such collections to digital format in a way that facilitates reuse and enhancement by the broad scholarly community over time–that weaves primary content into a web of commentary, criticism, scholarship, and instruction, and links it to other related content without regard to institutional or geographic boundaries, while preserving the integrity of the digitized representations. We need a new vision of opening up historically inaccessible special collections and linking them to both the existing and developing base of scholarly publication.

A GLOBAL CALL TO ACTION

While individual libraries will have to make difficult choices about resource allocation based on local programmatic objectives, it is clear that the scale of the transition to digital collections is beyond the ability of any individual library to manage independently. We need the development of coordinated national and international programs to manage the digitization of the out-of-copyright (and perhaps even much of the still in-copyright) published literature held in libraries, which forms our scholarly and social heritage.

It is also essential that we establish a viable economic framework to support the opening of the range of special collections held by libraries nationally and internationally, and to help institutions that hold such collections to avoid simply becoming publishers (perhaps in alliance with commercial firms) seeking individual economic advantage in a new, highly entrepreneurial marketplace of digitized materials. The extent to which the national and international communities can successfully put such programs and frameworks into place will have a major influence on the development of local strategies.

Beyond the specific concerns of libraries as managers of these collections, we must not lose sight of the fact that the transition of collections to digital formats represents a unique opportunity to rethink the way in which these collections are organized, structured, presented, and managed to serve more effectively the worldwide community of scholars for whom the libraries hold these collections in trust. The networked information model is tremendously compelling. Tomorrow's digital collections must move beyond static, closed "artifact publishing" models to accommodate the more flexible and dynamic networked information environment in which the management of collections may simultaneously include or at least facilitate continuous publishing.

NOTE

1. R.E. Lucier. "Embedding the library into scientific and scholarly communication through knowledge management." In *Designing Information: New Roles for Librarians*. Urbana-Champaign: University of Illinois Press, 1993.

Mapping the Intersection of Selection and Funding

Nancy E. Gwinn

The question of how libraries can develop a program of systematic funding capable of supporting a sustained digital-reformatting effort and meeting institutional priorities for what should be digitized is not easy to address. While thinking of this earlier in the week, I was also listening to a CD of Stephen Sondheim hits. Ethel Merman's familiar, huge voice belted out tunes from her hit *Gypsy*, which, as you all know, is based on the life of the famous stripper Gypsy Rose Lee. "You gotta have a gimmick," an older and wiser stripper tells a young Gypsy, "if you wanna get ahead."

Of course her kind of gimmick–dazzling lights, or even pizazz–is not what libraries are necessarily after. The digital world already has plenty of pizazz. The question is, how can libraries frame or shape programs that will attract funding, whether from external sources or redirected from internal budgets already stretched thin, sufficient to warrant the time and energy required? Are we even ready for systematic funding if it becomes available? And if so, what is our gimmick?

Libraries have been down this road before, of course, when they began to look for systematic funding for preservation microfilming. The same question arose of the contention between what foundations and the federal government were interested in preserving and what local institutions saw as their preservation priorities. This conflict was never completely resolved, nor will it be in the new digital world unless the procedures become so easy and the costs so low that external funding support for digital projects is not required. There are no ready answers to these questions.

Nancy E. Gwinn is Director, Smithsonian Institution Libraries, Smithsonian Institution, formerly Assistant Director, Collections Management, at the Smithsonian Institution Libraries.

[Haworth co-indexing entry note]: "Mapping the Intersection of Selection and Funding." Gwinn, Nancy E. Co-published simultaneously in *Collection Management* (The Haworth Press, Inc.) Vol. 22, No. 3/4, 1998, pp. 143-149; and: *Going Digital: Strategies for Access, Preservation, and Conversion of Collections to a Digital Format* (ed: Donald L. DeWitt) The Haworth Press, Inc., 1998, pp. 143-149.

Libraries can be proud of what has been accomplished in the reformatting programs of the last 15 to 20 years, both in terms of the product (over 700,000 rescued brittle books) and raising public support for and awareness of the paper deterioration problem. We should take our success in that arena seriously. It may be instructive to see if experience can provide any ideas that will work in the digital world. Then we can look at what makes the digital world different and what might affect funding and support.

FACTORS IN FUNDING PRESERVATION MICROFILMING PROJECTS

Microfilming as a preservation technique has been around since before the Second World War. Prior to 1980, several large institutions—the Library of Congress, the New York Public Library, Yale and Columbia universities among them—devoted substantial sums to in-house microfilming programs and collaborated with other institutions.[1] But in the 1980s, with the advent of serious, big-ticket consortial programs like those of the Research Libraries Group and the Committee for Institutional Cooperation (basically libraries of the "Big Ten" universities), along with the National Endowment for the Humanities' newspaper project, interest in and funding for preservation microfilming leaped forward. Thanks to intense lobbying by the Council on Library Resources, the Commission on Preservation and Access, and the research library community, in 1985 the U.S. Congress began annual funding of preservation programs with the intent of appropriating approximately $20 million a year for 14 years to support preservation of an estimated 3.3 million brittle books. Other federal agencies and private foundations joined in the effort.[2] What factors appealed to these funders?

- Although microfilming was a well-known technology, the library community defined the standards, procedures, and quality-control programs that distinguished commercial microfilming as carried out in the banking and insurance industries from what was needed for long-term preservation and usability of microfilm; library commitments to adhere to these standards ensured a satisfactory product and assured funders that their money would be well spent.
- Institutions and national agencies joined forces to mount a powerful and persuasive argument with Congress and the public that focused on the loss of cultural heritage to the nation generally, and not on the needs of individual institutions to save their specific collections.

- Institutions showed a willingness to cooperate and made a point of not duplicating efforts, so funders could be assured they would not be asked to rescue the same books over and over.
- Libraries successfully prevailed on RLG and OCLC to carry more preservation information in their bibliographic databases, to promulgate standards for it, and to share information through tape loads of records for microfilm master negatives.
- Reporting requirements that included bibliographic control of the microfilm copies and contribution of records to the RLIN and OCLC databases further assured funders they were getting full value for their dollars, that is, that the product would become publicly known and accessible.
- Libraries educated vendors who produced preservation microfilm and therefore increased their numbers, capacities, and reliability. Librarians even created one high-production, nonprofit microfilming facility (originally called the Mid-Atlantic Preservation Service [MAPS], now Preservation Resources, Inc.) specifically to respond to the needs of libraries and archives.
- The problem was made to seem manageable, that is, filming 3.3 million volumes would suffice; the project was not seen as a black hole without a bottom.

One other factor has always been implicit in raising funds for microfilming, mandatory in terms of federal resources but always an important factor elsewhere: The institution was expected to share the costs of the project and, in some cases, to find a way to continue it after the funding period ended. Whether that has happened, or is happening, in these days of declining resources is at best problematic.

FACTORS IN FUNDING DIGITAL REFORMATTING PROJECTS

Many of these same characteristics will have to be present before libraries and archives can expect to develop systematic, not research and development (R&D), funding for digital reformatting. Here is a lineup of needs:

- We must satisfy funders and ourselves that appropriate standards and procedures exist–basically, that repositories know what they are doing technically and at feasible cost and that an institutional infrastructure, both technical and administrative, is in place to handle digital projects over the long term. A number of already funded R&D projects are moving towards this goal.

- We must use powerful arguments for converting collections to digital form that do not seem self-serving. This is the attraction of subject-based collaborative efforts, or of the "great collections" or "core collections" ideas, which imply that the activity can be done once and serve for all. In other words, avoid the black hole syndrome.

- We will need to ensure that various projects will not duplicate efforts, so that funders will not feel they are being asked over and over for the same thing (I call this the how-many-19th-century-dime-novels-really-need-preserving? syndrome)–and, of course, there is also the practical matter of spreading limited resources as far as possible.

- We must be clear about whether libraries are using digitizing to extend access to already preserved material, to substitute for our preservation efforts, or to create new aggregations of materials. Preservation microfilming projects promised both, preservation *and* better access, in one project–powerful justification for funders, who could see the long-term benefits. This duo of benefits is not so clear-cut in the digital world, where long-term preservation is not yet a given. What kind of return will funders receive for their investments?

- On the other hand, digital projects provide attractive and flexible opportunities. Digitizing allows for grouping disparate resources, even parts of materials, in new ways without worrying about the whole. While the linear format of microfilm mandates striving for completeness of a journal run or multivolume set, in the digital world, for example, chapters of books, journal articles, pamphlets, photographs, and other items on a single subject can be easily digitized and packaged together–and additional material added later with no damage to the whole. Is this sufficient to entice funding? Again, what return on investment are we promising?

- Once past the experimentation cycle, we will need to ensure the widespread access and retrievability of digitized items over time. This means not only enhanced access to the digitized forms themselves, but also links to online catalogs and other forms of the material.

Three other points will also weigh more heavily in developing funding for digital projects than perhaps they did with microfilming. One is *visibility*. Everything libraries do in the digital world will be more visible to more people. This may enhance greatly the role of librarians as information providers, but it also will leave them more vulnerable to criticism. Librarians ignored user complaints about the difficulty of using microfilm because there was no better solution, but also because they had control: Microfilm was not used outside of the library, and library staff could facilitate its use. Personal mediation will not be as easy, or even possible at times, in the use of digital resources.

The second point has to do with *use of digitized materials*. A powerful argument for microfilming was that once a book had been "rescued," it would be forever available for potential use. Once the microfilm was cataloged and stored, nothing more was required except perhaps an occasional inspection. However, digitized files need to be refreshed, possibly reformatted for new equipment, or otherwise tinkered with in an ongoing program. Will we be willing to take on that work and expense for files that are seldom, if ever, used? Evaluation of past use of materials proposed for digitizing may become much more important as justification for funders.

The third point is *public enthusiasm*. To a certain extent, libraries both raised and capitalized on it to support microfilming programs by concentrating on the *goal*–rescuing our cultural heritage before it was lost–rather than the *method*. Funding for preservation microfilming has survived as a line item in program funds at NEH, even if the staff has been reduced, because that argument is still valid. Enthusiasm for the method is already there in the digital world because there are public activities using electronic files that the general public can relate to, for example, home shopping and electronic mail, and the media are constantly reporting on digital services and the Internet. In the rush to capture that enthusiasm for the method and promote it within a broad swathe of the scholarly community, especially the humanities, libraries and archives must not fail to define their goals if they want to add scholars' voices to the quest for funds.

This creates an opportunity to borrow some techniques from the museum world. To make the case for funding, much as a museum exhibition team does, libraries will have to pay much more attention to identifying the audience, projecting the usefulness of what is being captured in digital form, involving advisory or focus groups in the selection of targets, and evaluating the results. In some instances, potential users will have to be educated and trained in this new format.

Digitizing programs are forcing us to look at traditional means for offering information in new and flexible ways. At the same time, our heightened awareness may extend beyond traditional sources of funding support. In this brave new world, students with computers in their dormitory rooms are already receiving much of their information in digitized form. Far more than microfilming, certain digital reformatting efforts derive from curriculum needs and thus could be attractive to foundations or other organizations primarily interested in education.

There is also increased opportunity to develop an income stream through productive partnerships with the commercial world, including university presses. Precedents are visible in the CD-ROM products already available from museums and libraries and in publisher-developed projects to put journal back files on line. The hunger for images in the academic world was clear to me when I attended the 1994 American Studies Association annual conference to demonstrate a Smithsonian Institution Libraries experimental CD-ROM of images taken from rare books. The most frequent question was, where can I buy this? If there had been a stack of CDs on the table, they could have sold for $75 each! Of course, producing marketable digital collections has to be approached with care and in full recognition of the amount of staff time and resources required to develop a sound commercial product.

And that raises the issue of competition. Libraries have a clear field in microfilming projects, with only a few commercial vendors operating in this area–and those vendors need our collections. Libraries simultaneously are the market for the product–they have the machines to read and print from the film. For digital products, libraries still have the collections, but they will be competing with many more types of institutions and products. Opportunities abound for collaboration, for joining library-owned texts and images to those in archives and museums in new and complementary ways. Such projects must also compete internally for scarce funds, of course, and with the traditional library operations that must continue.

Getting the projects started is just one aspect that requires funding. As Peter Graham suggests, long-term funding of digital libraries will require active long-term care and maintenance far more than does storage and reproduction of microfilm. He encourages institutions to exploit different fiscal tools, such as endowments, consortial lease and purchasing of shares, and selling access to businesses or other clients to provide for continuing maintenance costs.[3]

In closing, I suggest that in the quest for funding to sustain digital-reformatting efforts, there are some "gimmicks" that librarians with their special skills are in the best position to develop and employ. First is the infrastructure that will make digital libraries organized, easily accessible, and archivally sound; and second is a built-in user population to investigate, involve, and make excited about what can be usefully done in both traditional and yet-to-be-discovered ways with this new carrier of knowledge and information.

NOTES

1. For historical background, see Pamela W. Darling and Sherelyn Ogden, "From problems perceived to programs in practice: The preservation of library resources in the U.S.A., 1956-1980." *Library Resources and Technical Services* 1981;25:9-29; and Nancy E. Gwinn, "The rise and fall and rise of cooperative projects," *Library Resources and Technical Services* 1985;29:80-86.

2. Nancy E. Gwinn, "The fragility of paper: Can our historical record be saved?" *Public Historian* 1991;13:46-47.

3. Peter S. Graham, "Requirements for the digital research library." *College and Research Libraries* 1995;56:336.

What Will Collection Development Do?

Samuel Demas

The potential information technologies to transform the methods of scholarship and scholarly communication is so far-reaching that it will likely force the retrospective analysis of a significant portion of the existing printed record. There will be great pressure to carefully select parts of the printed record and publish them anew in digital form. The question addressed by this symposium is by what criteria, methods, and processes will it be decided which parts of the universe of print will be privileged by digital conversion for enhanced access and preservation.

Traditionally, selection of content is the first step in the process of collection building, and it sets into motion a whole series of questions, activities, and operations that result in integration of the selected item into the library's resources and services. Selection is informed and conditioned by knowledge of the related implementation issues and the library operations that are affected. This portion of today's program sets the context for selection for digital reformatting. We will explore the issues and trends in the key domains involved with implementing decisions to reformat: technology, access, copyright, and preservation. We will be treated to a survey of the state of the art by specialists in these areas.

What might collection development specialists do to develop the criteria, methods, and processes necessary to address this massive selection challenge? While it is inevitable that librarians will play some role, along with people from other professions, in reselection of the print universe, I believe this will happen regardless of the role collection development, as a subspecialty of librarianship, chooses to play.

Will collection development provide vigorous and imaginative leader-

Samuel Demas is Head of Collection Development and Preservation at the Mann Library of Cornell University.

[Haworth co-indexing entry note]: "What Will Collection Development Do?" Demas, Samuel. Co-published simultaneously in *Collection Management* (The Haworth Press, Inc.) Vol. 22, No. 3/4, 1998, pp. 151-159; and: *Going Digital: Strategies for Access, Preservation, and Conversion of Collections to a Digital Format* (ed: Donald L. DeWitt) The Haworth Press, Inc., 1998, pp. 151-159.

ship, rising to the challenge of reinventing selection methods in the electronic era? Or will it default to a conservative, incremental approach, in effect continuing to nibble around the edges of a major intellectual challenge?

CHANGING ROLES, CHANGING CONTEXTS

What will collection development do? My title is a slight modification, used with the author's permission, of the title of a recent article by Michael Buckland speculating on the future role of collection developers if the importance of local collections is reduced by the increasing availability of networked resources and the development of national, regional, and virtual collections.[1] His conclusion is that the need for selectivity, for qualitative, systematic decision-making will not be reduced in the digital library.

A key assumption in my remarks today is that the need for qualitative, balanced, systematic, and efficient selection methodologies has never been greater. Another assumption is that we must frame selection in a context much broader than that of local collections. We will continue to select for local needs, but selection will increasingly serve much broader needs and interests. This will be most evident in the selection of electronic resources and in the related area of selection for conversion.

As a collection development practitioner with years of experience selecting print and electronic materials for preservation and for current use, I believe the currently accepted methods of selection are inadequate to this epic selection challenge. Most of the precedents available to build on are in the realm of selection for preservation. While these methods have some potential application, I believe they are inadequate to the daunting task at hand—which is nothing less than *reselecting* major portions of the collections we have built over centuries, for preservation and for enhanced access. The inadequacy of current preservation selection practices is due to their avoidance of materials that may be protected by copyright and their inherent focus on the holdings of individual library collections rather than on the literature of a discipline as a whole.

So what will collection development do? Nibbling around the edges involves searching our stacks for interesting special collections, whether they be pamphlets, monographs, popular literature, periodicals, maps, or whatever, for collections of the papers of important individuals and institutions, and any of a myriad of other interesting caches of materials. We already know how to do that. We are less practiced at lifting our sights beyond the horizons of our own collections, thinking in terms of analyzing and mapping the literature of whole disciplines, identifying whole bodies of literature for conversion and preservation and setting priorities among them.

REINVENTING COLLECTION DEVELOPMENT

My basic thesis is that the successful evolution of librarianship requires a renewed emphasis on updating the principles and practices of collection development to incorporate new technological realities and expanding our focus from local collections to whole disciplines.

The basic facts are:

- We in collection development have an awesome task ahead of us.
- We do not have a particularly innovative track record in updating and expanding selection methods as the information landscape changes.
- We cannot do it alone.
- The rest of the profession is becoming impatient for us to play a more dynamic leadership role in selection for conversion, preservation, and the development of the digital library.

Collection managers have been noticeably absent from the table as our colleagues in preservation have struggled to develop the remarkable preservation infrastructure which exists today. We have provided them with only the vaguest sort of direction, assistance, and leadership about the fundamental question of *what to preserve* with the array of techniques they have developed and refined. Similarly, we have been slow and not particularly imaginative in integrating the selection and evaluation of electronic resources into our daily lives and into our professional practices and principles.

Two of the most important challenges to collection development are to figure out how to select resources published anew in electronic form and to tell our colleagues what portion of the printed universe we think should be converted to digital form and why. Indeed, our most compelling professional imperative is to reinvent the processes and methods of selection, lifting our sights above the horizon of individual library collections in terms of content and developing methods for selecting among the many format choices offered by new technologies.

Selection is about choices–choice of content and choice of format. Technology promises an incredible degree of flexibility in moving among formats and a bewildering array of options for storage and delivery. And herein lies a fundamental problem for collection development. When the qualitative, content-based dimension of selection is overlaid with the challenge of deciding format issues, the number, complexity, and fluidity of the variables boggle the mind. Choice and flexibility are good things, but too much choice and too many uncertainties engender paralysis.

The complexity and uncertainty inherent in the issues we face have somewhat paralyzed collection development. To overcome this paralysis, collection development must focus on what is uniquely in our domain: developing criteria, algorithms, and guidelines for making decisions about the form and content of collections.

Four issues are important in reinventing collection development to address the challenge of systematic selection for digital conversion:

1. The interplay of technology and selection.
2. The relationship between selection of form or format and selection of content.
3. The role of librarians in selection for conversion.
4. Methods of selection and the need for a more holistic approach to selection.

Interplay of Technology and Selection

There is a tendency in librarianship to allow consideration of format options and access capabilities to take precedence over systematic evaluation of content. Enthralled with the latest technology, we make seat-of-the-pants selection decisions to hop on to a technological train we fear may leave us behind. This is understandable, perhaps even necessary, while we are experimenting with new technologies, but it must be overcome as we "mainstream" new technologies.

As an example, recent preservation history has been driven largely by the development and funding of various technologies and treatments. As new techniques emerge, we organize ourselves accordingly and select materials to be treated with the technique currently in favor. Barrow's ground-breaking work on deacidification[2] and the development of conservation and repair programs in the U.S. raised hopes that we could preserve documents in their original formats, spawning the serviceable "use and condition" approach (that is, focusing on treatment of deteriorating materials in high demand) to selection for preservation. The "great collections" approach to reformatting grew out of major funding for microfilming; this massive effort has been to some extent at the expense of developing other approaches to preservation selection and treatment. In the past few years digital conversion has dominated the preservation landscape, almost to the exclusion of refinement and application of other essential techniques in the preservation tool kit.

These swings of the pendulum caused by new technologies are perfectly natural, and each technology eventually takes its place among the growing array of format and treatment options at our disposal. Digital conversion and network delivery are nothing more than powerful new tools to use in implementing selection decisions.

At the end of the day, the information world is about content. And as librarians, we cannot afford to lose sight of the rational sequence of selection decisions:

1. Identify information content that has value.
2. Determine the nature of use it will receive, level of access required, and degree of longevity desired.
3. Find the format(s) that best achieve those requirements.

Selection of Content and Form

In theory documents can be selected in a technological vacuum, that is, strictly in terms of the value of their contents and without regard to the medium on which the information will reside or the mechanism that will deliver it. In practice, the physical characteristics of the information, how it will be used, and the level of access we wish to provide are impossible to ignore in making a useful selection decision. The trick is to marry the components of content and form when selecting materials for digitization. For example, what are the characteristics of print publications which make good candidates for digital conversion and why?

To answer this question I find it useful to break a complex bundle of selection questions into at least two parts, drawing a distinction between two overlapping domains: content and what Ross Atkinson has called *goal qualities.*[3]

The first consideration, *content,* involves intellectual significance, which is an assessment of qualities such as importance, authority, uniqueness, timeliness, and demand. Qualitative selection is difficult, and not a lot of models and methods have been developed for use in selection for digital conversion. But it is the traditional domain of collection development, and our past practices can certainly be adapted to the new technological possibilities.

Goal qualities are the set of qualities we wish to achieve or emphasize in reformatting a document. Broadly speaking, these include *fidelity* (to the original), *utility* (level and type of access to provide), *longevity, security,* and *portability.* We cannot necessarily achieve all goal qualities for any given document at a price we can afford. So we must set priorities, emphasizing those goal qualities we find most important.

This is the part of the selection process that is paralyzing collection development. And no wonder. We have little experience thinking in so many dimensions, juggling so many selection variables. And the technological options for achieving these qualities are still moving targets. This is the area where collection development needs the most help from other parts of librarianship, and from other professions.

Who Decides What to Convert?

What role will libraries play? Publishers, scholarly societies, computer and telecommunications companies, and librarians and archivists, to name some key players, will eventually sort out their respective roles in deciding what part of the print universe to convert to digital form. As in the print world, a partnership of the scholarly and research library communities will strive to apply broader public interest criteria than the private sector would through market forces when determining what will be preserved and converted for digital access.

Buckland describes selection fundamentally as the choosing of documents on the basis of two criteria: expected demand and perceived value. He suggests that in the future collection developers will place more emphasis on perceived value in selecting materials to digitize than on demand.

This perspective may be helpful in considering our role in selection for conversion. Value-based decision-making is the core of the *art*, as opposed to the *science*, of building research collections. Selecting the materials in highest demand is not terribly difficult. Identifying works of potential current value and/or long-term interest requires considerably more knowledge, skill, judgment, and discrimination. The private sector and scholarly societies will quickly convert high-demand materials for digital access once adequate copyright protection and profitable payment mechanisms are in place. Research librarians will advocate conversion of lesser-used, more obscure, alternative, or specialized materials—in other words, materials judged important to scholarship for reasons other than high demand.

In addition to selecting for library-initiated conversion, we will work to influence other players in their selection of documents for digital conversion. We have traditionally played this role by advising our own institutions in their selection of locally produced documents to convert, by participating on publishers' advisory boards, by recommending titles for reprint and reformatting, and, of course, by voting with our acquisitions budgets. We should not underestimate our ability to influence the digital conversion decisions made by other entities.

How to Decide: Methods and Issues

Precedents for selection for conversion come primarily from our experience with selection for production of microfilm and paper facsimiles for preservation. For these purposes we have developed a number of useful practices, including:

- Use and condition—we reformat deteriorated materials that are in demand.
- Local priorities—we focus on materials of strong local interest, such as institutional records, local and regional histories, and local industries, authors, notables, etc.
- "Classic bibliography" model—we select materials corresponding to qualitatively selected published bibliographies.
- The "great collections" or vacuum cleaner approach—we film the contents of one or two of the most extensive collections on a subject rather than preserve everything published on a topic.
- Genre-based programs—we film a genre of materials, such as the National Endowment for the Humanities-funded National Newspaper Program and the National Agricultural Library-funded project to film land grant and experiment station publications.
- Core literature—we film a segment of the total literature of a discipline based on input from and priorities set by scholars in that discipline.

Each of these methods has contributed to the national preservation effort and has continuing value. But many of us now sense that there must be a better, more holistic way to approach this fundamental problem of librarianship. What is lacking in this grab bag of selection methods is an organizing principle that can bring clarity and direction to our efforts. Among the organizing principles suggested are selection by discipline, geography (that is, by country or region), genre, chronological periods, agency of publication, language, and various combinations of these.

Organization by discipline has many advantages—practical, intellectual, and political—and will probably prevail for selecting materials of scholarly value. However, this is the time for trying other approaches, developing a variety of strategies, mixing and matching them. The challenge is to determine which combination of strategies works in each discipline to lift us successfully above the level of selecting from our own collections, to see the information landscape as a whole, and to make selection decisions within the framework of an overall disciplinary plan.

This is the professional imperative of collection development in the research library context: To fashion, through a variety of concrete projects, a series of cohesive, discipline-based intellectual frameworks within which to organize our individual and collective selection efforts. I hope collection development will take a leadership role in developing rational, national cooperative plans for selection of literature for preservation, for provision of enhanced access through digital conversion, and for building a network of national and international digital libraries.

NOT A PIPE DREAM

This may sound like a collection development pipe dream. But we have evidence from our experience in the agricultural sciences literature that it is achievable. Based on the experience of the Mann Library Core Literature Project and the work of the U.S. Agricultural Information Network in devising the National Preservation Program for Agricultural Sciences Literature, I have compiled a one-page handout entitled "Requirements for a Disciplinary Plan." In addition, I have brought for your perusal an example of holistic mapping and analysis of the literature of a discipline, the seven-volume *The Core Literature of the Agricultural Sciences* (Wallace C. Olsen, ed., Cornell University Press, 1991-1995).

This is an example of what I think collection development should do. Through an intellectually sound process involving hundreds of scholars in each discipline, we can identify a critical mass of content which is clearly of enduring significance to scholarship. We can then work with our colleagues in preservation, access, technology, law, and publishing to find and implement the best format in which to deliver and preserve these qualitatively selected bodies of literature. This, I hope, is what collection development will do.

I predict that many discipline planning efforts will emerge over the coming decade. These pioneering efforts will provide a variety of models and techniques for librarians and scholars to use and adapt in their work towards a more holistic, cooperative approach to collection building and maintenance.

NOTES

1. Michael Buckland. "What will collection developers do?" *Information Technology and Libraries* 1995 (September):155-159.
2. W.J. Barrows. *Permanence/Durability of the Book: A Two-Year Research Program.* Richmond, VA: W.J. Barrows Research Laboratory, 1963.

3. Ross Atkinson. "Introductory remarks: Some qualities and implications of digital preservation." Unpublished manuscript of a talk delivered at ALCTS Preconference on Electronic Technologies: New Options for Preservation, New Orleans, June 24, 1993.

The Technology Context

Ricky L. Erway

APPLICATION OF TRADITIONAL APPROACHES

Library professionals have a wealth of experience to build on as we turn to digitizing our materials. We already know how to effectively identify, store, and retrieve information to serve our researchers' needs. We need only to adapt and apply our skills to the digital realm.

The practices we have used to create microfilm surrogates, for instance, encourage adhering to standards, capturing at the highest resolution feasible, and optimizing legibility while retaining a sense of the artifact, and are equally valid in the creation of digital surrogates. The steps we take to prepare materials for microfilming are appropriate for preparing materials for digitizing. In the area of establishing capture requirements and verifying that these requirements have been met, Cornell University has made real progress in modifying and applying the standards for assessing microfilm resolution quality to the digital-imaging process.[1]

Another successful practice, the creation of finding aids to provide local access to archival collections, offers even greater value when made accessible over the Internet. When digitized, the finding aids provide remote access to a vast number of archives at a greater level of detail than has traditionally been available to the remote researcher. UC Berkeley has forged the way in its 1993-1995 finding aid project,[2] and many archives and organizations are helping to carry this work forward to result in a widely accepted standard in the library, archive, and museum worlds.

Collaboration on standards among libraries, educational institutions, government, and the private sector will be critical in ensuring that information digitized by one entity can be accessed and retrieved by

Ricky L. Erway is RLG Member Services Officer for Digital Initiatives.

[Haworth co-indexing entry note]: "The Technology Context." Erway, Ricky L. Co-published simultaneously in *Collection Management* (The Haworth Press, Inc.) Vol. 22, No. 3/4, 1998, pp. 161-167; and: *Going Digital: Strategies for Access, Preservation, and Conversion of Collections to a Digital Format* (ed: Donald L. DeWitt) The Haworth Press, Inc., 1998, pp. 161-167.

another. The University of Michigan Conspectus project is making real advances in developing a "smart" interface to help users discover appropriate resources.[3]

Other traditional library practices need merely to be transferred to the digital world. Columbia University started us down the path that led to the adoption of the MARC 856 field for linking to digital objects. Catalog records are now acquiring links to digital finding aids and surrogates. Librarians' experience with location-independent naming will help in the organization and retrieval of digital resources.

Participants in the RLG Digital Image Access Project implemented different approaches to hierarchical metadata and studied the effect of integrating the results.[4] Libraries' current automated systems will serve as starting points for future systems that will offer better navigation of the various levels of cataloging and various types of digital objects. The major leap from card drawers to local OPACs positions us for a minor hop to worldwide Internet accessibility for library users–already well underway at many institutions.

AREAS WHERE WE NEED HELP

A few years ago, I was asked to identify the areas most in need of attention to enable large-scale library digitizing. Scanning bound volumes and scanning from microfilm immediately came to mind. Within a year, a face-up bound-volume scanner was introduced and a couple of vendors were offering grayscale scanners for 35-mm film. (Complementary investigations at Yale and Cornell are exploring the relative merits of scanning from microfilm and producing microfilm from scanned images.[5])

Today I would say that the area most in need of attention is service bureaus that are capable of digitizing library collections.

Most institutions are discovering that even if they want to take on in-house digitizing projects and have the resources to do so, they cannot possibly handle every type of project. The requirements are simply too demanding.

Bound-volume scanning requires different equipment than microfilm scanning, which is different from that required for photograph scanning, which is different from that for document scanning. Even if your library could afford all the equipment and provide the CPU power and the requisite disk space, staff has to be trained on all the equipment and processes–a tremendous undertaking. And, because of rapid changes in the industry, equipment and software need to be upgraded or replaced frequently, often necessitating retraining. If searchable text is desired, you need OCR software or a pool of typists. If you want to do SGML encoding, you need specialists not only trained in SGML but able to interpret and apply the codes correctly. On top of all this, you need quality assurance staff who can ensure that the work meets requirements.

This is not to say that contracting out projects to service bureaus is effortless. You need library staff who understand the technology well enough to set specifications and describe what is required. You also need contracting expertise. And you still need the quality assurance staff.

While there are many service bureaus, most are primarily set up to do sheet-fed, high-speed scanning for jobs like forms recognition for entering orders and massive office-record scanning. They do OCR with about 99% accuracy (that is about 20 errors per page). Some provide offshore keyboard entry which can provide better accuracy. Those few that offer SGML-encoding services are accustomed to applying prescriptive coding to normalize newly created technical documents for government and industry.

Our materials challenge these approaches. We need service bureaus that can do onsite capture. They need to have nondamaging equipment and become sensitized to the special handling required for precious materials. They need to understand the significance of standards in our projects; a proprietary system that works very well is of little use to us if it is not compatible with other systems. They need to recognize that libraries, museums, and archives are interested in representing the nature of the original document, not in "fixing it" so that it conforms to an arbitrary standard. For SGML encoding, they need experience with the descriptive coding we want to reflect the nature of the wide range of materials in our care. And service bureaus need to understand that because of the massive volume of our materials and our increasingly limited budgets, we can digitize each batch of materials only once–at a high level of quality and in such a way that digitized versions will be useful into the future.

And maybe the most important thing they need to know is that we will have a steady stream of work for them if they can meet our criteria.

THE PRIVATE SECTOR AND DIGITAL DEVELOPMENTS

Because the private sector has larger and better-funded digitizing projects than we do and was able to get underway before we were, it has been able to influence the development of goods and services related to digitizing. In some areas, this has been a great boon to library digitizing.

The most mature digitizing practices are in the music industry. The commercially driven procedures for digital mastering and replication for distribution are increasingly being applied to reformatting. After further settling of compression and storage media standards, audio archives will be happily converting sounds to bits on a grand scale.

Similarly, the need to scan tons of office documents using the fax standard to format and compress bitonal page images has resulted in an abundance of software, hardware, and service bureau choices, which is useful for libraries that have recent, black-and-white (not grayscale) documents that can be sheet-fed, scanned, and effectively OCRed. The scanned office document image is often the end state and the file format header allows storage of a lot of information.

Digitized photographs, on the other hand, are not so straightforward. A digitized photograph is likely to end up printed on glossy paper or integrated into something else, so there has been a more cavalier attitude about format standards and the need to store information in the file header of these materials.

Kodak's immersion into photo digitizing (PhotoCD™) has had a huge impact. Its prominence advances our undertakings by creating a broader market for useful software tools and storage devices, as well as increasing the public appetite for access to digital images. But in other ways, its proprietary format has created barriers for us, as do most proprietary nonstandard systems, in manipulating the images, writing compatible software, etc.

At the far extreme, television, movie, and graphics endeavors have propelled digital multimedia developments, but with no focus on preserving the digital elements. Most of these activities are production oriented–details about the creation of the parts of a whole are unimportant as long as the whole ends up on a standard analog medium that can be played in movie houses or our homes.

While there are many incremental improvements that will make our work easier–faster capture devices, improved compression, greater storage capacities, and decreasing costs–there are just as many significant advances being made at the user end, such as faster modems and improved display and printing devices.

If the library-archives community joins together to convince vendors and service providers that there is significant business for them in the library world, we can better influence developments to meet our special needs.

CAUTIOUS NEXT STEPS

There are many things we can do to further our own cause.

Procedures

- We should consider adapting the methods we use in the conservation and preservation of individual items so that they accommodate future digitizing of those items and optimize effective capture while minimizing damage to the artifacts.
- We need to implement objective methods for measuring quality and performing quality control.
- We should consider when it is appropriate to think in terms of access quality rather than replacement quality in cases where we will also conserve and retain the original.
- File sizes that result from high-quality capture make compression necessary rather than optional. We need to understand the impact of compression on preservation-quality digital reproductions.
- We need to learn how to do SGML markup efficiently with the eventual goal of turning this task over to a reliable service bureau.
- Now that we have a sense of the effort and costs involved in converting and encoding texts, we need to select our conversion projects carefully in order to make the best use of our resources.

Standards

- We need to build on the work of the joint RLG and Commission on Preservation and Access task force to establish best practices for long-term digital archiving.[6]
- We need to work with the Internet Engineering Task Force (IETF), the Corporation for National Research Initiatives (CNRI), OCLC, and others to come up with a standard URN approach to naming digital objects that is independent of their locations.[7]
- We need to have a significant voice, building on the efforts of the Group on Electronic Document Interchange (GEDI), in discussions about what information needs to accompany digital objects–and how information in, for example, TIFF headers or TEI headers relates to bibliographic records, finding aids, and other metadata.

Technology

- We need to accept that there will not be an ultimate storage media solution. We need to wisely select the most appropriate media from which we can easily migrate our data as better storage devices and media become available.

- We need to provide users with access to appropriate workstations and worry less about the current equipment limitations in their homes and dorm rooms. Hardware companies will do their best to ensure that our users have fast processors, high-resolution color displays and printers, and fast modems. While we are bending over backwards to accommodate our users' technological shortcomings, they will have upgraded their equipment.

- We need not spend a lot of time worrying about digitizing motion or accurate color capture; industry is hard at work on these. We need only wait and then build on their efforts.

- Finally, we need to work with vendors (service bureaus and equipment manufacturers) both to convince them of a market and to communicate unmet needs.

SELECTION OF MATERIALS FOR DIGITIZATION

Selection of materials for digitization is the area in which our expertise is unsurpassed and we can best apply traditional practices.

We should consider materials on their own merit and utility to researchers—not on the basis of ease of digitizing. While theoretically it makes sense to select materials based on what is now possible and easiest to digitize, we do not want to preclude materials that will challenge us to address new digitization issues.

Once we have selected appropriate materials, we need to remind ourselves that users still need ways to filter out the "noise" of unwanted documents and to hone in on materials of interest. They, knowingly or not, rely on information professionals to select, sort, label, codify, coordinate, and provide the information they depend on.

The next technological advances of interest to us are likely to be improved ways users can access the marvelous things we have made available to increasingly larger audiences. If we build on our experience, we can overcome many of the obstacles and improve researchers' access to the myriad of information that is almost within their grasp.

REFERENCES

1. Anne R. Kenney and Stephen Chapman. *Tutorial: Digital Resolution Requirements for Replacing Text-Based Material: Materials for Benchmarking Image Quality*. Washington DC: Commission on Preservation and Access, April 1995. See a related presentation at Web address: http://www.uky.edu/~kiernan/ DL/kenney.html

2. Berkeley Finding Aid Project Web address: http//sunsite.berkeley.edu/FindingAids/

3. For information about the Conspectus and other University of Michigan Digital Library publications, see this Web address:
http://www.si.umich.edu/UMDL/publications/umdlpubs.html

4. *RLG Digital Image Access Project: Proceedings from an RLG Symposium.* Patricia A. McClung, ed. Mtn. View, CA: Research Libraries Group, 1995. Available from The Research Libraries Group, Inc.

5. For information about the Cornell/Yale projects: Anne R. Kenney, "Digital-to-microfilm conversion: An interim preservation solution," *Library Resources and Technical Services* 1993;37(4):380–101; and on digitizing microfilm, see this Web address: http://www.xerox.com/show/case_studies/yale.html

6. *Preserving Digital Information: Report of the Task Force on Archiving of Digital Information.* Washington DC: Commission on Preservation and Access, May 1, 1996. Also available at this Web address: http:/www.rlg.org/ArchTF/

7. IETF URI working group Web address: http://www.ics.uci.edu/pub/ietf/uri/index.html

The Access Context

Margo Crist
John Price-Wilkin

"There is nothing more difficult to take in hand, more perilous to conduct, or more uncertain in its success, than to take the lead in the introduction of a new order of things." So said Machiavelli in *The Prince*, and we might contemplate whether the digital environment represents a new order of things for us in libraries. Certainly with regard to access, we have many entirely new options and possibilities to consider.

CONCEPTS OF USER ACCESS

Before looking at the access strategies in use or development for digitally reproduced material, let us consider access in the paper-based environment and what we know about the ways users tap and utilize information in their work. Authors and publishers have for years packaged works in ways to support and assist access by readers and researchers. As a publisher friend reminds us, books and journals are, after all, a type of package and a type of technology.

These "packages" offer a table of contents to frame the entire work. They provide emphasis and structure to the thoughts being offered and lay out the development of the ideas and themes through chapters and headings. Footnotes clarify text through explanation and direct citation. Bibli-

Margo Crist is Director of Libraries, University of Massachusetts at Amherst, formerly Assistant Director for Public Services at the University of Michigan Library. John Price-Wilkin is Head of Digital Library Production Services for the University of Michigan Library.

[Haworth co-indexing entry note]: "The Access Context." Crist, Margo, and John Price-Wilkin. Co-published simultaneously in *Collection Management* (The Haworth Press, Inc.) Vol. 22, No. 3/4, 1998, pp. 169-176; and: *Going Digital: Strategies for Access, Preservation, and Conversion of Collections to a Digital Format* (ed: Donald L. DeWitt) The Haworth Press, Inc., 1998, pp. 169-176.

ographies provide citations of relevant works, context for the material, and authority to the effort.

Librarians have for years facilitated even further the ability to find ideas and works in a targeted way. We have provided access points and identified attributes through our cataloging practices and the use of Library of Congress subject headings or MeSH headings. We have developed control for variance of names, bringing items together under like headings and names through authority files. We have grouped physical materials together on same or related topics through classification and related shelving practices to enhance browsing possibilities and other chances of discovery. We have developed pathfinders as guides to resources by discipline or topic to enable researchers to navigate through enormous collections of material.

Over the years, there has been significant research on how our users learn and use information and information systems. Studies look at how people build their own information systems, their own "personal constructs" for creating knowledge.[1] Users are not passive, as we have learned, but give meaning to information based on these personal constructs. Information seeking is about filling gaps in those personal knowledge systems.[2,3]

How well are we helping users fill the knowledge gaps? We know that people who enjoy searching our OPACs tend to like the results more![4] We know that people seek out information that is the most accessible. Studies have also shown that researchers will follow habitual patterns that include tracking citations from articles or books they read and browsing in rather serendipitous ways.[5] How do we as librarians envision replicating that kind of environment in the digital world?

"Why convert a text to electronic form unless one can do more with it than with the printed version?" asks Raymond Smock, former president of the Association for Documentary Editing.[6] If we take his question to heart, we may want to assume that we need to keep all of the access mechanisms described here in addition to adding more. Dr. Smock suggests the value of hypertext links. We suggest that we may need to go much further than that.

Let us assume that all of the access strategies listed above should continue in the digital environment and that we want to include even more flexibility for the scholars who tell us they want to work in more free-form ways to fill the knowledge gaps they identify! They want the possibility of moving around in a work or group of works in the same manner as browsing through books or journals–flipping pages, capturing themes, making notes, noting authors whose additional work they will review, and so on. They care about the overall content of the work, the readability level, the availability of charts as well as the author, title, and date of publication. They want a critical mass of relevant work to explore. And they want it all to be fluid and quick, which, of course, is not the case in the paper world.

One approach to creating the digital information environment would be to assume that the most important thing to do is digital capture–a snapshot of each paper page, if you will–and do as much of it as possible at the best quality possible. We suggest that this is not nearly enough to meet the challenge of Dr. Smock's question. It would not allow readers/researchers to easily navigate through the text nor certainly to jump from place to place. Even introducing keyword or Boolean searching is a limited answer to the desire for easy navigation.

APPROACHES TO MAINTAINING ACCESS POINTS

To serve our users well, we must question assumptions about what is possible and seek approaches for access and organization that both maximize the features of the computer display and carry forward the best characteristics of print. What, then, are the approaches that maintain the access points identified? What types of access efforts enable the user to maintain a sense of a work's structure while also navigating easily through the more detailed subject matter?

One approach is to mark the text electronically so that any application can recognize headings, chapters, footnotes, as well as keywords in the text to maintain the structural codes that current books and journals give us. Suppose standards were developed for this type of description to allow for sharing and publishing of documents electronically. All of this does exist in SGML, a descriptive markup system. A number of tools and applications are built on the use of SGML. One takes the pathfinder concept from the past. The Berkeley Finding Aid Project has given new shape to the possibilities for the "pathfinders" we all remember by coding them via SGML to give the digital framework to collections that are not digitized.[7]

Another approach builds on the "relevance research" of the library field and uses the digital environment in ways that allow keyword searches to be analyzed and refined by relevance rankings. (Relevance research explores how relevant search results are to the needs/inquiry of the searcher.) Yet another approach allows a search to be run against a thesaurus appropriate to the discipline for which the search is targeted and alternative terms could be automatically offered.

All elements of access that have been cited–text structures coded for access, attribute identification, grouping by subject, enhancement of browsing, control of names for variance–are part of the types of systems that are evolving (Figure 1).

FIGURE 1. Access Strategies

Authors/Publishers	Librarians	Possible Digital Tools
Table of contents Chapter/section headings Footnotes		Descriptive markup
	Cataloging of attributes Subject headings Shelving practice	Relevance ranking Hypertext
Bibliographies	Pathfinders	Digital pathfinders

These approaches also begin to move us beyond the access models we have built around the limitations of print and the book form. Our imaginations have all been sparked in recent years by World Wide Web clients. Few people knew about the World Wide Web before Mosaic came along, but then that software was immediately hailed by *The New York Times* as the "killer app." We began to glimpse what would be possible in the delivery of networked information. Home pages by libraries, institutions, companies and individuals are everywhere now, offering easy access to files of information, images, video clips, and sound. Information can be modeled in the electronic space so that users can see many parts simultaneously, see the structure of the document in hierarchical displays, and browse forward and back (between notes and prose) without opening different windows. These features are almost taken for granted less than three years after that newspaper article, and our sights are set much higher. We hear the seemingly incongruous phrase *three-dimensional space* used when talking about the two-dimensional field of our monitors, and we have to wonder what will come next (next after java, the current wonder application, that is).

Tools that best model the admirable characteristics of print technology are probably those based on an understanding or representation of structure in the electronic "book." Browsers such as DynaText and SoftQuad Panorama use an understanding of the organization and function of the text to give the user an understanding of the relationship of the parts to the whole. These packages create a virtual table of contents by identifying headings or titles of sections and subsections, arraying them as pointers into the text. The user can see a representation of the whole while navigating the parts, and is therefore always provided with a sense of where he or she is in the work. This rendering of the forest view alongside the trees is done dynamically by extracting organizational elements from the text. That is, headings for chapter titles and section titles are drawn from the text; relationships are reflected in the nesting of heading elements. This is possible with SGML.

Similarly, the structure-aware interface, Lector, provides the reader with a flexible representation of the text–a multifaceted representation that can be modified instantly depending on need. For example, a lengthy dictionary entry from the electronic version of the *Oxford English Dictionary*–16 screens of text–can be represented as a simple dictionary entry (without quotes) for one user, but as a full-fledged historical resource with quotations from the word's earliest use through time for another user by simply selecting what to suppress. Another selection allows, again, the forest or skeleton view of all the definitions of a word or phrase so that the user can get a sense of the organization of this section and the user's location as well.

As with DynaText and Panorama, Lector relies on a recognition of the organization of the information, using that organization to help the user get situated in a sea of bytes.

These relatively modest interfaces demonstrate some of the more valued characteristics of print technology. The user can more easily navigate the electronic text than was possible with paper-based text. The sense of the text as black box–all-I-know-is-what-I-see-before-me-now–is avoided as the user is provided with these relatively simple navigational aids.

As we advocate the needs of the user, we should continue to stretch our sense of the effective methods and possibilities for presentation of information. Suppose that a search could be handled by a highly specialized set of agents that profiled the user and his or her information-seeking behavior and also the digital collections available and even offered mediator agents that could navigate between the two? This is the concept of the University of Michigan NSF Digital Library.

Are there even more flexible and expressive ways of presenting the information space of a single book or of our collections? J. David Bolter and Michael Joyce, the developers of a hypertext authoring environment called Storyspace, suggest the possibilities. They continue to push the notions of hypertext to heights the World Wide Web and Smock can perhaps only imagine. The intellectual work can be conceived of as a web of relationships. Storyspace uses that notion of a web to visually represent relationships and facilitate navigation. The user sees ideas, chapters, and even information resources spread before him or her in a multidimensional space, allowing easy hypertextual navigation from idea to idea, from closely related notions to far-flung, unrelated ideas.

Ultimately, the malleability of text will be the biggest boon in helping us make the most of the computer screen's small space. Hypertext links are one facet of this. Still more important will be the sort of basic structural encoding that is the foundation for programs like Lector or Panorama. This sort of flexible text will enable the user to see text variously, to see only what is needed, and to see both the forest and the trees. By separating structure from style, the text can respond to the needs of the moment, looking different for different purposes. By concentrating on structure and function in organizing our digital collections, we will build in the sort of flexibility that will aid navigation and multiple, individualized approaches. Inflexible electronic text may well be the microfilm of the new information age–useful for direct replication but unable to support flexible inquiry and knowledge creation.

THE INTERSECTION OF ACCESS AND SELECTION

How does this discussion of current, emerging, and future access possibilities for digital resources shape how we choose *what* to digitize? Several areas should be of major importance to us as librarians, and they are offered here as a list of assumptions:

- The decision regarding *what* to digitize is absolutely interconnected with the question of *how* we digitize it.
- Digital capture will not ultimately be sufficient. We need to move at once to the assumption that digitizing must provide, up front, the structures for access. If we fail to effectively organize the newly created digital materials, we will be limiting our users to cumbersome access systems that lose even the virtues we find in the traditional print environment. We also risk the strong possibility of creating a divide in digital collections, with some collections waiting for the appropriate access mechanisms to be added later.
- Because strategies for access will change, standards should be developed around the structure of the data and text being captured. If we agree that the characteristics of the traditional book–the browsable organization that lets us see parts as well as the whole–are desirable, we should seek mechanisms and standards that allow for variation in applications and tools intersecting with the structures.
- Some selection criteria for digitizing will need to be different from those for preservation selection. We will need to change from focus-

ing on artifactual value or even valuable intellectual content and institutional strength to creating a body of related digital material that constitutes a sufficient critical mass to have real impact on scholarship even if that body is uneven in terms of "value." The Making of America project being pursued by Cornell University and the University of Michigan with support from the Mellon Foundation offers a model here since its main prerequisite for selection of materials to digitize is to create a collection that is thematically related and will receive significant use. They are embracing the critical mass hypothesis.

- The access strategies will only be useful if the body of digitized materials is big enough and cohesive enough to truly impact scholarship. Funding for both the development of those digital collections and the access tools that will make them central for researchers should be pursued in tandem and in incremental ways that ensure the usefulness of both over time.

THE ULTIMATE QUESTION

Although we have shown some exciting tools and approaches to access, no one is fully using this type of access creation–descriptive markup or otherwise–in digitizing collections beyond prototypes. The expense of doing so has been a deterrent for everyone. However, as we grapple with the issues of quality and quantity of digital reformatting, we must also face realistically the user expectations regarding access in the increasingly unfettered digital environment. If it is true that researchers are influenced by what information is most accessible to them, the issue of access needs to be central to our selection process. Selecting collections then becomes a challenge that is a variation on our themes of the past. The question we will leave with you is only slightly different from the one we have endlessly asked: How do we offer the largest possible set of digital materials that is central to the research or study being done *and* offer it in a high-quality presentation that is accessible to the user?

NOTES

1. George A. Kelly. *A Theory of Personality: Psychology of Personal Constructs.* New York: Norton, 1955.
2. Carol C. Kuhlthau. *Seeking Meaning: A Process Approach to Library and Information Services.* Norwood, NJ: Ablex Publishing, 1993.

3. Brenda Dervin and Michael Milan. "Information and needs and uses." *Annual Review of Information Science and Technology* 1986;21:3-33.

4. Prudence Ward Dalrymple and Douglas Zweizig. "Users' experience of information retrieval systems: An exploration of the relationship between search experience and affective measures." *Library and Information Science Research* 1992;14:176-7.

5. Stephen Stoan. "Research and information retrieval among academic researchers: Implications for library instruction." *Library Trends* 1991;39(3):238-57.

6. Raymond Smock. "What promise does the Internet hold for scholars?" *Chronicle of Higher Education* 42 (4):B2 (September 22,1995).

7. Daniel V. Pitti. "Access to digital representations of archival materials: The Berkeley Finding Aid Project," from *RLG Digital Image Access Project: Proceedings from an RLG Symposium*. Patricia A. McClung, ed. Mtn. View, CA: Research Libraries Group, 1995.

The Copyright Context

Robert L. Oakley

This discussion of copyright issues and the digital library of the future will cover three major areas. First we will examine what the Copyright Act currently provides. What can you now digitize with confidence and where are the limits? We will then consider the state of the debate on the creation, use, and distribution of digital images in the library and archives community. Lastly, we will address the question of how libraries and archives might be able to proceed with digitization even if a work is protected.

COPYRIGHT LAW TODAY

The Copyright Act protects original works of authorship that are fixed in a tangible medium of expression. With regard to "original works of authorship," the Supreme Court has held that the white pages of the phone book do not meet the test because they lack sufficient originality (*Feist Publications, Inc. v. Rural Telephone Services Co. Inc.,* 499 U.S. 340 [1991]). There you have the first answer to what you can safely put into digital form: You can digitize the white pages. Actually, though, the Feist case is important because it has called into question the copyrightability of many databases in which the creative element might be lacking but which, nonetheless, are the product of significant work or investment. Because of a fear that such databases are now ripe for piracy, the information industry has called for the creation of a new system of protection–outside of copyright–for databases. So, while you could scan the white pages and other

---

Robert L. Oakley is Director of the law library and Professor of law at the Georgetown University Law Center.

© 1995 Robert L. Oakley.

[Haworth co-indexing entry note]: "The Copyright Context." Oakley, Robert L. Co-published simultaneously in *Collection Management* (The Haworth Press, Inc.) Vol. 22, No. 3/4, 1998, pp. 177-184; and: *Going Digital: Strategies for Access, Preservation, and Conversion of Collections to a Digital Format* (ed: Donald L. DeWitt) The Haworth Press, Inc., 1998, pp. 177-184.

similar data files now, you might want to follow the development of this proposal. (Such a proposal was, in fact, introduced into Congress as H.R. 3531 in May 1996.)

More relevant to the main purpose of our discussion is that the works of the United States government are specifically excluded from protection. Many of these documents are badly deteriorated, would be important candidates for conversion, and there is no copyright issue at all concerning them. Please note, however, that I said works of the U.S. government; I did not say government documents, generally. Under the Copyright Act, the states may copyright their works and many of them do. That is a quick summary of what is protected–original works of authorship that have been fixed, but not works of the U.S. government and not databases wholly lacking in originality.

For How Long Are the Works Protected?

This is the first and, for our purposes, probably the most important limitation on the rights of owners. Protection does not last forever. There is a whole series of rules on this issue, but you should know that for works created recently, since 1978, protection lasts for the life of the author plus 50 years, or for corporate or anonymous works, it lasts for 75 years from the date of first publication. For works published before 1978, the rules are complex. But what you can know with some certainty is that if a work is older than 75 years, that is, published in 1920 or before, it is in the public domain and safe to digitize.

Works that were published between 1921 and 1964 may or may not be in the public domain. All of those works should have renewed their copyright after 28 years. If they did not–and studies seem to show that the vast majority did not–the work is in the public domain and you may copy them freely. If they did renew, the works are protected for 75 years from the date of publication. Regrettably, the only way to determine whether the copyright was renewed is on a title-by-title basis. Works published after 1964 but before 1978 have their copyrights renewed automatically, and you should presume that they are protected for 75 years.

To sum up, works published in 1920 or before are in the public domain. Works published since 1964 are protected. The years in between are a gray area in which most works are probably in the public domain because they did not renew their copyright. How you proceed with such works depends on how much of a risk taker you are. You should also be aware of a proposal now on the fast track in Congress to extend all these terms by 20 years. This proposal is expected to pass and, if it does, will create a 20-year moratorium on any new works coming into the public domain.

The Copyright Owner's Rights

To understand what you can do with works that are still protected, you need to understand just a little more about the bundle of rights given to a copyright owner. The owner of a copyrighted work is given five exclusive rights, including:

- The right to reproduce the work, that is, to make copies of it.
- The right to prepare derivative works (interesting question how this right applies in the digital age).
- The right to distribute copies.
- The right to perform a work publicly.
- The right to display a work publicly. It is important to understand some of the current debate to know that the right to control the public display of a work was specifically added to allow copyright owners to protect their work in the electronic environment.

Without more in the Act, many of the things we, as librarians, want to do would appear to infringe on one or more of these rights. But the Act provides several limitations on these rights that are important to us.

With regard to copying, for example, Section 108 provides a safe harbor for some library copying. It gives us the right, within certain limits, to make copies for interlibrary lending, for personal research or study, and for preservation. Where does digital reformatting or the creation of a digital library fit into this section? Regrettably, I can find nothing in this section that would authorize large-scale projects to digitize protected works and retain them for future use.

First, all copying done under Section 108 must be single, isolated copies. In no event are multiple copies–such as might be required to meet preservation standards–allowed. Second, in the case of interlibrary lending or copying for personal use, the law specifically provides that the copy must become the personal property of the user. This provision is clearly intended to preclude the retention of an additional copy by the library. Third, the preservation sections permit the copying of complete published and unpublished works under certain circumstances and the retention of the copy by the library, but those copies are limited by the Act to copies in "facsimile form." Facsimile form is defined in the legislative history to mean paper or microform, that is, not digital.

If the safe harbor provisions of Section 108 do not permit what you want to do, the only thing you have to rely on is "fair use" under Section 107. If the purpose of the copying is for preservation, I think it is possible to make a case for digital reformatting as fair use on the grounds that the purpose meets a public need and that, for the most part, the works in question are old and out of print so that the copying does not interfere with the market. Outside the preservation context, the case for digital reformatting as fair use is more difficult. The entire work is being copied to be used, presumably, in the same manner and as a substitute for the original. Under those circumstances, the copyright owner is likely to insist on compensation, and a court would probably not find fair use.

REPORT FROM THE WORKING GROUP ON INTELLECTUAL PROPERTY

How does all this change under the recommendations of the white paper recently issued by the Working Group on Intellectual Property of the National Information Infrastructure? Regrettably, not very much.

The report does make a few recommendations that help libraries, especially those libraries involved in digital preservation. Unfortunately, it does little to help in the more general quest for the creation of digital libraries. In fact, many believe that the report and its recommendations do more harm than good because they set the stage for the substantial undoing of fair use, for significant incursions into individual liberties, and for setting limits on access to information.

Let us consider the positive side first. The Working Group on Intellectual Property signaled an intention to help the preservation effort by recommending a series of changes to Section 108 of the Copyright Act. They recommend that the two preservation sections–for published and unpublished works–be amended to explicitly allow for preservation using digital techniques. This change is needed because the preservation sections now exclude the use of digital methods, confining libraries to preservation copying using only paper or microfilm. Moreover, the working group recommends that Section 108 be changed to permit a library to make three copies of a work, with no more than one of them in use at any one time. Again, this change has long been sought by the preservation community to allow it to make an archival copy, a use master, and a use copy of a particular work. Although the specific proposals made by the working group need refining, the purpose–to allow for digital preservation–would be an important step forward.

The report–but not the recommended statutory changes–also has some general language about extending the Section 108 exemptions to include digital copying "for certain purposes." For example, the working group speaks positively about using electronic techniques to engage in interlibrary "borrowing," so long as it is not a substitute for a purchase. In almost the same breath, however, they substantially negate that idea by saying that in a world of electronic licensing, what constitutes a substitute for a purchase will be very different from the paper environment that existed when the Act was passed. When all is said and done, therefore, about all the working group recommended for libraries was digital copying for preservation purposes, allowing up to three copies to be made, of which only one could be in use at any one time, the others to be archived.

Despite these limited positive recommendations, some substantial concerns are raised by other parts of the report.

First, the report recommends expansion of the distribution right to include transmissions. This is important because previously the electronic rights of owners were covered by the display and performance rights, both of which must be "public" to be actionable. By this recommended change, the working group would give owners a claim over all electronic transmissions, both public and private. Since transmission of a work to a single offsite user by a library could well be described as "private," this recommendation could have a major impact on a library's ability to achieve the goals of this conference. The report describes this change as a minor clarification. But there is no equivalent clarification of electronic fair use rights. As a result, this proposed change would disturb the balance between the rights of owners and the rights of users and should give us all pause.

The report also refers favorably to the trends toward licensing and encryption of protected works. It goes so far as to suggest that licensing may become the modern substitute for a subscription. In this, the working group may actually be right. But, the combination of licensing plus encryption will give copyright owners total control–a total monopoly, if you will–over the information. There will be no fair use. Everything will either be paid for or done with the explicit permission of the publishers. I cannot help but think that such total control by copyright owners is not good public policy. How libraries respond to the trend and negotiate collective licenses on behalf of their users is critical to whether libraries will continue to play their traditional role, or whether libraries become just another place where you pay per view.

Finally, the notion of keeping track of what people are reading raises enormous questions about privacy and intellectual freedom. Every library association has stood firm on the issue of confidentiality of library records, and a national database on the reading habits of individual Americans is not one that will go down well with librarians or the American public.

So those are some of the trade-offs. The recommendations of the report would give us the ability to do more with digital preservation. But it also raises profound and troubling questions indeed, and most of the library community seems likely to oppose the report, despite the progress made on preservation.

STRATEGIES FOR THE FUTURE

As you see, what you can do to digitally reformat protected materials under the current law and even under the proposed changes to the Copyright Act is limited. If that is the case, how should you proceed?

I assume you are not satisfied with the limited categories of material we have identified so far as being in the public domain, and you want to begin digitizing newer works, including works not really old enough to be considered for preservation, for distribution over a campuswide network. Here we enter much more difficult territory, territory that will entail risk to you and your institution unless you do it correctly.

I am not going to tell you that you cannot do it. I am going to tell you that if you venture into this area you must be prepared to work with publishers and their representatives and to deal with the uncertainties of their publishing future as they see them. In general, this is going to mean seeking permission, working with publishers, and possibly paying royalties. To the extent that you do not do these things, you would be well-advised to set aside a fund to settle with the publishers when they come knocking on your door.

Recently I spoke with publisher representatives and a representative from the Copyright Clearance Center. The first thing I learned will not surprise you at all. Collectively, publishers are very worried about this thing we so glibly call the digital library. In fact, although they know they need to do something to take advantage of the technology, they worry about making their works available in digital form at all. They fear that once a work is available on the Internet, there will be no way to control its use or make any money from its subsequent distribution. The passage of time may alleviate these fears but, for now, many publishers are not likely to loosen their hold on their works.

If collectively publishers are nervous, individually many of them are looking for ideas and help, and they are willing to consider a variety of options to help them move toward their own digital future. To a large degree, these publishers have lost interest in negotiating with libraries about fair use, electronic document delivery, and electronic reserves because they believe that by using digital techniques, these are all things they can and will do themselves in the future under license agreements with libraries. If libraries can provide document delivery services for journals in their collection, so too can the journal publishers. If libraries want to have a digital library of current materials, publishers can license the digital version along with selling the print version. If libraries want to preserve historic materials, publishers can maintain their back lists in electronic form. In effect, there is no reason for books ever to go out of print because they will always be able to be printed on demand and delivered directly to the user, either electronically or in hardcopy.

This scenario ought to make you nervous for the future because it fits so neatly together with the licensing and pay-per-view schemes promoted by the Working Group on Intellectual Property. But for the purposes of this symposium, this approach may suggest some opportunities.

The Conventional Approach

Certainly, the most traditional and straightforward thing to do is to write for permission and be prepared to pay a royalty. That sounds easy, but the publishers are so nervous about the whole concept that they are not going to want to give you permission unless there are a whole lot of strings attached: no works for which they see any likelihood of a future market; no works that might be used in a course pack from which they might get royalties; no works that you might put on a network and make available beyond your local user community, no works that might get incorporated into a multimedia work, and so on. Nonetheless, if you are prepared to enter into these discussions with publishers, you may get permission to digitize some works. Given this one-title-at-a-time type of scenario, however, the process is not likely to be efficient or allow for large-scale digitization of the historic record.

The Joint Venture Approach

The second suggestion I have, therefore, is to think differently about the permission process. Most publishers do not yet have a significant digital back file. This situation presents an opportunity for librarians and publishers to work together collaboratively in their mutual interest. Rather than simply writing for permission to make a digital copy, you should consider proposing a series of joint ventures—working cooperatively with individual publishers—to begin a massive conversion process to accomplish the goal of retrospective digital conversion and at the same time to provide publishers with a digital back file of their works.

You have the publisher's back files in your libraries. You are also willing, I take it, to devote the time and effort to a project for digital conversion. At the same time, most publishers would like to have a digital file of their works. These mutual objectives would appear to form the basis of an agreement. Libraries could agree to scan the works of a certain publisher in their collection in return for a right to use the digital files.

How those agreements between libraries and publishers might be negotiated will be critical to the success of the venture. Libraries could provide the digital conversion but insist on the right to provide some level of access to the information. Publishers, on the other hand, would obtain the digital file for their own use, but would naturally insist on retaining the ability to resell the work and to have an appropriate market that was not undercut by the library distribution system. All in all, however, this kind of approach to the publishing community seems likely to me to lead to success.

The Copyright Clearance Center Approach

Finally, a third approach is through the Copyright Clearance Center (CCC). The CCC has not yet ventured into the digital environment, but they are anxious to do so. Because of the collective nervousness of the publishing community, the CCC is uncertain how to grant limited rights to digital copying, how to track uses, how to charge in an appropriate manner, and how to ascertain an appropriate amount to charge. As noted before, they are also nervous about granting any digital copying privileges to libraries because of the potential for loss of control over the work.

However, I talked to a representative of the CCC, and they would welcome specific, limited projects as a way of beginning to move into the digital environment. "Bring us a project," she said. I take that as an open invitation. Again, it will be crucial how any such agreement is negotiated. Obviously we will want to obtain the ability to digitize the works we feel are important and make them available to our users. On the other hand, the CCC will be sensitive to the potential for lost revenues, and we must be aware of their concerns. Any proposal presented to them would need to begin to answer the questions I identified a minute ago. Who would have access? How would compensation be provided—through an annual license fee or through a transactional tracking mechanism? What would the fees cover—all uses or only uses in which permanent copies are made? How would publishers protect themselves against the making of second generation copies that might be distributed outside the agreement with the library? All of these are questions that would need to be answered, but I believe the CCC has opened the door to engage in a dialogue that could lead to a mutually satisfactory conclusion.

The Preservation Context

Tamara Swora

As we move to incorporate various types of digital technologies into our menu of reformatting options for library and archival materials, we need to understand changing roles and directions in key areas, especially in our preservation operations. This kind of taking stock is timely because we must understand how to select materials for conversion to digital media and begin to devise formal selection procedures that responsibly serve our institutions and collections. In large part, my comments will draw on experiences with the preservation reformatting of retrospective book and paper collections in libraries and archives, since this is where standards and infrastructure are in place. My remarks may not apply to all preservation operations nor to all institutions since approaches to preservation selection and treatment vary from institution to institution.

In the last decade, the preservation community has established national standards for almost all parts of the reformatting processes we use in preservation microfilming and also for preservation photocopying. The development of these standards was largely driven by cooperative preservation microfilming projects and national support through the National Endowment for the Humanities. What became a national effort began with the first RLG cooperative microfilming projects and culminated in the de facto standards set forth in the RLG preservation microfilming guidelines, the well-known preservation manual edited by Nancy Gwinn, as well as standards for preservation photocopying. We have also developed complex selection procedures for preservation reformatting. All of the knowledge and skills we have gained are critical to the expansion of preservation work into the digital environment. However, for us to be most effective in

Tamara Swora is a digital conversion projects coordinator for the Library of Congress's National Digital Library Program.

[Haworth co-indexing entry note]: "The Preservation Context." Swora, Tamara. Co-published simultaneously in *Collection Management* (The Haworth Press, Inc.) Vol. 22, No. 3/4, 1998, pp. 185-191; and: *Going Digital: Strategies for Access, Preservation, and Conversion of Collections to a Digital Format* (ed: Donald L. DeWitt) The Haworth Press, Inc., 1998, pp. 185-191.

applying and sharing what we know, we will need to make some changes in how we think and accomplish our conversion work. For example:

- We need to rethink or reengineer our selection and production procedures to make them relevant in a digital environment. The infrastructure that presently supports preservation reformatting can and must be adapted if it is to support the production of digital products. This reengineering of the known will allow preservation to continue to occupy the prominent position it has historically enjoyed in reformatting.

- Much broader collaboration and partnerships both inside and outside our institutions are essential if selection decisions and plans for conversion are to be effective and responsible.

- The preservation community has long been the champion of the physical item or object and been less concerned with how or if it will be used. This important advocacy must continue, but it no longer is sufficient. We also need to consider content and its use in the electronic environment. Until recently, our thinking has begun with selection (largely triggered by poor physical condition) and ended with defining the product (microform, photocopy, or reproduction with limited access). In digital reformatting, we must learn to think first about defining the content as a product, considering how it will be disseminated and used, and then selecting materials for conversion. To many of us, this may seem like putting the cart before the horse.

- We must take an active role in influencing the design and development of appropriate equipment, particularly scanners, so that selection for digitization need not be limited by currently available hardware.

- We must also shift our attention to access as the dominant objective. In many of our preservation reformatting programs, we may be required to move away from our traditional priority of selecting materials at risk because of their physical condition to materials where use is the decisive factor. Digital technology forces us to consider access before preservation because image presentation, delivery, and storage are computer driven. Also, it may be important to remember that digitized materials in a network environment are always available for use, or as someone recently phrased it, "Pixels never sleep on the Internet."

- We fully understand and have educated library managers about the high costs associated with preparation, conversion, and delivery of reformatted materials. We must now all understand that although some of our conversion costs may decrease over time, the work surrounding current and emerging conversion technologies is similar, also resource intensive, and equally costly.

- We in preservation need to remain viable players in the digital world by learning the meaning of quality in the context of digital imaging so that preservation can offer such expertise in selection for digitization.

BROADER COLLABORATION AND PARTNERSHIPS

If our preservation operations are to successfully employ digital conversion in reformatting and flourish in the digital world, much broader collaboration and partnerships, both inside and outside our institutions, are essential for selection decisions, conversion plans, and cost plans to be effective and responsible. A great benefit to strong collaboration is that our colleagues will also share the responsibility, now and in the future, of our difficult selection decisions.

Within our institutions, assuring a responsible approach in these mostly uncharted waters requires the participation of special individuals–technical gatekeepers or bridge people who will contribute information that informs our work and helps us make sound decisions. We need to identify, nurture, and support these colleagues. They build links to people outside our institutions whose expertise becomes essential (for example, computer experts, imaging scientists, and even technical experts within the entertainment industry).

A crucial element in building technical partnerships is training preservation and associated staff in the technologies surrounding digital imaging. The evolution of national practices in preservation reformatting and our ability to influence standards development only occurred after we had people who understood microphotographic, photographic, and photocopying technologies enough to separate the technical wheat and chaff and apply the best approaches to reformatting our collections. Although we are now beginning to influence the development of digital-imaging practices and standards, we still need more people to communicate and translate our needs to the imaging and communications industries.

Preservation can expand internal collaboration in selection. When collections (as opposed to individual items) are considered for preservation, preservation and collections development staff can convene a selection, planning, and editorial group for a digitization project. For example, a typical assemblage might include staff with expertise in preservation, collections development, cataloging, acquisitions, copyright, computing, and digital conversion. These people have an investment in the future of the item. Singly, each might make different decisions, but together they make negotiated, consensus-based decisions that work to the benefit of all.

Formal collaboration and partnerships external to our institutions are also needed. In preservation microfilming and preservation photocopying as well, we have raised consciousness about our specialized requirements, albeit arduously, with the imaging industry. We should continue these relationships so that we may drive the design and development of appropriate equipment, including computer hardware and software to serve our materials.

A key area for collaboration is in the design and production of scanning equipment which handles our materials as gently as is mechanically possible. Development of such equipment is a collaborative activity, and the importance of the participation of conservators cannot be overstated. They must take an active role in the design and development of appropriate scanners, particularly for scanning of bound items and rapid throughput of unbound sheets in less than pristine condition, so that selection for digitization need not be limited by scanning hardware. Much to the surprise of many of us who struggled to have edge photocopiers, face-up photocopiers, and similar microfilm cameras developed, the imaging industry has already begun to market custom scanners for library applications, so this is an opportune time to make our needs quite clear.

We also have a golden opportunity to influence the direction of imaging and publishing through companies that are patiently, but persistently, seeking content from our collections for their products.

A NEED TO RETHINK CURRENT PRACTICES

As we begin to reengineer the known we must rethink our current practices so that they facilitate rather than complicate or hamper future scanning, thus helping to keep costs down. This becomes significant when we decide that conversion of an item will produce an intermediate reproduction which in turn will be used to generate multiple and successive end products now or in the future.

We need to rethink procedures also because some are based on a linear sequencing that is characteristic of human-readable materials and of the microfilm medium. In the digital realm, we need to abandon linear thinking as we develop new work flows and access tools. To reassess procedures, we also need to consider some of the following questions, which are prompted by previous experience.

- Will we follow any kind of searching procedure to avoid digital duplicates?
- Will we seek to fill in missing material from other institutions for our digital items?
- Should we be using explanatory targets or anomaly targets?
- What kind of technical targets are needed to evaluate quality?
- Should we produce guides to contents of an image file for serials?
- What kind of quality review procedures will we use for digital images?

THE MEANING OF QUALITY

For the preservation community, to keep our place at the table we need to learn the meaning of quality in the digital-imaging context. As I mentioned earlier, we have consensus-based standards and practices in place that currently form the reformatting infrastructure. They ensure that preservation microfilm and preservation photocopies can be used as replacement copies, allowing us to discard materials with almost a clear conscience.

To make use of digital conversion as a replacement medium and thereby facilitate selection decisions, we need to work through numerous issues in which preservation could play an important role. For example, preservation can take the lead in devising digital-imaging standards by defining what constitutes a preservation-quality image as opposed to an access-quality image. Although we are using digital technologies mostly to produce surrogates at this time, until we have a standards framework in place and archiving practices established, the preservation community could begin to accept, reject, or interpret the existing standards. We could incorporate them into product design during selection by defining and providing options or models for what is required to produce surrogate (access quality) and replacement (preservation quality) digital copies. Such models could be developed for:

- Books with line art and no illustration.
- Purely textual materials of a certain size.
- Text with illustrations integrated into the text.
- Handwritten materials.
- Sheet music, etc.

Digital product models could also set forth requirements for appropriate scanning resolutions–perhaps one for storage (preservation quality) and one for display (access quality)–compression, use of grayscale, and color. They could also define the meaning of facsimile in the context of digital conversion by answering such questions as, when we scan books, must we represent true color, original size, the look and feel of the book, covers and endsheets, original size, blank pages, etc.?

Although there is general agreement that scanning from the original enables the best possible capture, when that is not possible, a reproduction continuum or digitization chain (as it has been termed by Peter Robinson) is built.[1] In such a continuum, we move from higher-quality reproductions through increasingly lower-quality reproductions, and generational loss is assumed to occur at each point in the continuum. Intermediate products or copies are produced for a variety of reasons, chief among them to produce a digital image at some point in the chain. However, if a digital image is expected to meet the needs of users, there should be as few intermediate conversion or reproduction steps preceding it as possible. A straightforward example of a conversion chain is to begin with the original, then use microfilm or a photograph as an intermediate, and then produce a digital image. In this process, preservation staff can analyze typical reproduction chains to better determine loss and apply that information to the selection process.

To assure that we are producing fine quality reproductions, we must continue to use our standard national practices in the production of original (first-generation copy) microfilm, so that microfilm can serve as an intermediate (surrogate) or original (replacement copy) in the transfer continuum, thereby minimizing generational loss and operational costs. For example, quality requirements we have established should permit the use of preservation microfilm for future scanning. However, if we reduce these requirements and produce film that is lower in quality, when we scan such film, we likely will be able to recover the image electronically, but the custom scanning required will increase costs, increase conversion time, and compromise the quality of the digital version. Given the high costs for a full preservation microfilming work flow, we should do our best to produce the microfilm that may be a surrogate or replacement copy and that becomes the first reproduction in a reproduction chain.

CHALLENGE FOR THE FUTURE

Preservation administrators can play a key role in selection for digitization. For the past decade, we have had full responsibility for and controlled much of the supporting work in selection for preservation. Preservation had a solution to the problem of book and paper materials whose condition was compromised, and so preservation was often the focal point. We now have a changed role and may no longer be the major interface, within and outside our libraries, for reformatting or conversion. The challenge is to build on our existing expertise, bring new players into the work of preservation, and assure that we understand the fundamentals of these new technologies and apply them to effective decision-making in selection. Clearly we will have broader options and will be better able to serve our collections.

NOTE

1. Peter Robinson. *The Digitization of Primary Textual Sources.* Oxford: Oxford University Office for Humanities Communication, 1993.

The Collection Management Perspective

Linda M. Matthews

Building and managing collections is always about choices. Digital technologies offer so many opportunities for reformatting and increasing access that we are almost immobilized by the array of choices. Go forth and digitize! But given limited time and money, choosing the best collections to digitize is a critical choice and a complex one. Issues of preservation, access, cost, importance to the research community, potential for broad use, and duplication of efforts must be addressed.

A library's collections are raw materials from which we can create new products in digital form. As with the creation of any new product from raw materials already on hand, we want to consider the inherent characteristics of these materials, how they are best used to create a new product that shows off their qualities to better advantage or that makes them more valuable to a wider audience. Ideally, we want the derivative product to be superior in important ways to the raw materials. Superior is a relative term and we need to be clear, as collection managers and curators, about the factors that make a well-chosen digital product if our time, money, and collections are going to be used.

Collection managers and curators look at collection assets from many different perspectives. Collection managers and selectors responsible primarily for general collections will likely be primarily concerned with the value of a digital product for the local institution's curriculum and faculty research. They will also be concerned with coordinating digital projects in a cooperative collection development environment so that digital research collections are built in a planned, not scattered, way with a clearly defined and unifying purpose for collection building. Special collections curators,

Linda M. Matthews is Head of Special Collections at the Robert W. Woodruff Library of Emory University.

[Haworth co-indexing entry note]: "The Collection Management Perspective." Matthews, Linda M. Co-published simultaneously in *Collection Management* (The Haworth Press, Inc.) Vol. 22, No. 3/4, 1998, pp. 193-197; and: *Going Digital: Strategies for Access, Preservation, and Conversion of Collections to a Digital Format* (ed: Donald L. DeWitt) The Haworth Press, Inc., 1998, pp. 193-197.

while also concerned with university teaching and research potential, will likely be equally focused on the broad scholarly uses of a digital collection outside the particular institution and with promoting new uses of unique or rare collections in the scholarly and public arena. For most special collections, some 50% of research use is by persons from outside the home area or home institution. Both perspectives, local and global, must be taken into account. Public institutions will think of their collections in terms of public and political benefits in the budget process, and all of us must look at the broader component of our work that can be defined as the "greater public good."

Collections have public relations value, obvious scholarly value, and hidden or undiscovered value. Some archival and rare book collections, for example, may have marquee value for an institution as well as significant, perhaps untapped, research value, "show horses" as "work horses." Some have no marquee value but are nonetheless important because they form a core of significant research and teaching materials that should be more widely known and available. We cannot focus solely on the "great collections." Hidden gems may offer the potential for opening new avenues of research. Would digitizing these collections bring materials of broad research use to a wider audience or make them more accessible through expanded searching options?

FACTORS IN PROJECT SELECTION

Collection managers and curators will look at their collections from many different perspectives when considering digital projects. The following will weigh heavily in a decision.

Ownership and Copyright

Legal ownership and copyright issues in collections of manuscript and printed materials must of course be addressed immediately before other considerations. Manuscript collections may present particularly difficult problems for literary rights as will photographs, art work, and other graphic materials. Printed materials under copyright protection must obviously be cleared. For archival and manuscript collections, legal ownership and donor restrictions will also weigh in the decision. Donor approval, if needed, may be easily obtained but must be considered as a possible obstacle in the decision-making process.

Broad Research Value

Obviously, the scholarly importance and research potential of a collection for a variety of communities is an essential factor. The more potential communities that may benefit from the collection's greater accessibility, the broader value a digital version will have. The cost of digitizing may preclude a project that focuses on a collection of narrow research interests no matter how important that collection may be for a particular subject specialty.

Local Research Value

For those in a university setting, the importance of the collection for faculty research and teaching at the institution may drive decision-making. Given funding considerations and the importance of building resources in collaboration with an institution's academic program priorities, collection managers must always look at the local community and its needs. When these needs coincide with a broader good to the scholarly community at large, the decision for digitizing a particular collection gains greater weight, particularly when funding must come from institutional resources.

High-Demand Collections

The current demand for access to and use of a collection may be so great that a digital version will relieve custodial and reference concerns and bring the collection directly to the user without the intermediary of the archivist or librarian. Thus, digitizing a heavily used collection will benefit the library staff who must service the collection, the user who may have to travel distances to consult the collection, and the materials that are suffering from use. A collections curator will work with the reference staff and preservation officer to identify these collections.

Unique Collections

A collection that is unique (as with an archival collection) or unduplicated elsewhere in its variety and scope, and also holds research significance for a broad audience of users, will be high on a list of possible digital projects since it would bring one of an institution's treasures to a wider audience, benefiting both the research community and promoting the institution's rich collections. The value of digital collections for advancing an institution's mission and reputation as a research center cannot be overlooked by collection curators who spend their time and institutional resources in building those collections.

Availability in Other Formats

Collection curators will also look at the availability of a collection in other formats. Although digital reformatting can provide improved access, would we want to digitize a collection that has already been microfilmed? Given the many choices to be made in digital projects, the added value of digitizing would have to be significant to warrant this expenditure of money and time. A good preservation microfilm of a collection makes that collection accessible through interlibrary loan, reduces wear and tear on the originals, and preserves the materials in a medium in which preservation standards have been established. Digital formats at this time are not preservation media.

Collaborative Collection Building

The opportunity and likelihood of collaborative ventures in building digital collections around a subject area or theme would weigh heavily toward a digital project, contributing to a long-standing goal of collection managers, at least in the rhetoric, of cooperative collection building. The significance of a particular collection in relation to other collections of similar materials or on a related topic at other institutions would give promise of collaborative digitizing projects and the development of a digital collection made up of significant holdings at several institutions. The likelihood that a digital version of materials will add to a growing mass of collections in a digital form in a particular subject area will be of importance to collection curators.

Size of User Community

Relating to all of the above, we need to be assured, or relatively certain, that there is a user community for these digital collections that will make the expenditure of funds and effort worthwhile. While there are preservation issues to be addressed, digital reformatting is primarily an access tool to bring collections easily to a broader audience in a searchable form not available through the original format or in microfilm. Is the user community large enough to justify the cost? Despite the oft-described difficulties in using microfilm, are there not times when microfilm is a suitable and appropriate choice, based on the user community and its needs as well as preservation considerations?

Funding and Budgeting

The collection manager will also be concerned with the budgeting for digital-imaging projects. How much money can the institution commit to digital projects and from what source will the money be found? If digital projects primarily augment collection resources by providing collections in different formats for new means of access, are they primarily an acquisitions cost? Will acquisitions funds be used and at what cost to ongoing acquisition of new materials? How does the digital project fit into library and institutional priorities? If there is an impact on funding allocations that affect acquisitions, how will the collection manager look at the digitizing question?

Long-Term Considerations

Given the unstable nature of digitized formats, what weight do we give to considerations of the long-term availability of these digitized collections? Collection curators will weigh factors of a collection's condition and preservation issues when considering the purchase of print and non-print collections. The long-term costs of maintaining digitized collections should also be given consideration since it will be a part of the total cost.

NO EASY DECISIONS

Five different collection managers and curators, like appraisers of a collection's market value, may look at a list of collections, consider all of the above factors, and come up with five different priorities for digitizing. There are almost no easy decisions. Cost is always a factor, since digitizing costs vary greatly depending upon the materials to be digitized and the indexing required. Research value and a broad user audience, including the use at the curator's own institution, are obviously key factors. Making our decisions in a collaborative way, knowing about other digitizing projects and other related collections that might make up a collaborative project, and learning from shared experiences are all keys in considering digitizing projects from a collections viewpoint.

The Public Services Perspective

Karin Trainer

Library mission statements, TQM (total quality management) manuals, and customer service outlines all proclaim that the user is what drives our library decision-making, and yet, I ask, why didn't we engage them in this panel directly? We have had a couple of people from industry at this symposium; why are there no users?

I jest, of course, and pretend that complicated issues can be rendered simple to make a point–despite our professional credo and a great deal of lip service, we have not in fact found a way to directly incorporate users into the decision-making processes that we have used for reformatting.

What are some of the ways we can give users more influence over what gets selected for reformatting? First, we can just ask them. Along these lines Gerald George, former executive director of the NHPRC and former director of the American Association for State and Local History, was engaged by the Commission on Preservation and Access (CPA) to consider, among other things, how scholars might be called upon to play a larger role in preservation initiatives. In a report issued in July 1995, George points to the growing number of digitization projects and wrestles with what he calls the macro and micro models of scholarly decision-making in preservation decision-making, where *macro* represents organized efforts to consult scholarly organizations and associations about material in their disciplines, and *micro* represents conversations and consultations with scholars on local campuses.

Perhaps predictably, he concludes that both models are useful. One of his concrete recommendations pertaining to digitizing, however, is the

Karin Trainer is University Librarian at Princeton University. At the time of the symposium she was Associate University Librarian and Director of Public Services at the Sterling Library, Yale University.

[Haworth co-indexing entry note]: "The Public Services Perspective." Trainer, Karin. Co-published simultaneously in *Collection Management* (The Haworth Press, Inc.) Vol. 22, No. 3/4, 1998, pp. 199-203; and: *Going Digital: Strategies for Access, Preservation, and Conversion of Collections to a Digital Format* (ed: Donald L. DeWitt) The Haworth Press, Inc., 1998, pp. 199-203.

creation of a register of digital library projects similar to RLG's register of material targeted for preservation microfilming. It is interesting to think about why he advocates this. Without such a register, he asks, how can scholars tell if the right things, the things capable of supporting their teaching and research, are being digitized?

In addition to drawing users into campus-based selection processes (and here no magic is needed–committee structures, focus groups, surveys, just talking to people, all of the things we do already come to mind), we can take heed of users' voices by putting the material they actually use closer to the top of our list of projects for consideration for reformatting. This of course is exactly the opposite of the approach we have been taking with microfilm formatting. In a helpful article, Paula De Stefano of New York University reminds us that "employing a use-based method of identifying candidates for filming has never been pursued seriously as a legitimate vehicle for selecting titles to add to the national collection of microform masters despite the fact that when queried, preservation professionals strongly advocate its merit."[1]

And, finally, we can put users at the center of our reformatting decision-making simply by finding out more about them–the users. In order to take user preference and behavior into account when planning and implementing digital projects, we need more reliable data about those preferences and behaviors. Despite the fact that we are surrounded by digital projects–prototypes, pilot projects, testbeds, call them what you will–we know amazingly little about who uses the existing digitized files, their purposes in using the files, their level of satisfaction, or the changes they might care to recommend. I suspect that we actually do know some of these things, but for perfectly benign reasons we have not shared them with each other. I also am sure that many project directors intend to do this work; they just have not gotten around to it yet. But in any case, we are now at a point where we are casting about for additional projects and hoping to create new operational models, but we do not yet have much data.

One of the challenges we have to face is sorting out the distinction between studying something to death and studying it enough. In fact, we also know amazingly little about who makes use of the Internet on our campuses. Much of the information we have comes from surveys commissioned by commercial interests seeking to find ways to use the Internet for profitable business transactions.

Last week, for instance, CommerceNet, a consortion of over 130 electronics, computer, financial services, and information service companies, released the results of a Nielsen poll it commissioned on the demographics of Internet use. It found, among other things, that 11% of the total adult population of the U.S. and Canada have used the Internet in the past three months (or claim they have), and that the amount of time devoted to Internet use is now equal to the total playback time of rented videotapes. The typical World Wide Web user, according to the poll, is male, upscale, professional, and well educated.

What is most compelling about this survey is not so much its particular findings but its rationale. This is an excerpt from the preface of the survey: "Understanding the demographics, attitudes, and interests of Internet users and how they differ from nonusers is essential to move the business industry forward." And I think it is essential to move our digital project and implementation planning efforts forward too.

Since, as I have noted above, there is not much data to suggest what users want in terms of a digital library, or even whether they want a digital library at all, my remarks that follow on the criteria we might employ in selecting material for digital projects are based solely on my own observations and M.B.T.A. (aka management by talking around). My assumptions underlying these criteria are as follows:

- Users want to be self-sufficient; they don't want to waste time; and they want to work where and when it is convenient to them.
- Digital projects, however carefully selected and designed, will not be productive unless we can provide our users with the appropriate tools and environment, such as reliable and well-designed network access, intelligently designed interfaces, powerful capabilities for intellectual access, the ability to generate high-quality output, and so forth.
- The context in which we are creating these resources must be understood to be one of limited financial resources, which puts on us the extra burden to make sure the work we produce is of the greatest possible value to the users.

Those are my assumptions. Here are the three most significant criteria I would apply from the user's point of view (and my user of course is the academic user):

- *Significant impact.* If we are going to make the investment we should aim to select the content with the potential for having a substantial effect on as many users as possible. Margo Crist and Nancy Gwinn and others have already addressed this, so I will not hammer it into the ground except to offer one more rationale for consciously selecting material with broad appeal: Research and testing, in light of what I said earlier, can be carried out much more fruitfully when there have been enough users to monitor and measure.

- *Appropriate format.* When selecting among collections at this early stage in the digitizing process, it is foolish to focus on material whose physical dimensions and distinctions do not lend themselves to being easily and accurately viewed within the limits of today's software and hardware. Full-scale architectural plans, for instance, which even in thumbnail form cannot be seen in their entirety on the monitors most users are likely to own or have access to, could fall to the bottom of my priority list as might any object where absolutely faithful color capture is necessary for its study.
- *Intellectual access.* We are not doing our users any favors when we give them what Clifford Lynch referred to as a "vast mountain of bitmapped images" without the appropriate organization and tools for searching, sorting, and filtering.

These are the values and criteria I will bring to the selection exercise. Before turning to the next panelist, though, I would like to highlight several other challenges in the arena of digitization. I have already suggested that our lack of information about users and their preferences is a problem that needs to be addressed. We also need to do much more work on shared technical and descriptive standards. And, as described in the joint RLG/CPA report on archiving digital images, chaired by John Garrett and Don Waters, we face an enormous task in making digitized data permanent and thereby allowing us to assure our users and ourselves that we are making long-term commitments to the secure existence of this data which we have just so expensively and carefully converted.[2] How many more digital projects does it make sense to initiate before we are confident that we can retain the content we have just captured? And, finally, do we know enough about the economics of digitized information to be certain we are getting the best return for ourselves and for our users from our investment?

In the end, the most challenging assignment facing the people in this room may not revolve around making decisions about selecting material for digitization but in creating the collaborative structures that are necessary to address the questions I just posed. The reason I make the point to this particular audience is that we as a group have a long and successful history in collaboration. I would like to suggest that this be added to our agenda.

NOTES

1. Paula De Stefano. "Use-based selection for preservation microfilming." *College and Research Libraries* 1995;56:409-418.

2. *Preserving Digital Information: Report of the Task Force on Archiving of Digital Information. Commissioned by the Commission on Preservation and Access and The Research Libraries Group, Inc.* Washington, DC: Commission on Preservation and Access, 1996. Also available at this Web address: http://www.rlg.org/ArchTF/

The Systems Perspective

Dale Flecker

I preface my talk today with two caveats before moving on to a discussion of the issues that systems professionals need to consider in evaluating digitization projects and a very broad (and brief) cost/benefit analysis of the projects under consideration in this exercise.

An inherent problem in discussing long-term digitization projects is that the incredible current rate of change in technology means that anything we say today might not be true tomorrow. This is my first caveat. We have probably all encountered projects in recent years where technological change between conception and implementation has made the original approach obsolete and perhaps has forced significant midcourse correction. Not trusting my powers as a seer, and being suspicious of assertions about how technological "silver bullets" will solve today's technical problems, I will limit my observations about technology to the relatively near-term future.

My second caveat: I have a strong prejudice for the electronic service model being built in American research universities today. Most of you are probably comfortable with the assumption that our automation efforts should be oriented towards delivering services and information over networks, and that if possible we should deliver these equally well to users remote from our libraries and those within the library's walls. We have to recognize, however, that there are other models for electronic information delivery. I regularly encounter people, particularly from abroad or the commercial publishing sector, who remain strongly oriented towards CD-ROM as the delivery vehicle for digital information. That is not my point

Dale Flecker is Associate Director for Planning and Systems at the Harvard University Library.

[Haworth co-indexing entry note]: "The Systems Perspective." Flecker, Dale. Co-published simultaneously in *Collection Management* (The Haworth Press, Inc.) Vol. 22, No. 3/4, 1998, pp. 205-211; and: *Going Digital: Strategies for Access, Preservation, and Conversion of Collections to a Digital Format* (ed: Donald L. DeWitt) The Haworth Press, Inc., 1998, pp. 205-211.

of view. I believe that the digital library is essentially a network application, and my talk today will be from that perspective.

ISSUES IN PROJECT SELECTION

Most of the systems issues involved in selecting digitization projects can be organized loosely into two categories: those concerning users and those concerning the materials. I will start with the users:

User Software, Hardware, and Network Capabilities

If we convert a given set of materials, will a large enough percentage of the target audience have the infrastructure to use it? It is too easy for us to sit in a campus office in Cambridge, Ann Arbor, or Palo Alto and assume that everyone has or will soon have the necessary hardware, software, and network facilities to make use of what we provide. All around us people are sitting at Pentiums or PowerMacs with well-configured Web browsers connected over Ethernets to the campus backbone and the Internet.

Much of the world, however, is not like that and will not be for some time. There are large scholarly populations not on networks at all or on networks that seem to move bits through molasses. Applications that look great in my office can become unusable when the response time for a World Wide Web transaction is measured in minutes not seconds. Likewise, those spiffy high-resolution images are of little use to someone whose technology limits them to a character-based interface or whose workstation lacks the speed or memory to gracefully handle what we can deliver. On average there remains today quite a gap between the technical infrastructure of the high energy physicist and the average Byzantine historian.

User Access, Access Restrictions, and Security

Which potential users will have the right to access the converted materials? How will the system know who may and may not use the data? Many materials have restrictions on use–the example in our set is #8, the social reform collection,[1] which says "access is restricted–apply at repository." If the user is remote, how is that application accomplished? If the curator grants permissions how is that decision to be implemented in the system? Security systems for information resources are still pretty crude in most libraries and universities. If one needs to do more than limit access to those with an on-campus network address or to those represented in a campus directory file, there are significant difficulties. Policies that require collection-by-collection security or that restrict access by type of use (scholarly vs. commercial) or by class of users ("legitimate scholars only") are going to be difficult to enforce.

Recovering Costs from Users

With some hesitation I raise an issue that increasingly lurks in the back of my mind: Will we need to bill users? I could probably make this point somewhat palatable by pointing out that our candidate collections today include some that have copyrighted materials whose owners might well want recompense for use. But, frankly, I think billing is a broader need and that we are going to find ourselves soon wanting to recover costs from at least *some* of the users of *some* of our resources. Like security, billing systems are in a primitive state on most campuses today and are nonexistent when you cross the campus boundary. If billing users is likely to be an issue for a collection, the time may not yet be right to convert that collection.

Next, the systems issues involving the materials to be digitized:

Intellectual Access

Can we provide appropriate intellectual access? There are actually two issues here. First, if we make a collection or body of materials available, will the target users find them? Some collections, such as #1, the Susan B. Anthony materials, are probably not too bad in this regard. A few well-constructed records in the big bibliographic databases, some references in updated versions of guides to research materials in women's studies, etc., will probably lead a significant percentage of potential users to the collection. I was tempted at first to also use the example of #7, *Puck* magazine, but on further reflection this example actually brings up another interesting issue. Certainly we could lead users to a digital version of *Puck* from union catalogs like OCLC or RLIN. But isn't it likely that campus-based users will start with their own catalogs, in which they will commonly find a paper or microfilm version? What will take them on to our at-your-fingertips version? This is one of the key issues in the construction of virtual libraries, and one I suspect we are not close to solving.

The second access issue is that once users locate a digitized collection or publication, will they be able to easily locate the relevant *part* they wish to use? In today's world, at least, flipping through a large collection or publication online to find the appropriate part is problematic–in user time and effort and in network load. This is an area where potential projects will vary enormously. Some materials lend themselves to reasonably "fine grained" access. Journal articles, for instance, for which tables of contents and standard abstracting and indexing sources provide good reference, can be arranged in a system for efficient access. For some books, a small amount of structuring of the digitized images can make tables of contents and indexes useful tools for quickly locating appropriate parts. Detailed inventories, indexes, and folder lists will provide adequate access to some archival collections. For certain visual materials, digitizing itself provides improved access through the use of thumbnail images.

Other materials, however, offer significant access problems. Collection #4, slavery pamphlets, which is presumably unarranged and makes no mention of a finding aid, worries me as does the large amount of hard-to-index materials in #5, the Walter architectural archive, with its many volumes of diaries, account books, and personal papers.

The Appropriateness of Digitization

Will digitization add value? Some of us assume that the digital form of something is automatically better. Digitization, after all, should bring at least the advantages of remote access, replication, and manipulatability. But we should be careful to articulate the added value for each individual project. Some materials will profit from remote access or manipulability; for others it may not be a great advantage (you can manipulate the image of a page of text but not often to any great advantage).

I mentioned the added value in browsing visual materials that can be gained through digital techniques. There are times the digital format of an item is easier to use (compare browsing images in a slide collection to using the same materials online), but also times when it is harder (for example, display technology for oversized materials can be extremely cumbersome–those oversize maps in #2, the Pennsylvania Railroad collection, are problematic in this way). Digital image enhancement can make certain materials more legible in digital form than they were on paper. But I wonder about those 15,000 dime novels in #6. If we were able to convert them to full-text form, it is easy to imagine enhancements in both access and analysis. But if they were simply converted to bitmapped image form, do we add much advantage over simple microfilm?

Conversion Difficulties

Will the materials be difficult to convert? Conversion difficulties are related to the form of the original and the target format. If our product is to be a digital image, oversize materials present difficulties (note those elephant folios in #2, the Pennsylvania Railroad collection). So does poor physical condition (look again at #2) or tight bindings. If we are trying to convert to full-text form via OCR, things like typeface, poor page contrast, and complex layout (such as that of most newspapers) present difficulties. One needs to consider each project individually in terms of the precise nature of the originals, the intended format, and the capabilities of available conversion agencies.

Scale

Scale is an issue that might not be obvious to the newcomer. Systems with large databases or heavy transaction loads are qualitatively different from small systems. The appeal of small demonstration projects is that they allow you to learn about and solve the particular problems of a new application before having to tackle the complexities of scale. If you lack experience and infrastructure, start small.

Standards and Formats

Are the standards in place to convert the materials wisely? We are at the very beginnings of the digital library age, with only the dimmest understanding of the optimal formats for digital library content. Unless we are discussing a research or demonstration project, we need to ask whether we know today what the appropriate target format is for a specific set of materials. Are we certain that digital image is in fact the appropriate format for many textual materials? If we are dealing with complex documents, do we know how to structure the components, which elements to keep separate, how to label the parts, etc.? It will be easy for the next several years to make serious mistakes in format. Given the difficulty of funding conversion in the first place, reconverting to correct for a bad guess will be problematic.

Printing over Networks

Are these materials very likely to be used in printed form? If so, is the infrastructure in place to enable users to print? Anyone who has heard many descriptions of early digital library projects is familiar with the recurring theme of the serious and unexpected difficulties of printing over networks. This is another area in which the infrastructure on most campuses is still quite primitive and the state of interinstitutional service even worse. If users will need more than a simple page printout from their workstation and cannot do their printing in a given location over which the library has control, printing is a very serious worry.

A BRIEF COST/BENEFIT ANALYSIS

In my years in automation I have spent a lot of time doing careful cost/benefit analyses of potential projects, and such analyses are especially necessary and appropriate with digitization projects. Like the majority of target materials we have considered digitizing at Harvard, the materials we are discussing today largely fall into the category of special collections materials. We choose such materials for a variety of reasons: Frequently they are unique to our institutions, in some cases they are our real jewels, they are materials we cannot expect others (particularly those in the commercial sector) to convert, and so forth. Equally important, I suspect, they frequently present little or no copyright problem. Those are all good reasons. Nonetheless, concentrating on these materials worries me. My concern is simple: Are the economics sound? Can we cost-justify these projects?

Digitization is expensive–even to convert relatively straightforward materials (and many of these materials are hardly straightforward). And conversion cost is only half the issue–once converted we face perpetual costs for ongoing maintenance of the digital copy. For materials such as these, it will be very difficult to ever back away from such ongoing support.

So what we are talking about is costly. That by itself is not bad, but the cost issues for these materials are greater than average. For example:

- We have already mentioned the effect of format and condition on the difficulty of conversion.
- Frequently we are talking about materials that are voluminous, meaning there is much to convert, much to maintain.
- For such materials, the costs of digitization are largely incremental–we do not throw away the originals to save ongoing housing costs.
- As discussed, I suspect that to be useful in the current environment many of these collections will require that we provide additional intellectual access, adding to the cost. Unlike some other kinds of materials, we cannot rely on independent indexers to provide such access.

- Many of these collections are embedded in institutions or in parts of institutions that are already strapped financially, making the additional economic burden even more problematic.

Therefore, the cost issue is worse for these materials than average. How about the benefits? There, too, I see problems. With a few exceptions, we are not dealing here with what most of us would call heavily used materials. Generally these are the raw materials of scholarship, materials requiring special skills to use, appealing to the specialized researcher rather than the general run of undergraduates or the curious public. The users are scattered geographically and institutionally. Usage is sporadic. And so on. So we have here higher than average costs, representing ongoing incremental expenses for financially strapped institutions to serve a small, specialized, highly distributed user base. That should give us pause.

NOTE

1. [Editor's note.] As a closing exercise, symposium participants were given a list of thirteen collections from RLG's RLIN database. After reading the collection descriptions, they were to choose the collection most meriting digital conversion and the one least meriting digitization. The numbers and collection titles cited by Flecker in this essay correspond to the numbers and titles of the thirteen collections on the list. See *Selecting Library and Archival Collection for Digital Reformatting,* pages 91-98, 147-155.

The Preservation Perspective

Barclay W. Ogden

Considerations regarding the role of digitization in preservation fall into two groups: preservation considerations when digitization is used for conversion of documents to digital media, and considerations in the preservation of natively digital information objects, that is, research resources not only created in digital form, but which must remain in digital form in order to be used as originally intended.

CONVERTED DOCUMENTS

The considerations that apply when digitization is used for conversion of documents to digital media include the following:

Surrogates and Replacement Copies

The conversion process should capture sufficient information to enable the digital document to serve at least as a surrogate for the original document, thereby reducing demand for (and wear and tear on) the originals. Conversion that achieves a relatively low level of information capture (for example, low-resolution hard-to-read text) enables images to serve as finding aids to the originals, but often cannot satisfy even casual use, thus increasing demand for the originals.

For originals at risk of damage or loss during the conversion process, the conversion process should capture sufficient information to enable the

Barclay W. Ogden is Head of the Digital Library Research and Development Department of the University of California, Berkeley Library.

[Haworth co-indexing entry note]: "The Preservation Perspective." Ogden, Barclay W. Co-published simultaneously in *Collection Management* (The Haworth Press, Inc.) Vol. 22, No. 3/4, 1998, pp. 213-216; and: *Going Digital: Strategies for Access, Preservation, and Conversion of Collections to a Digital Format* (ed: Donald L. DeWitt) The Haworth Press, Inc., 1998, pp. 213-216.

original to be succeeded by the digital copy since there may not be a second opportunity to subject the originals to the conversion process.

Maintenance Through Time

Access to the digital file must be maintained through time and changes in technology for retrieval and display. The life of magnetic media is relatively short, apparently less than a decade; files must be refreshed, that is, copied from one medium to another to avoid information loss due to deterioration of the medium. Additionally, changes in hardware and software technology used for retrieval and display require that files be migrated from one technology to another, rather than simply refreshed. Obsolescence of technology due to rapid development poses a considerable threat to continuing access to information. Further, unlike refreshment, which exactly duplicates the original file, migration risks changing the digital file to conform to the requirements of the new hardware and software used for its retrieval and display. The promise of exact copies through the use of digital technology well may remain unfulfilled.

Document Integrity

Maintaining the integrity of the document throughout the conversion process needs to be ensured to avoid the loss of essential information, a consideration in digital conversion no different than conversion to film or to preservation photocopy. However, due to the ease of changing digital documents, authentication of digital files must be addressed more rigorously than ever has been necessary in the analog world. Without a widely accepted and utilized means of authentication, the digital researcher will be at the mercy of unreliable source information.

Nondamaging Digitization Process

The digitization process should be nondamaging to the original documents. Until we understand better than we do now levels of information capture required for research, until we develop a management strategy for refreshment and migration of digital information, until we are confident of the integrity and authenticity of the digital information we use, the prudent step would be not to use digitization to preserve materials that will be damaged by the digitization process.

The Preservation Decision

Finally, and perhaps better a first consideration than last, there is no need for any preservation action, including digitization, unless the materials are at risk of either wear and tear from large amounts of use or of loss to deterioration. At this time, digitization appears to have a preservation role in reducing use of originals (minus authentication), but appears not to be suitable for preservation of information that is preserved in no other form.

NATIVELY DIGITAL INFORMATION OBJECTS

The second group of considerations apply to preservation of natively digital information objects and are in part the same as using digitization for conversion.

No Conversion Required

We need not be concerned about information losses from the conversion process. For information created in the digital environment, there is no need for a conversion process.

File Refreshment and Document Integrity

Refreshment of files raises issues of integrity to be addressed by quality-control routines, which themselves can be automated. Authentication of files of natively digital information objects is a problem identical to the authentication problem for files resulting from conversion.

Maintenance Through Time

Migration of natively digital information objects presents all the problems of migration of converted information, and potentially many more, because unlike paper- and film-based documents, information objects created in the digital environment can include added functionality essential to their value, such as cumulation (for example, an online catalog), linkages to other documents (for example, hypermedia), and interactivity, that is, the ability to change in response to outside forces (for example, video games). As information objects migrate from one combination of hardware and software to another, the probability of losing functionality appears high; documents whose essential value resides in their functionality may prove to be the greatest preservation challenge of the digital medium.

NEW CHALLENGES

Margo Crist in her presentation intriguingly suggested that documents should be selected for conversion on the basis of their likelihood of having their value enhanced in digital form. Such added value could be created by adding functionality, such as machine searchability for greater access, and linkages to references. Converted documents then would become more like natively digital information objects and acquire their additional preservation problems as well. As digital media transform information into more useful and more exciting modes, preservation will become increasingly challenging, and the links between our information future and information past increasingly less certain.

Institutionalizing Digitization

Nancy S. Allen

A GLANCE BACK BEFORE MOVING FORWARD

The reformatting precursor to digitization is, of course, microfilming. This route has been tackled by many institutions and received critical support from funding agencies both private and public. It has worked to the extent that the intellectual content of tens of thousands of pages from books, periodicals, newspapers, and archival collections have been rescued from oblivion. It has not worked, however, by one critical measure. Few libraries and repositories have made this means of preservation an institutional priority, and the reasons for this must be examined.

The Art Serials Microfilming Project of the Research Libraries Group provides an example. The goal of this collaborative effort of academic and museum libraries was to preserve volumes of 19th- and early 20th-century art periodicals printed on brittle paper and containing black-and-white illustrations. RLG staff wrote the successful NEH grant and administered the project. The now defunct RLG Art and Architecture Program Committee developed the candidate list by checking the major bibliographies in the field and eliminating those titles which had already been filmed. The lists were circulated, and the participating libraries examined and reported on the condition of their run of each title. When this information was pooled, RLG staff assigned titles to each library, and the work of preparing, shipping, filming, and examining for quality control commenced.

The end result could be likened to successful surgery. The goal of reformatting journals significant to the study of art and architecture–in time and on budget–was achieved. Alas, the patient died, which is to say

Nancy S. Allen is Director of Information Resources at the Museum of Fine Arts, Boston.

[Haworth co-indexing entry note]: "Institutionalizing Digitization." Allen, Nancy S. Co-published simultaneously in *Collection Management* (The Haworth Press, Inc.) Vol. 22, No. 3/4, 1998, pp. 217-223; and: *Going Digital: Strategies for Access, Preservation, and Conversion of Collections to a Digital Format* (ed: Donald L. DeWitt) The Haworth Press, Inc., 1998, pp. 217-223.

that few, if any, of the libraries involved turned the experience of this project, initiated externally, into an ongoing reformatting effort within the institution.

The lessons learned may be valid whether we are talking about art or astronomy, architecture or agriculture. Experience indicates that selection dictated by the collective group does not promote institutional commitment. Hastening the demise of the physical book, an inevitable outcome of microfilming, put most art library directors at odds with staff, scholars, faculty, curators, and students for whom immediate access to a particular book seemed to rank as a higher priority than the preservation of vast portions of mankind's documented knowledge. Within the library, the preparation, quality control, and cataloging requirements of the effort created unfunded staff demands. Finally, there was that troublesome matter of the outcome. Researchers everywhere prefer holding books to cranking microfilm. In short, the correctness of the cause was not compelling enough to convince those outside the library profession that institutions should commit staff and resources to reformatting projects that destroy materials before their time.

CURRENT POSSIBILITIES

Budget constraints within universities and cultural institutions have had a negative impact on institutional commitment to preservation microfilming. Action motivated largely to benefit an external community becomes harder and harder to justify. When the responsibility to preserve collections for national and international scholars has to be evaluated against the information needs of the institution's immediate constituency, large-scale ongoing microfilming projects are hard to sell. Institutions lacking the funds to accomplish all their goals inevitably place collaborative "greater good" projects lower on the list of priorities.

Digital preservation projects provide the opportunity to address many institutional goals at once–the added-value concept that has been addressed at this symposium. Although microfilming has reduced the wear on high-use originals, the medium has been a poor substitute for the original because it has failed to attract a similar high use. Scanned texts, on the other hand, have the potential of increasing physical access, if "handling" the virtual book can be termed physical access, because many can view it at once, and it can be delivered anywhere the reader chooses. When electronic preservation takes its place alongside an array of electronic initiatives within an institution, it promotes access to the whole information object–to bibliographic citations, indexes, images, and full text. This route provides the opportunity for librarians and scholars to embed links to other information, which greatly enhances intellectual access to both high- and low-use collections.

INSTITUTIONAL COMMITMENT

Building an institutional commitment requires building an internal constituency. With the technology in flux and long-term issues of refreshing still difficult to settle, what will convince administrators that digital preservation must be funded? If we approach digitization as we do collection development, it may be easier. Candidates for selection, whether for acquisition or digital preservation, may be best identified if we ask ourselves how well they address the overall teaching and research mission of the institution. This argument may be more compelling than selection based on the needs of the most seriously deteriorated books. Cooperative collection development projects have largely failed, in spite of diminished book-buying power in many libraries, because they tend to pit the needs of any given institution against the requirements of the group. Books held locally have been easier to put in the hands of our users, who find it far less satisfactory to learn that a consortial partner owns the book they want. In the virtual library it becomes far less important which library physically owns the digital book. Scholarship becomes increasingly reliant on how we build, generate, preserve, and provide access to digital files than on how we shape and develop collections of printed materials.

Our administrations also need to understand the budget implications, including the articulation of initial costs and analysis of long-term digital file refreshing. They must understand the issues of media deterioration and technical obsolescence. The plan and cost of ongoing migration of digital preservation files can be integrated into the future technical environment of the institution to provide context and perspective on the budget impact.

As digital preservation is "sold" to our administration, a plan for evaluation of these efforts can help strengthen the argument. Currently, the body of literature and collective experience on digital preservation can ensure positive results on the technical aspects of the work. Within each institution, however, the true success of digital projects will be measured by how the preserved materials are to be used. What is the audience for the materials selected for digital preservation? Is the display, retrieval, and delivery of the digital file satisfactory to them? How well do they integrate use of this digital information with other digital resources available to them? If we can frame this discussion on a cost/benefit basis, our administrators will be more likely to understand and accept the plan. Librarians will have to prioritize the cost of digital projects against that of traditional operations. With level or decreased spending mandates, materials, services, or staff might have to be sacrificed to fund digital preservation.

STAFF

As we build the constituency for digital preservation projects, the staff of the library must not be overlooked. Change is difficult to legislate, and the success of digital preservation projects will depend on the commitment and participation of staff. They must acquire a high level of technical understanding and experience to undertake project planning and gain the necessary expertise to carry out these new initiatives. Most staff find such an investment in their training and professional growth to be an incentive. It is surely part of the cost of institutionalizing digital preservation. Work responsibilities will have to be reestablished if existing staff will be devoted partially or fully to this new initiative. In some cases the difficult choices regarding what the library may stop doing so it can start doing something new will have to be made and clearly articulated to staff to convince them that the objectives are realistic.

SCHOLARS

There has been considerable discussion regarding microfilm reformatting projects among scholars. The Commission for Preservation and Access has convened seven scholarly advisory panels to address the matter of selection and issued a report earlier this year summarizing the variety of methodologies recommended. One clear message is that scholars lack enthusiasm for the medium of microfilm. How can we now build enthusiasm for electronic reformatting projects? Perhaps it is necessary to shift the selection methodology to include more emphasis on what scholars require for their immediate research and teaching needs. Can digitally preserved texts increase use of collections if scholars integrate these texts with other electronic information including images, primary source documents, citation indexes, and large raw data files? Do we, or they, understand how they use information now and could use digital files in the future to better support their original research and the creation of instructional packages? When our scholarly constituency becomes a stakeholder in the selection process, support for institutionalizing digital preservation will likely soar above the previous level of interest in efforts producing a microfilm end product.

PROJECT FUNDING

The primary financial model for preservation microfilming has been project-based funding. We know that many of these one-time projects have enhanced staff expertise and created microfilm that can be used within the library and microfilm masters that can be copied for and distributed to other institutions, copyright permitting. We also know that this model has not translated into ongoing projects supported by operating funds. Given that grant funding may be difficult to identify for preservation projects in the late 1990s, new financial models for digital projects must be developed.

BUDGET REALLOCATION

One method of funding the start-up and ongoing costs of digital preservation is through budget reallocation. This forces difficult decisions about what to cut. At the Museum of Fine Arts, Boston, the legitimacy of acquiring new works or art when so much of what we currently own is in need of conservation is often discussed. In libraries, is there a similar link between acquisition funding and preservation? It is a drastic thought that we could be investing more in preserving and promoting our existing collections and less on new acquisitions, but the preservation needs of the collections for which we care require drastic action.

In the electronic age perhaps there are other areas where traditional operations and services can be eliminated or curtailed to divert funding to digital preservation. Are there ways to outsource aspects of technical services? Will we forgo binding journals and come to rely on digital archives to supply missing back issues, saving on both bindery expenses and staff devoted to this labor-intensive aspect of library operations? Will we save space and money by destroying originals when digital files exist as replacements? None of these cost-saving measures come without some negative impact, but where incremental funding is unavailable, such options may have to be exercised.

COST RECOVERY

Another model for funding digital preservation is recovering costs, or at least partial costs, from users. Many librarians still have difficulty putting a price tag on information, yet the practice is well established. Individual library patrons have long paid for photocopying, access to online indexes and databases, and, more recently, searching the RLIN database. Will they pay for access to digitally reformatted books, and what might be the price structure? Pricing based on the number of pages follows the standard photocopying model. Many of the microfilm projects funded by the NEH have reformatted secondary sources, which may or may not be rare. If selection for digitally reformatted material in the future includes a high proportion of rare books and unique archival documents, the value of the information to scholars may be gauged to determine the fees for accessing the digital files.

Another fee structure focuses less on content than on the transferability of information. What is the speed of information delivery worth to a scholar? This is in essence the same matter as the value of next-day delivery versus first class mail. When the information being accessed is image, not text, another added-value opportunity occurs. Accessing a relatively low-resolution image will cost one amount while downloading a high-resolution image file, suitable for reduplication, may cost much more. This is basically a marketing issue. Can we select at least some of the material we digitize carefully enough to reap some financial pay back for its use?

PRIVATE/NONPROFIT PARTNERSHIPS

All nonprofit organizations are scrambling to establish funding support from private sector corporations. In the past, project funding for educational and cultural institutions was easily obtainable through corporate support programs. Now the ability to attract corporate funding often requires the establishment of partnerships between the library or museum and the for-profit company. Does this situation create constraints or opportunities for libraries seeking to fund digital preservation? Many microfilm projects have been the result of partnerships between the repository and the publisher. Unfortunately, these projects, at least in the arts, have resulted in rather random selection of materials that the publisher has somehow judged to be commercially viable. Successful partnerships in the future must have a better division of labor and responsibilities. Clearly the repository that owns the content and has the direct link to the users must select materials for digitization. Publishers, on the other hand, may front the costs of image capture and market the electronic product. Profits, when they are turned, can be shared. This idea is by no means new. Since 1988, the Harvard University Library's James B. and Esthy Adler Preservation Publishing Fund has been used to encourage the institution to form partnerships with commercial publishers for filming and marketing, while the university does the selection and bibliographic work.

WORKING TOGETHER

The benefits of collaboration can also help reinforce institutional commitment to digital preservation. The Research Libraries Group will continue to be a driving force in preservation of our cultural heritage. With the enormous complexity surrounding the technical aspects of scanning, compression, creating embedded information links, storing, transmitting, and ensuring forward compatibility, only a handful of libraries have developed the expertise to embark on large-scale digital projects independently. Working together within the context of RLG we can continue to learn from one another, find financial incentives for collaboration, contribute to an international effort to preserve brittle books, and contribute to a worldwide virtual library that offers new ways to teach and undertake scholarship.

SELECTED BIBLIOGRAPHY

Commission on Preservation and Access and Research Libraries Group. *Preserving Digital Information: Draft Report of the Task Force on Archiving of Digital Information.* Version 1.0. Washington, DC: Commission on Preservation and Access, 1995.

Gerald George. *Difficult Choices: How Can Scholars Help Save Endangered Research Resources?* Washington, DC: Commission on Preservation and Access, 1995.

Harvard University. Task Group on Collection Preservation Priorities. *Preserving Harvard's Retrospective Collections: Report of the Harvard University Library.* Cambridge, MA: Harvard University, 1991.

Christy Hightower and George Soete. "The consortium as learning organization: Twelve steps to success in collaborative collections projects." *Journal of Academic Librarianship* 1995 (March): 87-91.

Index